Canadian Business Strategies
for Winning in the Borderless World

GLOBAL
PURSUIT

Other Books by Susan Goldenberg

*Hands Across The Ocean: Managing Joint Ventures
(With a spotlight on China and Japan)*

Trading: Inside The World's Leading Stock Exchanges

The Thomson Empire

Canadian Pacific: A Portrait of Power

Men of Property: The Canadian Developers Who Are Buying America

Canadian Business Strategies
for Winning in the Borderless World

GLOBAL PURSUIT

Susan Goldenberg

McGRAW-HILL RYERSON LIMITED

Toronto   Montreal

Global Pursuit: Canadian Business Strategies for Winning in the Borderless World

First published in 1991 by
McGraw-Hill Ryerson Limited
300 Water Street
Whitby, Ontario, Canada
L1N 9B6

1 2 3 4 5 6 7 8 9 0 TRI 0 9 8 7 6 5 4 3 2 1

Printed and bound in Canada

Cover design: Stuart Knox/Matthews Communications Design

Canadian Cataloguing in Publication Data

Goldenberg, Susan, date
  Global pursuit

Includes index.
ISBN 0-07-551304-8

1. Business enterprises – Canada.   2. International business enterprises – Canada.   I. Title.

HD2809.G65 1991   338.8'8971   C91-095001-6

To my parents
and
my grandfather, Edward Dworkin,
a global business pioneer

ACKNOWLEDGMENTS

This book is based primarily on interviews with executives at 100 large and small Canadian and foreign-owned companies across Canada. The people who spoke to me are exceedingly busy and travel a great deal to build up their international business. Yet, they graciously and generously gave me considerable time. Moreover, they willingly spoke of their setbacks as well as successes in order to help others. I am extremely grateful and thank them very much.

S.G.

C O N T E N T S

Foreword   *xiii*

1. *Planning To Go Global*   1

   When ready to go global, cost, preparatory research,
   government assistance and awards, market differences
   in tastes and regulations, distributors, management,
   examples of companies that had setbacks and/or
   revised their strategies.

2. *Global Niche Strategy*   35

   Value to small and medium-sized firms. Importance of
   product uniqueness, marketing skills, clearly defined
   tight focus, controlled growth. Examples of industrial
   and commercial niche firms.

3. *More Niche Strategy: Consumer Products*   55

   Niche consumer products and services: sample
   companies. Importance of not neglecting Canadian
   market. Importance of recognizing different tastes in
   consumer and retailer buying. Advantages and
   disadvantages of establishing foreign operations.

4. *High Technology*   70

   Buoyant world outlook for high-technology growth.
   Generally small size of Canadian high-technology
   firms. Product, marketing, and management strategies.
   Why Canadian firms acquired by foreign companies
   believe they benefit. Examples of Canadian global
   successes and setbacks in: computer hardware; computer software; engineering, medical and scientific
   instrumentation; telecommunications.

5. Big Canadian Companies   100

Production, planning, marketing, and management
strategies. Setbacks that are useful for firms of all sizes
to examine. Companies covered: Alcan Aluminium,
Bombardier, Dominion Textile, Federal Industries,
Magna International, the Molson Companies,
Noranda, Northern Telecom, Nova.

6. The Role of Foreign-Owned Subsidiaries   131

The impact of foreign ownership on the economy;
examples of foreign ownership that saved, expanded,
or curtailed Canadian companies; Japanese
investment in Canada.

7. World Product Mandates   163

Importance to survival in Canada of foreign
subsidiaries. Benefits and drawbacks. Strategies to win
and maintain manadates by subsidiaries of Du Pont,
General Electric, General Signal, Honeywell, IBM,
Pratt & Whitney, Rockwell International, and Upjohn.

8. The Soviet Union: Opportunities and Problems   191

Attractions of Soviet market; advantages of Canadians
in doing business in USSR; problems regarding
bureaucracy, infrastructure, foreign exchange, worker
productivity; examples of Canadian firms doing
business with the USSR and how they handle
problems.

9. Increasing Canada's International Competitiveness   213

Canada's strengths and weaknesses. Why some
companies have left Canada in order to survive. How
others have strengthened themselves through
productivity improvement and training programs to
increase competitiveness. Examples.

APPENDIX A: FEDERAL GOVERNMENT ASSISTANCE

International Trade Centres   242

Program for Export Market Development (PEMD)   244

Business Opportunities Sourcing System (BOSS)   244

World Information Network (WIN) for Exports   245

Export Development Corporation   246

Canadian International Development Agency (CIDA)   247

Export Orientation Programs   247

International Trade Data Bank   248

Canadian Commercial Corporation   249

APPENDIX B: FEDERAL GOVERNMENT AWARDS FOR EXPORTING AND BUSINESS EXCELLENCE   250

APPENDIX C: PROVINCIAL TRADE ASSISTANCE   252

APPENDIX D: ASSISTANCE AVAILABLE FROM ASSOCIATIONS, BANKS, AND CENTRES FOR INTERNATIONAL BUSINESS STUDIES   254

Index   259

Tables

Canadian Exports by Country xviii

Canadian Imports by Country xix

Number of Canadian Firms That Export xx

Where Canadian Firms Export xxi

Foreign Direct Investment in Canada and Canadian Direct Investment Abroad 134

Foreign Direct Investment in Canada and Canadian Direct Investment Abroad: Ranked by Top Ten Countries 135

Thirty Largest Foreign-Owned Companies in Canada 136

Foreign Control of Canadian Manufacturing 139

Leading Exports — Leading Imports 216

Labour Costs and Productivity 224

FOREWORD

"The competition no longer is the factory next door but one halfway around the world."

Hugh Hamilton,
Senior Executive
during Northern Telecom's
formative international years

·For their own sake as well as for Canada's, Canadian firms must become more competitive globally. Not to do so is to avoid today's business reality, a reality that will become even more pronounced during this decade and into the rapidly approaching twenty-first century. Due to the lowering of trade barriers and continuing advances in transportation and communications, we now live not in a local, nor a national, nor a regional economy, but rather in a truly global one. Consumers can make their purchasing decisions on a comparitive basis worldwide, and companies can produce and sell wherever they have a financial advantage instead of confining themselves to their home countries.

This globalization of business has vastly increased the opportunities to make money. But it has also added to the risks. In times of war, such as with Iraq in 1991, uncertainty about the future often causes business to postpone foreign as well as domestic expansion. However, in direct economic relations, Canada had little at stake in its dealings with either Iraq or the entire Middle East. As little as approximately 0.1 percent of Canada's trade prior to the outbreak of war was with Iraq, and Canada's trade with the Middle East amounted to only about 1 percent of the whole. Far more serious to Canada, had the war lasted longer, would have been the potential harmful economic impact on the United States, its major trading partner.

Instead, as it turns out, the war paid off handsomely for Canadian companies, as well as for those in other Coalition countries that fought Iraq. Although Canadian firms will make much less in Kuwaiti reconstruction contracts than the leading Coalition participants, especially the United States, they will earn millions of dollars.

Even in peacetime, no nation's market is safe from infiltration by foreign competitors. With companies around the world now regarding other countries' markets as fair game, domestic corporations can no longer complacently view their homeland as their personal domain. In this struggle for economic superiority, only the best will survive. With almost 30 percent of our Gross National Product derived from trade and more than 25 percent of the labour force working in industries that produce goods and services for export, the future of every Canadian depends on our country being among the best. While it *is* among the better, it is some distance from the best.

Canada does rank high in several key categories. It is the world's seventh-largest trading nation and eighth in Gross National Product. It also has some special leverages in the global economy. Canadians are regarded as less overwhelming and aggressive than Americans, and are gaining a reputation for flexibility and speed in response to specialized requests from customers.

As a result, Canada's manufacturing exports grew from 32 percent of the total in 1979 to 44 percent by 1989, and Canada's share of manufactured exports to other developed countries has expanded from about 3.8 percent in 1975 to approximately 5 percent in recent years. Nevertheless, Canada continues to suffer trade deficits in manufactured goods with the exception of paper and wood products which have substantial surpluses and food items which have a slim one.

Moreover, Canada's gain in exports to other developed countries lags far behind the rise from 12.3 percent to more than 16 percent recorded by Japan, the country in the lead in this significant indicator of trading strength. Canada is unlikely to overcome its manufacturing trade deficit in the near future, considering that only 25 percent of the country's manufacturers export.

In addition, our international competitiveness is severely harmed by higher labour costs, lower productivity, and less innovation than in many other industrialized nations. Furthermore, even Canada's biggest corporations are minuscle compared to the world's giants. Not one ranks in the world's 50 largest companies. By contrast, there are 17 in Japan, 14 in the United States, 7 in Germany, and 3 in Italy, which is just ahead of Canada in world trade.

The attractiveness of our exports also has been undercut by the long duration of steep interest rates and by the appreciation in the value of the Canadian dollar versus the American. Since the United

States is the principal foreign buyer of Canadian goods, a strong Canadian dollar strikes at the core of our aspirations to increase our international trade.

With globalization becoming the standard way of conducting business, Canadian companies must upgrade themselves to world-class calibre. This does not necessarily entail international sales; a company with only domestic customers must have a global perspective to withstand foreign competitors more capably in its home market. However, many advantages exist for fighting rivals on an around-the-world basis. These include economies of scale due to a larger market base, financing of a subsidiary in one country with profits from another, and a hedge against economic and political risks through the ability to shift manufacturing and sales operations, if necessary.

"Sales of commodities have been global for a long time, and those of manufacturing and services are becoming global; therefore, the competition is globally oriented and Canadian companies must learn to compete against those that are often larger or more broadly based geographically," advises Paul White, a senior management consultant at Toronto-based Hatch Associates. Hatch exemplifies this conviction: started in the 1960s as a one-person enterprise, the engineering and management consulting firm now has 800 employees in Canada, the United States, and England.

Another significant benefit that Canadian firms attain from going global is access to a much larger market. On its own, Canada is too small a marketplace; although in area it is the world's second largest nation, it is only thirty-first in population. Thus, it cannot provide the opportunities to achieve the volume of growth essential for Canadian firms to be globally competitive. Similarly, the Canadian market is not large enough to support the amount of research and development needed to create the new technologies that are critical to our country's future. Therefore, Canadian high-technology firms stress that it is imperative for them to go global in order to be foremost players.

Provided they plan carefully and target their strategy, small firms, as well as large ones, can become globally successful; there are many examples in this book. "No firm is too small to go global. If you are resourceful, you can become global quickly," asserts Eugene Joseph, president of Montreal-based Virtual Prototypes, which develops software for aircraft and car dashboard control-and-display systems. He definitely knows whereof he speaks: created in 1980 by Joseph as a one-man concern, Virtual Prototypes now has 75 employees and does 95 percent of its business outside Canada.

For Canadian companies and their shareholders, going global has many advantages: new sales, a cushion against economic changes at home, and hence greater corporate profits that can be ploughed into research and development, as well as fatter dividends for shareholders. Perhaps more firms will follow the example of Newfoundland's Instrumar, which deliberately set out to prove that an internationally competitive high-technology company could be created at a considerable distance from the rest of Canada and world markets.

Started in 1979 with a meagre capitalization of eight dollars, St. John's-based Instrumar, which makes scientific instruments for quality-testing food, now obtains the bulk of its sales from exports to 15 countries. Founder and chairman Alastair Allan, a geographer and sea-ice researcher formerly associated with St. John's Memorial University, had a longtime interest in the factors that foster regional development. He wanted also to demonstrate that since natural resources, like Newfoundland's oil, are depleting commodities, "deriving wealth from creating things is crucial." An additional goal was to contribute to the development of infrastructure necessary to give rise to other high-tech ventures in Newfoundland: materials and parts, patent services, and financial support from banks and venture capital investors. "It would have been easier to locate in Toronto or Ottawa where such infrastructure exists, but I was interested in the mechanisms of stimulating high-technology development in Newfoundland, even though I knew there was virtually no local market and therefore we would have to go global," Allan says. Having successfully proved his thesis in St. John's, Allan recently opened a branch in a small Newfoundland community with high unemployment to ascertain if what worked in the city is applicable in this more remote locale.

To the extent that globalization generates profits, raises shareholder dividends, sustains jobs, creates new employment, and brings in added revenue to the government from increased tax payments, it is in harmony with Canada's national interest. But the global company — or stateless, as some economists refer to it — creates distinct problems too, and there are no easy solutions to them. Most significantly, globalization renders corporate nationality irrelevant in that global companies behave like citizens of the world, rather than tying their loyalties and priorities to their countries of origin.

They place their own interests first by manufacturing, buying supplies, and raising money wherever it is best for them to do so. While this attitude benefits balance sheets, shareholders and host countries, it can result in the export of jobs from countries where the cost of labour is high, like Canada, to countries where the cost is lower, a trend that is well underway. Thus, the message for Canadians is clear: they must work harder and better to counterbalance cheap wages in much of the world.

Globalization also requires substantial adjustment by managers because a global company is run far differently from a multinational one. In the multinational system, foreign subsidiaries operate as autonomous, distinct businesses. By contrast, in global companies strategies are centrally co-ordinated so as to create cohesiveness and cost efficiencies, eliminate duplication, spark more rapid decision making, and build a sense of team effort.

To survive in this decade's and the next century's savagely competitive international business arena, Canadian firms must draw up an economic battle plan. They must become thoroughly knowledgable about markets, suppliers, distributors, customers, competitors, national regulations, exchange rate fluctuations, and changing world demographics. They must also be capable of projecting trends so as to be prepared for the future. Morever, they must not be deterred by setbacks because these are an inevitable part of the learning process.

Canadian business people have amply shown already that they can compete strongly internationally. For the well being of Canada, becoming more competitive internationally should be a vital part of our national agenda.

CANADIAN EXPORTS BY COUNTRY
(Ranked by latest year)
(Millions of Dollars)

Top Ten, as of Most Recent Available Year, with Comparisons for Past Years

	1990		1989		1988		1985		1980		1975	
	$	%	$	%	$	%	$	%	$	%	$	%
Total	140,989	100	134,843	100	133,904	100	115,911	100	74,228	100	32,096	100
United States	105,090	74.5	98,703	73.2	97,530	72.8	90,344	77.9	46,825	63.1	20,939	65.2
Japan	8,172	5.8	8,797	6.5	8,708	6.5	5,745	4.9	4,370	5.9	2,115	6.6
United Kingdom	3,381	2.4	3,454	2.6	3,465	2.6	2,313	2.0	3,193	4.3	1,761	5.5
West Germany*	2,197	1.6	1,822	1.3	1,695	1.3	1,189	1.0	1,637	2.2	585	1.8
China	1,647	1.2	1,121	0.8	2,600	1.9	1,259	1.1	866	1.2	376	1.2
South Korea	1,550	1.1	1,651	1.2	1,194	0.9	775	0.7	504	0.7	79	0.2
Netherlands	1,450	1.0	1,542	1.1	1,392	1.0	929	0.8	1,428	1.9	471	1.5
France	1,273	0.9	1,231	0.9	1,186	0.9	714	0.6	997	1.3	332	1.0
Italy	1,131	0.8	1,100	0.8	1,001	0.7	525	0.4	981	1.3	473	1.5
Taiwan	789	0.6	951	0.7	1,010	0.7	1,607	1.4	251	0.3	38	0.1

Source: Statistics Canada, "Exports by Country" Catalogue #65-003

*Effective October 1990, Statistics Canada lists as GERMANY, combining West and East Germany.

Note: For its country export tables, Statistics Canada uses merchandise trade statistics covering the physical movement of goods as reflected in Customs documents.

CANADIAN IMPORTS BY COUNTRY

(Ranked by latest year)

(Millions of Dollars)

Top Ten, as of Most Recent Available Year, with Comparisons for Past Years

	1990 $	1990 %	1989 $	1989 %	1988 $	1988 %	1985 $	1985 %	1980 $	1980 %	1975 $	1975 %
Total	135,922	100	135,191	100	131,172	100	104,914	100	68,979	100	34,537	100
United States	87,803	64.6	88,104	65.2	86,020	65.6	74,377	70.9	48,414	70.2	23,486	68.0
Japan	9,517	7.0	9,563	7.1	9,268	7.1	6,113	5.8	2,792	4.0	1,205	3.5
United Kingdom	4,839	3.6	4,565	3.4	4,629	3.5	3,281	3.1	1,970	2.8	1,221	3.5
West Germany*	3,832	2.8	3,702	2.7	3,841	2.9	2,716	2.6	1,448	2.1	786	2.3
France	2,434	1.8	2,028	1.5	2,884	2.2	1,373	1.3	770	1.1	488	1.4
South Korea	2,251	1.6	2,441	1.8	2,270	1.7	1,607	1.5	414	0.6	166	0.5
Taiwan	2,109	1.5	2,352	1.7	2,256	1.7	1,286	1.2	557	0.8	182	0.5
Italy	1,953	1.4	2,012	1.5	1,954	1.5	1,331	1.3	609	0.9	379	1.1
Mexico	1,730	1.3	1,708	1.3	1,327	1.0	1,331	1.3	345	0.5	95	0.3
Brazil	789	0.6	1,131	0.8	1,193	0.9	808	0.8	348	0.5	170	0.5

Source: Statistics Canada, "Imports by Country" Catalogue #65-006

*Effective October 1990, Statistics Canada lists as GERMANY, combining West and East Germany.

Note: For its country import tables, Statistics Canada uses merchandise trade statistics covering the physical movement of goods as reflected in Customs documents.

NUMBER OF CANADIAN FIRMS THAT EXPORT

Number of firms exporting	9,972
Number of firms interested in new markets	2,934
Number of firms with over $50 million in export sales	225
Number of firms with $5–$50 million in export sales	950
Number of firms with $1–$5 million in export sales	1,657
Number of firms with $100,000–$1 million in export sales	3,029
Number of firms with under $100,000 in export sales	3,786

Source: Business Opportunities Sourcing System (BOSS) Industry, Science and Technology Canada.

WHERE CANADIAN FIRMS EXPORT
(by size)

Region	Number of Exporters	Number Interested in Exporting	Total
North America	9,062	7,545	16,607
Western Europe	3,731	4,594	8,323
Commonwealth	3,569	4,201	7,770
Asia or Far East	3,262	4,282	7,544
United Kingdom	2,380	2,864	5,244
Latin America	1,953	1,866	3,819
South America	1,269	1,808	3,077
Scandinavia	1,261	1,745	3,006
Eastern Europe	611	1,896	2,507
Middle East	1,162	1,192	2,354
Caribbean/West Indies	1,343	910	2,253
Africa	1,092	1,297	2,389
World-wide	103	1,837	1,940

Source: Business Opportunities Sourcing System (BOSS) Industry, Science and Technology Canada.

CHAPTER

1

Planning To Go Global

"I ask all domestic manufacturers I meet, 'Do you export?' If they say 'No,' I inquire 'Why not?' and stress that if they want to expand their business, they must export."

Donald Fell,
Chairman,
Fell-Fab

Canadian candy buyers have a fondness for maraschino cherry chocolates; liquor-banning Arab countries refuse to import them because maraschino is a liqueur. Canadian beer drinkers, like most worldwide, prefer lager; the British prefer maltier ales. Canada's paved highways can easily support heavy transport loads; the dirt roads of many Third World countries cannot. In Canada and the United States, equipment operates on 110 volts; in most foreign countries, the voltage is 220.

Canadian business people can quickly contact one another by local or long distance phone calls; in many parts of the world, telephone service is primitive. The French spoken in Quebec differs somewhat from Parisian French, just as there are variations in the English spoken in Canada, the United States, the United Kingdom, Australia, and New Zealand. And these are only some of the contrasts that must be learned in going global!

Canadian firms contemplating the international marketplace must weigh many factors. Getting started is expensive and breaking even takes at least two to three years. Going global is time-consuming and, therefore, harmful to family life; absences amounting to half a year are common, particularly in the early days of building foreign business. Decisions must be made as to how and where to go global. Should the route be via exports or direct investment? If direct investment, should it take the form of startups, mergers, acquisitions, or joint ventures?

Since the common theme of internationally active firms is "You can't be all things to all people," which of a company's products are most suitable for the global marketplace? Geographically, the firm must decide in which direction to head, bearing in mind that despite their proximity, the U.S. and Canadian markets are not identical; that some currencies such as the Soviet ruble and Chinese yuan are not readily convertible; and that entire regions cannot be regarded as homogeneous. For example, the Asia–Pacific region encompasses the vastly different areas of Australia, Japan, China, and India.

Deliberations about globalization must also consider future potential as well as present buying power. Moreover, financial prudence is essential. It is a common failing of companies that have experienced global success to jeopardize their future by chasing after expansion without paying sufficient attention to the consequent drain on capital. Such disregard inevitably leads to losses. In going global, as in developing domestically, basing spending on what has been earned, rather than on projections, is much more sensible.

Other important elements that must be considered are the vast variations in product standards and merchandise tastes, how to co-ordinate worldwide operations, and whether to sell directly through distributors, agents, or a combination. Distributors and agents are on-the-spot connections to a market, but careful selection, training, and supervision are necessary to ensure their commitment does not wane.

There is no all-purpose yardstick that companies can use to gauge whether they are ready to go global. One guideline is the qualifying criterion set by the federal government for its export market development financial assistance, called the Program for Export Market Development (described in detail later in this chapter). Applicants must have sales performance data for at least two years or annual sales exceeding $100,000. However, companies are described in this book that went global from their earliest days, since domestic demand for their products was limited.

In projects requiring vast resources, many companies prefer to be part of a consortium rather than bear the burden on their own. "International consortia provide the comfort of strength since the whole is stronger than the parts," enthuses Alan Curleigh, vice-president, contracts and international project finance at Klöckner Stadler Hurter of Montreal, an engineering consulting and contracting firm that has undertaken numerous projects in developing countries. "One partner contributes through parts in its home country being cheaper than those of the other partners, another through special technology, and a third through favourable financing arrangements," he continues.

While there is no across-the-board generalization as to when a company should consider itself globally ready, it can use a number of indicators to decide whether it has the desire, energy, and strength to go global. Government trade development officials stress that it takes at least two years to learn about customs documentation, freight packing and shipping, invoicing, and forms of payment (letters of credit,* rather than cheques, are standard with many Third World nations), as well as to prepare market analyses. Often, thousands of dollars must be spent to adapt products to the standards of other countries, as well as to their preferences regarding size and appearance.

Most importantly, no headway can be made unless the chief executive officer is enthusiastic and aware that it can take several years until a globalization program breaks even. "When I hired our first-ever export manager in 1987, he cautioned me that the export department would not make a profit for at least three years—and he was right," says David Ganong, president of New Brunswick candy maker Ganong Bros. Nevertheless, during those three years Ganong laid a strong international foundation, exporting to the United States, Japan, and South Korea, and exploring other Pacific Rim markets. It also opened a joint venture plant in Thailand, which proved almost instantly profitable. "It's vital to have the support of the head of the firm," says Christopher Wilkinson, the man Ganong hired as export sales and marketing manager. "Until there is solid corporate resolve to build up the international side, foreign business might as well be forgotten. Fortunately, David Ganong is totally committed to Ganong's globalization."

---

*A letter of credit is a letter or statement issued by a bank that authorizes the bearer to draw a specific amount of money from that bank or its branches or agents.

In addition, the international side must have the co-operation of the entire company, which is not easily achieved when it is but a minute portion of the business. "For the first five years, until our offshore sales reached $1 million, it was difficult to get employees to care if invoices or shipping documents were done wrong," recalls Glen Sluggett, international sales manager at Milltronics of Peterborough, Ontario. Milltronics, which makes measuring and weighing instruments, ventured into the offshore market in the late 1970s and now has sales exceeding $14 million from outside Canada and the United States. "At first, I felt like a pioneer chopping through a forest, but now people come to me with suggestions as to how to improve and speed up scheduling, shipping, customs clearance, and so on," Sluggett continues.

As Milltronics demonstrates, going global can greatly benefit the balance sheet. But because of the arduous effort involved and the many potential setbacks, companies should not be drawn into the global arena simply to be fashionable. As Hugh Hamilton, a senior executive during Northern Telecom's formative years, warns: "Canadian business people must decide whether there is a good reason to go global and if their product fits the international marketplace. They shouldn't go global simply because they believe far pastures are greener."

Going global requires patient, determined, thorough planning. (Please refer to the footnote below for lists of detailed guidelines provided at the end of this chapter.*) The addition of "International" to the company name is a simple yet highly effective tactic that makes the change in thrust from domestic to global very plain to employees and customers. So that the importance of succeeding internationally will permeate the entire workforce, many firms create a brief, rousing mission statement that is posted throughout their facilities, as well as distributed to employees. The following are excerpts from the statements of four companies that derive more of their revenue from outside Canada than from within.

Alcan Aluminium —Montreal-based; one of Canada's most global companies with operations on six continents.

"To recognize and seek to balance the interests of our share-

---

Common Mistakes by New Exporters, p. 24; Export Planning Checklist, pp. 25–27; Sources of Market Information, pp. 28–30; Form Letter to Trade Commissioners, p. 31; Planning Foreign Business Visits, p. 32; Creditworthiness of Foreign Customers, pp. 33–34. For government and other assistance, see pp. 241–258.

holders, employees, customers, suppliers, governments, and the public at large, while achieving Alcan's business objectives, taking into account the differing social, economic, and environmental aspirations of the countries and communities in which we operate."

Chemetics International —Vancouver-based; has seven hundred employees in Canada, the United States, and Sweden; involved in chemical, fertilizer, mining, and pulp and paper process engineering; derives 70 percent of its revenue from international sales.

"Our mission is to help selected manufacturing industries around the world to solve environmental problems and/or improve productivity by being the leading supplier of proprietary process technology and equipment."

Mobile Data International —Vancouver-based; derives 90 percent of its revenue from outside Canada.

"Our mission is to be a significant and profitable supplier of mobile data communications hardware and software products to businesses on the move within selected international markets by being responsive to customers' needs."

Positron Industries —Montreal-based; products include emergency response telecommunications equipment. Derives 85 percent of its revenue from international sales.

"To design and manufacture quality innovative equipment and systems and market these worldwide. . . . To ensure rapid sales growth and a broader market base by continuously developing new products that address clearly defined market requirements and reflect Positron's constant drive in research and development to achieve world leadership in technology."

While mission statements crystallize corporate objectives, they must be backed up by detailed research. For example, Chemetics concluded it could most readily excel through concentrating on technology that "has an advantage and is an improvement," explains President Stuart Harper. "The key to success is to be the best in selected technologies and systems, rather than average in a broad range." In keeping with this theory, Chemetics has developed a line of products that treat toxic, potentially flammable gases, disinfect water, and safely handle acid, all of which are targeted at the rapidly growing environmental protection market.

When Christopher Wilkinson joined Ganong Bros. in 1987 as the first-ever export sales and marketing manager in the more than one hundred years of the company, he began, not by globe trotting, but rather by carefully plotting strategy in his office. For background, he read voraciously: general magazines for overall world trade information, industry journals for trends in the candy business, and trade directories for lists of potential customers. As well, he obtained free federal government country-by-country booklets on pertinent economic facts, business conduct, and local statutory holidays which render trips futile since companies are closed.

Subsequently, to short-cut the process of trial and error, Wilkinson turned to the federal trade commissioner service for help. "They have their ears to the ground regarding business opportunities, and their assistance adds prestige to your inquiries," he says. Unlike its counterparts in many countries, Canada's trade commissioner service, which is attached to Canada's embassies and consulates around the world, does not charge for its services. Also, the officers are given intensive training in foreign languages, as well as in trade development procedures. Recently, the Department of External Affairs and International Trade, which administers the service, began posting newcomers for tours of duty at the government's regional international trade centres across Canada to learn firsthand in what areas Canadian businesses most need help and how to provide it.

The ways in which trade commissioners can help are many: the selection of effective local agents; credit and business information on potential foreign customers; advice on a country's trade and business practices as well as on licensing and joint ventures; intercession to help solve problems with duties, taxes, and foreign exchange; and recommendations of good translators and interpreters.

The "Government and Other Assistance" appendix to this book provides the addresses in Canada of the international trade development offices of the federal and provincial governments. In addition, it lists the sources of nongovernment assistance: industry associations, guidance that your bank can provide, and centres for international business studies. Many heads of small young firms complain that they lack the personnel and time to read through the government literature, fill out the paperwork for financial assistance, and submit to government cost recovery audits of certain types of financial aid. But surely they should make the time, considering the extensive help they can get. Moreover, their attitude is illogical since they expect people to find time to read *their* own promotional literature.

Of the government programs described in the "Government and Other Assistance" section, two are singled out here as basic to going global: the federal government's Business Opportunities Sourcing System (BOSS) and its Program for Export Market Development (PEMD). BOSS is a computerized data bank on the products, services, and operations of listed Canadian companies. Registration is free. Subscribers include the purchasing departments of Canadian, U.S., and other foreign companies. BOSS-listed companies are automatically included in "WIN Exports" (World Information Network for Exports), a computerized international sourcing system used as a reference by federal government trade development officials in their efforts to bring together Canadian companies and potential foreign customers.

PEMD provides funds annually to about three thousand companies for up to 50 percent of the expenses involved in participation in trade fairs, trade missions, market identification visits, project bidding, and the establishment of U.S. and overseas sales offices. The bulk of the money—59 percent—is earmarked for businesses with under $2 million in annual sales and another 17 percent is set aside for $2–$5 million businesses. It should be borne in mind that the government seeks full repayment for such assistance, albeit on a gradual basis. Sad to say, many companies refuse to repay, thereby depriving other firms of the opportunity to receive PEMD help. Between these ungrateful recalcitrants and those recipients who cannot reimburse due to losses in risky projects for which they obtained PEMD funds, the government recovers only about 35 percent of the annual PEMD payments.

Close to half the requests received by PEMD are for assistance to attend foreign trade shows, indicating that they are the most popular method among Canadian businesses for scouting foreign opportunities. However, careful selection is imperative, considering both the plethora of such shows, with ten thousand annually in North America alone, and the cost. Renting booth space and shipping exhibits are estimated by trade show veterans to represent only half their expenses. The rest of their bills are for hotel accommodation, meals, hospitality, advertising and promotion, and fees for show services such as electricity, plumbing, janitorial, telephone, and security. Therefore, budget-conscious Canadian firms try to get the most for their money by principally participating in large international shows. Local ones, they believe, can be handled capably by their on-the-spot distributors. In such cases, head office provides backup support—brochures, pictures of equipment—but little money; it tells distributors they can pay the bills from their profits.

Besides introducing your products to the world, international trade shows are valuable for the many contacts made. But as Ganong's Wilkinson emphasizes, it is "extremely important to follow up" to consolidate initial good impressions. On his return to Canada, Wilkinson writes to everyone he met, thanking them for visiting Ganong's booth and inquiring whether they will be attending other shows where their itineraries might mesh. He maintains these contacts on an ongoing basis through mailing brochures and press releases, so that distributors and customers "come to feel a part of the Ganong family. You can't just send your price list and say, 'Take it or leave it.' "

Companies interested in going global must invest in a telex and/ or facsimile machine to keep in constant contact with distributors, suppliers, and customers. For firms considering doing business with Third World countries, a telex is essential, since many lack the good telephone service basic to facsimile transmission. Courtesy, of which there is lamentably little these days, is another powerful tool to win and keep friends worldwide. "We all know how frustrating it is waiting for a reply; therefore, even if a definite answer is impossible because I am travelling to develop business or work on an order is still underway, I make it a point that inquiries receive immediate responses explaining the circumstances," says Richard L'Abbé, president, Med-Eng Systems of Ottawa. Med-Eng, which makes bomb disposal helmets, has grown from a shoestring operation in 1982 to an exporter to 50 countries.

Firms whose global aspirations encompass direct investment as well as exports have several options: startup branches, mergers, acquisitions, or joint ventures with foreign partners in research, manufacturing, marketing, or a combination of the three. Many of the world's most populous countries, including China, India, the Soviet Union, South Korea, and much of Central and South America either bar foreign companies or severely limit their scope unless they have a local partner. Joint ventures make possible the sharing of costs, risks, and expertise in technology and marketing. Because each participant has an ownership stake and, therefore, an interest in the profits or losses, the incentive to succeed is often greater than is the case with distributors and licensees who represent a number of firms and, consequently, cannot devote all their attention to just one. On the other hand, joint ventures, unlike mergers, leave the partners independent in their other activities, with the result that they are a mixture of allies and competitors.

Usually, joint-venture ownership is split 50:50, but this balance of power can deteriorate into dissension unless there is agreement on objectives and management style. Such was the unhappy experience of Electrohome, a manufacturer of video electronic products located in Kitchener, Ontario. What it regarded as "a marriage made in heaven" with a British parts supplier fell apart within months because management problems at the supplier disenchanted Electrohome. "For joint ventures to succeed, the partners must be of comparable size, balance one another in what they bring to the arrangement, and have similar outlooks," observes John Pollock, Electrohome's chairman, president, and CEO. "It is very difficult to find partners with complementary skills and assets. If a partner is too small, your side can end up as the banker; conversely, if too big, your company can get squashed."

Market selection and marketing are two more areas to which businesses with global ambitions must devote considerable attention. Canadian companies that are veterans of the international marketplace stress that success depends on a focused approach to target markets. They also point out that patience is vital because convincing potential foreign customers of your sincere interest in their market can take years. In addition, some countries erect invisible trade barriers to prevent unwelcome competition to their domestic firms. These barriers—local content regulations, voltage and testing requirements, and long drawn-out custom clearance procedures—can be as tough to overcome as actual tariff protection.

Moreover, due to them, obtaining economies of scale from manufacturing standardized products for worldwide sale is impossible. The only consolation is that overseas firms encounter some of these difficulties in selling to Canada. Another factor to consider is whether you find it morally acceptable to do business in countries where corruption is rampant, human rights are violated, or boycotts of other nations are the price for getting deals.

In order to build up foreign sales, exporters must be prepared to travel extensively. Government trade officials advise that one side of business cards should be translated. Some firms include a picture on the cards of the sales representative who will be making the trip and send the cards in advance with promotional material, thereby preventing embarrassment if the imagined and real appearance do not tally.

Veterans of the world business circuit readily admit that the glamour of globe-trotting is quickly erased by fatigue, loneliness for loved ones, and longing for regular hours and home cooking. Therefore, most say they find three weeks the maximum they can endure at any one time. Less than three weeks, however, is often pointless because of the time involved in getting to a place and, at the end, preparing for the home-bound trip. Besides being a physical strain, such expeditions also are a drain on finances. It is not unusual for one week to cost $10,000, taking into account plane fare, accommodation, meals, hospitality, and car rental. Thus, experienced international firms would rather postpone a trip than try to enter a market before they are fully prepared.

Another lesson they have learned is that big business can be derived from small markets. For example, Montreal-based Eicon Technology (systems for personal computers) has found businesses in Finland, with a population just one-fifth of Canada, to be among its biggest customers. All told, Eicon has sold more than three thousand units to the Bank of Finland (the nation's biggest bank), the country's railway, and the largest computer company. For its part, Ganong Bros. appointed an agent in Malaysia despite that country's low level of chocolate consumption. In so doing, Ganong was looking at the future, rather than the present, because Malaysia's standard of living and buying power are rapidly growing.

To get their message across, an increasing number of Canadian companies are creating catchy slogans that sum up their international aims as well as their products. For example, Fell-Fab, which is based in Hamilton, Ontario, makes coverings for airplane wings and seats, nuclear reactor insulating pads, storage containers, elevator protective pads, awnings, boat covers, tents, and newspaper carrier bags. It says of itself: "We cover the world." Klöckner Stadler Hurter describes its international engineering services as "Your direct access to the world market." Other firms print photographs of their equipment beside their address on envelopes.

Novices, and even long-established firms, too often assume they can transplant their successful Canadian formula to the United States. This assumption is erroneous; the marked differences in selling in Canada and the United States require tailor-made tactics for each country. Two well-known giant Canadian companies that paid the penalty for not developing specialized strategies are

Canadian Tire and Dylex, the clothing retailer whose chains include Fairweather, Tip Top, and Big Steel.

Canadian Tire withdrew from the U.S. market in 1985, three years after purchasing White Stores, a Texas automotive supplier chain. Canadian Tire had inaccurately judged White Stores as a duplicate of itself, since both were widespread groups carrying similar merchandise. But behind these superficial similarities were marked contrasts in store décor, layout, management, promotional methods, inventory control, and the degree of computerization (Canadian Tire used more sophisticated systems). They also differed in store locations: Canadian Tire's outlets are concentrated in growing metropolitan areas; White's at that time was under-stored in comparable-sized American cities.

Canadian Tire also fell into the trap of regarding a money-losing company as a worthy buy, because it was priced low. But, as we all know, if a deal seems too good to be true, it usually is. When all White's losses continued to mount, Canadian Tire realized that its apparent bargain was actually an albatross. By 1985, it was fighting a losing battle and retreated from the United States.

For its part, Dylex has had mixed results in the United States. The lesson that can be derived from its experiences is that a targeted strategy fares far better than an across-the-board one. In 1988, Dylex discontinued Brooks Fashion Stores and in the following year, Foxmoor, both middle-of-the-road women's wear chains, a segment of the market in which the competition is fierce. Conversely, Wet Seal, which is closely focused in merchandise and in location—casual moderately priced women's wear sold in the western United States and Florida—has grown from 18 stores in 1984 when Dylex acquired it to more than 90.

Another mistake is to take a high profile for granted. Because their names are well known in Canada, many firms believe they automatically will be well known in the United States. Such arrogance quickly leads to problems, as Montreal-based Sico, the largest Canadian-owned paint manufacturer, can attest. When it first entered New England under its Canadian trademarks, consumers steered clear of its paints because the names meant nothing to them. When Sico switched to "Sturbridge," the name of a community in southern Massachusetts, it began to do better.

Some Canadian companies prefer to sell outside Canada directly through their own sales force; others, with less money, prefer to commission locally based agents or distributors; and still others employ both methods. Distributors take title to the goods they handle; agents do not. Careful selection and intensive training are vital for success. "Finding suitable representatives is a problem for any major exporter, as is keeping their motivation on a high level; you have to keep the pressure on all the time," says Michael Roumi, export sales manager at Winnipeg-based Controlled Environments (Conviron), which makes agricultural research equipment.

The federal and provincial trade commissioners posted around the world can speed up the selection process through their recommendations in trade journals and advertisements; referrals by other companies are useful sources, too. Nevertheless, it is far easier for well-established Canadian firms to reach agreement with well-regarded foreign distributors than it is for newcomers who often are saddled with years of hiring and firing until a satisfactory lineup is achieved.

For example, it took ten years for Milltronics to develop a distributor network with which it was happy. International Sales Manager Glen Sluggett compiled a two-page "points of consideration" for deciding whether to hire a distributor. The points include:

- *Jurisdiction*: appointment for only one country
- *Products*: all Milltronics product lines must be carried; direct competitive products are forbidden, although Milltronics does hire companies that previously represented competitors, because of their experience
- *Targets*: annual, mutually agreed-upon targets plus five-year forecasts which Milltronics uses as a guide for production planning
- *Training*: Milltronics trains distributors at its Peterborough, Ontario, headquarters, as well as at their facilities

In most cases, distributors pay the travel fare to attend training programs in Canada, and their hosts take care of accommodation and meals. Generally, product training sessions last a day or so, while those on servicing can run for one to two weeks. Frequently, annual meetings of all distributors also are held. Regular follow-up is important, too, in the form of brochures (translated, if necessary), press releases, telephone calls, and facsimile and telex messages. "In effect, you must form alliances with your distributors," says Clive Milo, international manager at Ontario-based Edwards, a leading manufacturer of fire alarms and other signals. Adds Richard L'Abbé of Med-Eng Systems: "Agents and distributors should be treated like royalty because they are your eyes and ears abroad. You should visit them frequently and invite them to accompany you on visits to clients, thereby enhancing their prestige. In turn, they will be more zealous about promoting your products."

International success also largely depends on whether the right managers are chosen at home and abroad. As you will note, none of the companies described in this book, even if big, have large head-office staffs. In the case of the smaller firms, the owner-president doubles as international sales manager or, if there is such a manager, assists in the travelling and promotion. "Firms like to do business with the owners because they regard that personal contact as a guarantee for the deal," points out Fell-Fab's chairman, Donald Fell. Practising what he preaches, Fell spends much of the year in foreign countries drumming up business. When he is home at head office in Hamilton, Ontario, his son, who is vice-president of international marketing, embarks on the global circuit.

Companies with small international departments can still sell to much of the world, despite not being able to be everywhere at once. For instance, Conviron exports to 70 countries, but Michael Roumi and a technician who do the travelling for the company visit perhaps half these places each year. Generally, they alternate between Europe and the Far East. "It can be done with a limited staff, provided you have priorities as to what countries to concentrate on," Roumi advises.

Rather than parachute in Canadians, companies with foreign branches find it more effective to appoint nationals as heads of local operations and/or to transfer executives from one outpost to another to reap the most benefit from their expertise. For example, the wide mix of nationalities among Alcan's senior executives reflects the company's global nature. Chairman David Morton, now a Canadian citizen, is British-born and worked at Alcan in the United Kingdom for 23 years until moving to head office in Montreal in 1977. President Jacques Bougie is French Canadian. The British division is headed by a Canadian, and the American by an Englishman. The chief legal officer and the controller, located in Montreal, are from India.

To ensure that they select suitable managers for transfers from one country to another, an increasing number of companies put candidates through psychology tests to assess tolerance, flexibility, patience, adaptability, initiative, cross-cultural skills, and empathy.

They also take into account whether the executive has a happy family life, because the stresses of adjusting to a new culture can worsen already troubled family relationships.

Just as an increase in the number of non-Canadians in senior management serves to broaden companies' global perspective, the appointment to their boards of directors of knowledgeable people from other nations would also be beneficial. Unfortunately, few Canadian firms have cosmopolitan boards, and when they do include non-Canadians, they are apt to choose Americans or Britons. If Canadians are really intent on becoming truly global, they should extend board memberships to the Japanese and Europeans as well.

The recurring theme of successful Canadian-based international companies is that they pursue a tightly focused strategy. Most of them, however, learned the wisdom of this technique the hard way—through setbacks encountered by failing to delineate a clearcut plan. What follows are the experiences of five companies that represent the evolution.

Capsule Technology International (1990)

In its short life, Capsule Technology, a Windsor, Ontario manufacturer of capsules primarily used for pharmaceutical drugs, has undergone a rollercoaster ride. In 1986, just four years after its formation, it won three federal government awards: a Canada Export Award and Canada Business Excellence awards for marketing and entrepreneurship. Two years later, Capsule experienced its first-ever loss ($9.4 million) and recorded a debt of almost $7 million, compared to $480,000 the previous year. In 1989, as the losses continued, Capsule reverted to private ownership after two years of being publicly traded. Later that year, the company went into receivership.

Founder and owner Stephen Lukas then sold the company to a private Toronto investor, effective the beginning of 1990, which explains the "1990" in its name. Lukas was retained as president, but to restore Capsule to profitability, the new owner reduced head-office employment from 100 to 60, lowered management salaries, sold a branch plant in Nova Scotia, and placed another in Puerto Rico into U.S. "Chapter 11" bankruptcy protection while restructuring it. In addition, Capsule's product line was reorganized to items less costly to manufacture. All these efforts resulted in a 1990 profit.

It is Capsule's original main product that caused most of its difficulties. Initially, it concentrated on "turnkey" systems—the manufacture and installation of equipment, production tests, and the training of customers' staff. Unfortunately, every time Capsule sold such a system, it shrank the market for first-time sales. Also, its concentration on developing countries exposed it to downswings in their economies and to restrictions by their central banks on the allocation of limited foreign exchange reserves for exports. These errors in marketing strategy became glaringly evident in 1988. For the first time in Capsule's six-year history, it signed no contracts for international sales of equipment due to uncertain economic and political conditions in some countries and the inability of clients in other countries to secure sufficient funding.

What made the crunch worse was that it occurred just as Capsule completed its Puerto Rico manufacturing division. It was a sound choice of location, since many of the world's major pharmaceutical firms, attracted by Puerto Rico's tax incentives, have plants there. But Capsule could not begin production when the plant was completed because it was still awaiting required validation from the U.S. Food and Drug Administration.

Consequently, Capsule had to ship finished products from Windsor to Puerto Rico, cancelling out any expected gains from the Caribbean plant. The equipment it sent had been earmarked for international sales to outsiders, representing lost sales of $8 million. Simultaneously, Capsule's diversification in Canada into fish-oil capsules, made at a plant in Nova Scotia, turned out to be ill-timed; the plant came into production just as the fish market began to slump.

Capsule might have reined in its growth sooner if its accounting methods had been more conservative. "It expanded too quickly and spread too wide without sufficient financial backing and management strength," says Executive Vice-President Gordon Moore, a ten-year finance manager hired in 1988 to overhaul Capsule's financial systems. He forced Capsule to recognize potential problems faster by no longer deferring and amortizing costs associated with preproduction until production commenced. Instead, Capsule now charges them up in the year they occur.

Thanks to this more realistic appraisal of its finances and the pruning of its operations, Capsule became profitable again in 1990. The chief change on the production side was a shift from turnkey equipment projects to ways of adding value to the capsules themselves, a cheaper and safer diversification route. For example, Capsule now makes bath oil and vitamin-filled capsules, as well as liquid-filled ones that splatter on impact in war games. Thus, by refining its marketing strategy to less ambitious but steadier business, Capsule has strengthened itself.

Sico

Montreal-based Sico is Quebec's biggest paint manufacturer and Canada's second largest, following British-owned Glidden/C-I-L. Its experience shows the importance to a major Canadian firm with a straightforward product of going global. It also demonstrates the challenges. Established in 1937 with $450 in capital, Sico had sales of $208 million in 1989 when the company decided it must break free of its parochialism. To guide it into the global marketplace, it hired as president and CEO, Ed Prévost, previously head of Carling–O'Keefe Breweries in Quebec and then of Molson–O'Keefe in that province following the 1989 merger of the two brewers. Sico believed it would benefit from Prévost's experience, both because beer and paint are consumer products whose sales largely depend on image, and because his promotion of beer exports acquainted him with foreign markets.

Sico sells the bulk of its paint in Quebec, and Prévost's summary of the ramifications is applicable to many Canadian companies which are still principally regional, notwithstanding remarkable growth. "There is nothing wrong with being a regional company, but a public corporation is under pressure from its shareholders to grow and generate greater earnings per share," he points out. "Also, there is the element of pride that your firm's products are superior and, therefore, should be made available to a wider audience."

However, even more important than pride and pressure from shareholders is the question of survival in an overpopulated industry, a concern these days in many fields besides paint manufacturing. "The world's ten largest paint manufacturers, which now have 30 percent of worldwide volume, are expected to have 50 percent by the turn of the century," Prévost continues. "As this will largely be accomplished through takeovers and mergers, the number of players will decrease. For small to medium-sized firms like Sico, the danger of this absorption process is that they could be swallowed. We at Sico do not want this to happen."

Sico is weighing a number of strategies to preserve its independence. From the product viewpoint, it is examining which market segments offer the most growth potential. It is not an easy choice because, although paint is an uncomplicated product, it has to be formulated for many uses: electrical, automotive, marine, floors, walls; solvents, latexes, refinishes. There are also thousands of nuances regarding shadings. Recently, as part of its focusing, Sico became the distributor in Quebec and the Maritimes for a major U.S. manufacturer of industrial maintenance coatings, a new market segment for Sico. In research and development, Sico participates in two international trade associations, geared to small and medium-sized paint manufacturers, in which the funding of research is shared and the results distributed only to members.

When Prévost joined Sico, it already was selling to the United States, but just on a small scale. "To say that Sico has a U.S. operation when it merely covers New England and derives just 9 percent of its sales from there is stretching it," Prévost comments trenchantly. Nevertheless, despite the proximity to the United States, Prévost says it is imperative that Sico "not be seduced by the U.S. market to the point where it ignores others." Thus, he also is scouting opportunities in Europe where due to "insecurity in the industry, there are many firms searching to be bought."

Atco

With sales of more than $1 billion, Calgary-based Atco (portable shelters, oil and gas exploration, natural gas production, electrical power generation) is one of Alberta's biggest corporations. Starting in the late 1940s and continuing for 40 years, it also was one of its most global, ploughing its revenue from international sales into domestic expansion.

But now that it is a well-established, mature company, Atco no longer has to race here, there and everywhere for business, a costly endeavour since the supportive administrative structure cannot be easily dismantled when no big international projects arise. Having decided it will only pursue global contracts that will be of benefit instead of business just for the sake of business, Atco now relies on exploratory telephone calls as a substitute for expensive in-person visits that sometimes lead nowhere.

It also has determined it can be most competitive through concentrating its energy on Canada and the United States, and selecting offshore opportunities carefully. For example, it recently acquired a 45 percent interest in a newly formed British power-generating firm in order to gain a strong foothold in the U.K.'s recently privatized electricity industry. But most of its attention is tightly focused on North America. "As we pursued internationalization, we overlooked opportunities emerging under our noses," says Kingsley Purdie, group president, manufacturing and leasing, Atco Enterprises. The division, which makes portable shelters and oversees Atco's energy operations in Western Canada, accounts for 42 percent of overall net earnings.

Primarily, Atco failed to recognize the boom in the space rental business in the United States to a $1 billion industry, caused largely by the growing "special events" market such as conferences and conventions. Hitherto, Atco had concentrated on temporary accommodation for classrooms and construction crews. When it finally awoke to the possibilities in the United States, it dithered over whether to invest directly to have a major onsite presence.

"Even though the western U.S. is much closer than major cities in eastern Canada, the company had avoided investing there, save for small operations in California and Texas that it closed in the 1980s," Purdie says. "I kept arguing 'Do the Rockies run east and west?' in my effort to point out that southward expansion was a natural step to take." In 1989, Atco took a big step with its $12 million purchase of a southern California and Arizona space rentals firm. It was selected because the California portion of its business alone gave Atco access to a population equivalent to 60 percent of all Canada. Another U.S. acquisition is also likely.

Thus, although Atco still exports offshore, it has found in its version of "you can't be all things to all people" that the most lucrative market can be close to home rather than across the world.

Emco

London, Ontario-based Emco exemplifies two important aspects of global business planning. First, it demonstrates the value of targeted strategy. In Canada, Emco is the country's largest manufacturer of stainless steel sinks and faucets as well as of fibreboard products and the second largest of roofing. Such prominence could theoretically be used as a springboard into the international marketplace, but Emco has chosen not to do so. "Tastes in style differ," explains president and CEO John Brant. Also, Emco has been owned since 1973 by Michigan-based Masco Corporation, the foremost U.S. manufacturer of faucets, as well as a major producer of whirlpools, shower units, furniture, and fabrics. Thus, the only product line that Emco sells globally as well as domestically is its petroleum-related one. This line includes such equipment as service station nozzles, tank trunk fittings, tank monitoring devices, and marine loading arms. On average, these products, which have universally standard applications, account for approximately 9 percent of sales and 16 percent of profits.

The other significant aspect of Emco's international planning typifies a trend that likely will become more pronounced as business globalization increases: the location of worldwide headquarters in the country where the most business is done rather than at the corporation's base. Although Emco's petroleum-related products are manufactured in seven countries—Canada, the United States, the U.K., Germany, France, Japan, and Australia—and exported to one hundred, half of all sales are made in the United States. Thus, in 1985, Emco transferred its international head office from London to Raleigh, North Carolina, the site of its U.S. headquarters; the Canadian president of the U.S. operations was given the added responsibility of looking after non-U.S. activities as well. Like this executive, most of his assistants are Canadian. They are supplemented by an on-the-spot European marketing co-ordinator.

Brant cites several advantages from this relocation. "Expenses were cut because London no longer needed its international staff of four senior executives, and the elimination of what was regarded as interference has led to greater co-operation and aggressiveness," he says. In turn, the co-ordination has smoothed the process of new product development, essential in the petroleum-related business. "Fifty percent of our sales are from products that did not exist five years ago," Brant comments. Further, with the plants in each country encouraged to concentrate on what they do best, the Canadian division has been able to focus on lines in which it excels: short production runs of nozzles for specialty purposes, such as for planes and buses.

Combined, all these benefits flowing from Emco's restructuring contributed to 40 months of improved profit in the petroleum-related division. The division suffered a setback in 1989 due to one-time difficulties in the United States related primarily to the costs involved in the introduction of a new product, but since then it has rebounded.

When Masco bought Emco in 1973 from the prominent Ivey family of London, it pledged not to break up the company, and it has kept its word. In addition, it practises a hands-off approach. Only three of its executives are on Emco's 12-person board, and Brant reports to Masco only once per quarter over and above board meetings. Otherwise, Emco is on its own save for consulting Masco's European controller about tax and currency trends and its international marketing group for market analyses.

Fell-Fab

Established in 1952, Fell-Fab epitomizes the progression and tactics of small-to-medium-sized Canadian companies as they move into international markets. The company went global early in its history, evolving from local business in the Hamilton, Ontario area, to the national market in its fifth year, and into the international in its sixth. It succeeded through a tightly focused strategy: industrial protective coverings for airplane seats, wings, and baggage carts, as well as for boats, sports fields, and trucks; carnival and utility tents; nuclear reactor insulating pads; elevator protective pads; and storage containers for bulk products. Its market selection has been based on careful, realistic analysis. It is prepared to redesign products rapidly in order to satisfy customers' requests and differing requirements from country to country.

As a result, Fell-Fab now has sales in excess of $10 million, 60 percent of which is derived from exports, and the company has consistently had profits throughout its nearly four decades. Moreover, the company has won business achievement awards from the federal and Ontario governments, as well as from the Ontario Chamber of Commerce. But behind the prizes lies what founder and chairman Donald Fell describes as "a trudge—a long, slow process."

It began with Fell carefully appraising what countries have in common that would require coverings: a national airline or, if not, several big regional ones, as in the United States; chemical production; military forces; and a need to transport free-flowing materials such as water, grain, and sand. He deliberately identified several market segments so that any downswing in one would, he hoped, be offset by strong sales in the others. He also established realistic market share expectations as to the maximum business Fell-Fab could obtain from customers, in view of the fact that customers do not want to take the risk of buying from just one supplier in case it is shut down by a strike or fire, sells out, or closes down.

Just as important as deciding with whom he wanted to do business, Fell determined what market sectors he wished to avoid. For instance, he ruled out hauling liquid milk because it is difficult cleaning containers afterwards. He also does not ship wines since vintners frequently claim the flavour is harmed during transit. Nor does he handle products that are prone to liability lawsuits nor those he believes could discredit Fell-Fab's image.

Stressing that exporters must recognize the sharp difference between marketing and selling, Fell says he undertook extensive preliminary marketing analyses as to the most receptive places for Fell-Fab's products. Like most Canadian exporters, he began in the United States. In his case, he had the good fortune to start when the Canadian dollar was low in terms of U.S. currency. When it rose to a point where Canadian exporters were at a premium disadvantage, Fell went to other English-speaking countries. Then, when the dollar was again in Canada's favour, he returned to the United States. In recent years, as the dollar has climbed to what exporters regard as an uncompetitive level, Fell-Fab has elected to remain in the United States in order to maintain its market position. Today, as a mature company with exports to many countries, it can readily withstand adverse fluctuations in Canadian–U.S. dollar ratios.

Fell also expanded his international business gradually, rather than depleting his resources by going in all directions at once. Only after Fell-Fab was securely established during the 1960s and 1970s in the United States, the U.K., Australia, and New Zealand did he branch into Asia and Africa, doing so in the 1980s, and then into Eastern Europe, beginning with Hungary in 1988. Today, Africa is Fell-Fab's biggest customer, followed by the United States. How Fell developed business in Africa demonstrates the precision in market strategy that distinguishes successful exporters.

Like most people, Fell was well aware that Africa has a great need for the packaging and storage of food products. But he also realized that he had to acquire much more in-depth knowledge before proceeding. "I had to determine what they really needed, what they could afford, who could afford to buy it, and how fast we would receive payment," he says. "Receipt of payment takes much longer with Third World countries because letters of credit are used and it can take several months for them to be cleared. By contrast, clearance is much faster with U.S. customers since they pay by cheque."

Fell obtained answers to many of his questions from world food monitoring organizations and then visited Africa to gain his own impressions. As there are more than 50 countries in Africa, Fell decided it would be best to sell to a handful instead of attempting to cover the entire continent. He settled on five to begin with— Ethiopia, the Sudan, Kenya, Ghana, and Nigeria—and ultimately intends to export to 12 altogether. "Exporters must realize they can't cover everything because of the expense of exploring and building up business," he says. "Also, in developing countries, plane service is less reliable, which means you can miss appointments to which much planning was devoted. Appointments are hard to get and to replace, and it is expensive waiting around for them to be rescheduled." Another consideration is the stability of a country. "In Third World countries when governments change, it is usually a major upset and, as the saying goes, 'To the victors go the spoils,' " Fell points out. "Or the country's economy can slow down in the aftermath. Thus, exporters must weigh the fact that Third World nations need everything against the possibility of deals being harder to make due to government changes."

Selling to Africa has required Fell-Fab to be flexible in its designing, since products suitable for developed countries must be modified for Third World ones. For example, North American roads can easily support trucks carrying loads weighing 20,000 litres, but Ethiopia's roads cannot. Using its computer-aided design and manufacturing programming, Fell-Fab was able to ascertain within hours that it could easily scale down the size of its storage containers to an 8,000-litre capacity. It also had to redesign the containers so they would not be in danger of punctures from the huge thorns of African acacia trees.

Canadian companies that are proud of their global accomplishments should consider applying for the federal government's Canada Export Awards. Applicants must have at least three years of export experience, and branch plants as well as Canadian-owned firms are eligible. Since the award's establishment in 1983, 74 percent of the winners have been small-to-medium-sized firms. Another federal government prize for which exporters might want to apply is the Canada Award for Business Excellence. This is awarded for environmental protection, entrepreneurship, industrial design, innovation, invention, labour/management cooperation, marketing, productivity, quality, and small business. As with the Canada Export Award, both Canadian companies and foreign-owned subsidiaries are eligible.

Neither is a cash award; the winners receive plaques. (For more information on both, see page 250–51). Winners say the awards enhance their credibility and provide prestige, particularly in dealing with foreign governments and selling within Canada. Some, however, downplay the award in their foreign business, especially with the United States, because they do not want to draw attention to themselves as outsiders.

For Canadian businesses, going global can have great rewards, but as Donald Fell observes, "International markets are the most expensive and time consuming to develop." Hence, a clearly defined sense of purpose and of direction are vital for success.

COMMON MISTAKES MADE BY NEW EXPORTERS

1. Failure to obtain qualified export counselling and to develop a master international marketing plan before starting an export business.

2. Insufficient commitment by top management to overcome the initial difficulties and financial requirements of exporting.

3. Insufficient care in selecting overseas agents or distributors.

4. Chasing orders from around the world instead of establishing a base for profitable operations and orderly growth.

5. Neglecting export business when the domestic market booms.

6. Failure to treat international distributors on an equal basis with domestic counterparts.

7. Unwillingness to modify products to meet regulations or cultural preferences of other countries.

8. Failure to print services, sales, and warranty messages in locally understood languages.

Source: External Affairs and International Trade Canada.

EXPORT PLANNING CHECKLIST

The Market

- What are the tariff barriers, import quotas, and internal taxes for the product? Have they been subject to frequent changes in the past?
- What is the long-term potential, based on future growth, for each sector?
- Is there any domestic production, and how competitive is it?
- Who are the major foreign competitors and what is their market share? Which foreign competitor has the largest market share and why?
- In what areas, if any, does the product excel over the competition's?
- Does the cost of transportation, because of market conditions, make the product uncompetitive?
- Is the market politically and economically stable?
- Is the currency convertible?
- Are there government-imposed restrictions on foreign exchange availability?
- What are the possibilities of countertrade being demanded? (In countertrade, a sale to an importer is conditional upon a reciprocal purchase by the exporter.)

The Product

- Can the product be sold in the target market, or does a modification have to be made and at what cost?
- What size, colour, and design are preferred by the users?
- Will assembly have to take place in the target market, and is resident expertise available?

(cont'd)

- Will there be a need for after-sales servicing? If so, are there presently companies in the target market that can provide this service, or will locals have to be trained?
- If the product is new, has it been adequately tested?
- What are the packaging and labelling requirements?
- What technical specifications does the product have to meet in the target market?
- Does the product meet local health and safety standards?

The Price

- What is the bottom line on pricing and what is the profitablity at various pricing levels?
- Can the pricing match or better the competition and still have a healthy profit margin?
- If the pricing cannot match the competition, can it still sell because of product superiority, ability to deliver, and after-sales servicing?
- What are the normal terms of payment extended by competitors?

Distribution

- What methods of distribution are available in the country, and which is the most reliable and cost efficient?
- What markets are normally sought by middlemen in the industry?
- What promotional assistance is normally provided by middlemen?
- Who are the main importers? What are their reputations, capabilities, and financial strengths?
- Does the country specify the type of distribution allowed?

- Will an exclusive distributorship or agency enhance market potential?
- How are the goods to be packed for transportation?
- What types of carriers are needed? What are the transportation costs? How frequent and reliable are the various methods of transportation to overseas and domestic markets?
- What are the port and warehousing facilities like?
- Is there an agent capable of providing satisfactory technical services?
- Do competitors control the distribution channels, making market entry difficult?

Promotion

- What are the types and costs of advertising in the individual markets, and which are best suited to the needs of the product?
- What are the advertising practices of competitors? What percentage of their gross profit goes into advertising and in what media do they advertise?
- Where and when do trade fairs and exhibitions take place, and what opportunities exist for participating in them?

Source: *Export Guide—A Practical Approach,* External Affairs and International Affairs Canada.

SOURCES OF MARKET INFORMATION

Market Data

Tariffs, rates, import policy, customs requirements, product classification, internal taxes

Sources

- External Affairs and International Trade Canada
- Canadian Trade Commissioner Service
- Embassy/consulate of country in Canada
- U.S.A. only: *U.S. Customs Directory,*
                1301 Constitution Avenue N.W.
                Washington, D.C. 20229

Export/import statistics, quantities imported from various countries, main exports, growth in market

Sources

- Department of External Affairs and International Trade Canada (geographic trade development divisions)
- *Yearbook of International Trade Statistics.* New York: United Nations
- *U.N. Monthly Bulletin of Statistics.* New York: United Nations
- *Statistics Canada Merchandise Exports Annual.* Ottawa: Statistics Canada. Catalogue No. 65-202

Economic/Geographic

Economic indicators, income, purchasing power, domestic production, consumption, product usage levels.

Source

- *U.N. Statistical Yearbook Annual.* New York: United Nations.
- *The Monthly Bulletin of Statistics.* New York: United Nations.

Country

Basic information such as size, population, neighbouring countries, chief ports, air routes, business hours, holidays, currency, weights and measures, electric current used, languages, travel facilities, banks, business practices and customs, climate

Sources

- Guides for Canadian Exporters (various country titles available) from External Affairs and International Trade Canada
- *Overseas Business Reports.* Washington: U.S. Department of Commerce, International Trade Administration, Washington, D.C. 20230
- *The Times of London Atlas of the World*
- *Handbook of International Trade & Development Statistics* Supplement UNCTAD/GATT, Geneva, Switzerland

Distribution

Foreign importers, trading houses, distributors, agents, wholesalers, retailers, buyers, et cetera

Sources

- Trade or commercial directories published by the country
- *World Marketing Directory.* Write to: Dun & Bradstreet, Exchange Place, Jersey City, New Jersey, U.S.A.

Transportation, shipping costs, routes, sea and air shipping costs

Sources

- Freight forwarders: domestic and foreign
- Shipping companies
- Airlines

(cont'd)

Prices

Sources

- Monthly commodity price bulletin, UNCTAD/GATT, Geneva
- *Commodity Trade & Price Trends:* World Bank. Baltimore: Johns Hopkins University Press
- *Yearbook of International Trade Statistics*
- *International Financial Statistics.* Washington, D.C.: International Monetary Fund
- *Handbook of International Trade & Development Statistics.* Supplement available from the United Nations

Finance and Documentation

Financing of exports, foreign exchange, terms of payment, handling of documents, et cetera

Sources

- Export Development Corporation, 151 O'Connor Street, P.O. Box 655, Ottawa, Canada K1P 5T9
- Local bankers: domestic and foreign
- *Trade Financing.* Available from: Euromoney Publications Ltd., Nestor House, Playhouse Yard, London, EC4, England
- *Incoterms.* Available from: Canadian Chamber of Commerce handbook, International Chamber of Commerce, 1080 Beaver Hall Hill, Montreal, Quebec H2Z 1T2

Source: *Export Guide—A Practical Approach*, External Affairs and International Trade Canada

FORM FOR COMPANY LETTER
TO
CANADIAN GOVERNMENT
TRADE COMMISSIONER POSTS

(A directory of the posts, with names and addresses, can be obtained at an International Trade Centre office.)

1. *Brief History of Company*
    Provide company background information which will enable Trade Commissioners to evaluate experience and capability.

2. *List Products*
    Where available, enclose six copies of product literature. List the salient advantages of your equipment.

3. *Marketing*
    A brief description of domestic marketing organization, i.e., whether you currently market direct to retailers or use distributors, manufacturers' agents, et cetera.
    List main Canadian customers so that the trade commissioners understand the type of companies with which you deal.

4. *Price*
    Quote all prices Cost Insurance Freight (C.I.F.).

5. *Marketing Information*
    Detail the marketing questions you wish answered, i.e., who manufactures similar equipment in the area; is a similar product imported; in what volume and from where; who is main competition?

6. *Assistance*
    Spell out the type of assistance you require, whether it is recommended distributors, contacts in retail chains, et cetera.

PLANNING FOREIGN BUSINESS VISITS

To maximize the benefits of foreign visits, carefully plan every phase in advance. The Canadian trade commissioner can provide invaluable service in this area. Your product's competitive features, the anticipated export price, and promotional literature should be forwarded to the trade commissioner well in advance of the proposed visit.

Give the trade commissioner time to put together a list of suggested contacts and agents and distributors. Discuss the suggested contacts with Canadian exporters who are familiar with the market to obtain their views. Contact the Export Development Corporation to see if it has had any previous experience with potential clients, and request a Dun & Bradstreet report. Once you are satisfied that the contacts are reputable, set up the appointments, and do not hurry to see your customers right after landing in the country. It is important to be well rested and fresh when talking to prospective clients. Travel and hotel reservations should be confirmed before leaving Canada. Determine if you require a visa along with your passport to enter the country. It is wise to take a few extra copies of your photograph for visa purposes in the event you wish to visit a neighbouring country. In addition, take business cards, company letterhead, samples of the products (if feasible), descriptive brochures, pamphlets and photographs of the products, and a pocket dictaphone for recording notes as you travel.

Source: *Export Guide—A Practical Approach,* External Affairs and International Trade Canada

CREDITWORTHINESS OF FOREIGN CUSTOMERS

You must be sure of the creditworthiness of individual buyers and their countries. The evaluation of a country's risk is a basic step in the development of credit policy. Here are items that you need to know about buyers' countries. As this information is sometimes difficult to acquire, approach your bank or the Export Development Corporation for assistance.

A detailed assessment of the country along the following lines will indicate how stable a market it is.

Economy

- Gross Domestic Product and per capita income
- Balance of payments
- International indebtedness
- Currency convertibility
- Exchange controls
- Inflation rate
- Unemployment
- Trade agreements, including current trade with Canada
- Trade restrictions—import quotas and tariffs
- Customs rates, preferential treatment
- Level of industrial development
- Population size, distribution
- Skill and wage level of workforce
- Income distribution
- Labelling and packaging requirements

Political and legal Factors

- Form of government, stability
- Attitude towards foreign business, especially Canadian
- International credit record
- Fiscal and monetary policies

(cont'd)

- Tax laws and equity in their administration
- Fairness of courts, collectibility of debts

The next step is to evaluate your buyer's credit standing: major considerations are length of time in business, the size of operations and amount of importing, financial strength, credit rating and ability to pay.

There are numerous ways to find this information:

- The major banks, through their overseas branches and correspondents, can usually obtain information on any publicly owned company.
- The Trade Commissioner Service can tell you if the buyer is known to other Canadian companies and may put you in contact with local suppliers.
- You may directly contact exporters who have done business with your importer. Their comments are a good indicator of the buyer's overall reliability.
- Dun & Bradstreet International will investigate a foreign firm and submit a credit report. There is a charge for Dun & Bradstreet reports, however, and they are only as reliable as the information they can assemble from foreign sources.
- The U.S. Department of Commerce publishes the *World Traders' Data Report* with information on foreign firms, covering their size, operations, background, bank references, et cetera.

Source: *Export Guide—A Practical Approach* External Affairs and International Trade Canada.

C H A P T E R

2

Niche Strategy

"What with the Free Trade Agreement with the United States, post-Europe 1992, and the Far East bloc, unless Canadian business is lean, mean, and efficient, it won't survive. To survive, it must look at niche markets because overall, it lacks the economies of scale to compete against the U.S., Japan, and Europe."

Richard L'Abbé,
President,
Med-Eng Systems,
Ottawa

A substantial—and heartening—number of Canadian firms are niche-market pioneers worldwide and/or revenue leaders in a wide array of activities, ranging from industrial measurement instruments to bomb disposal protection helmets, tourist submarines, window blinds, sportswear, and housecleaning services. Niche strategy is specialization in narrowly focused products or service areas. Or as niche players like to say, they do not just sell equipment, they sell "solutions to problems."

Niche strategy is particularly suitable for small and medium-sized companies, and because most Canadian companies are in these categories, this strategy is vital to Canada's global economic prospects. According to the most recent analysis of Statistics Canada figures by the Canadian Federation of Independent Business, 97.6 percent of Canadian businesses are small (up to 50 employees),

2.2 percent are medium (50 to 499 employees), and only 0.2 percent are large (more than 500 employees).

Canadian niche-market companies that have gone global have done so for defensive and expansionary reasons. At home, they face difficulties that will not disappear and that are shrinking their competitiveness. These are a limited domestic market because of the relatively small Canadian population, the free trade agreement with the United States which has ended the sheltered era of tariffs, and the erosion of market share due to incoming competition from the United States and offshore companies. From an expansionary viewpoint, going global has advantages, too. Cyclical swings are cushioned: when demand declines in one country, it is often offset by increases in others. Also, going global diminishes vulnerability to the loss of a major customer at home or in a single foreign country. Then, too, it can mean significantly greater revenue and, consequently, increased employment at the Canadian operation, especially as most niche firms cannot afford U.S. or offshore plants. It is not unusual for niche companies that have gone global to derive as much as 90 percent of their business from outside Canada. Many owners stress that their businesses otherwise would have died or remained tiny.

Success abroad can also enhance credibility at home. Canadians often display an inferiority complex that manifests itself in amazement at Canadian skill. Frequently, Canadian entertainers, scientists, and businesses receive more acclaim abroad than at home. Then, they belatedly obtain domestic applause. Such is the experience of kidney dialysis machine manufacturer Medionics International of Markham, Ontario, which has won a federal government Award for Business Excellence, an Ontario Chamber of Commerce Award, and a Markham Board of Trade Award for product innovation. Medionics has pioneered in home use dialysis machines as well as information display units on them. Sixty percent of its sales are outside Canada, primarily to the United States. Medionics's president, Mahesh Agarwal, says that despite the many Canadian awards received by Medionics, domestic sales are harder to make than foreign sales "because our machines are sometimes dismissed as not as good since they are made locally, even though we were the first with a new approach and are regarded as leaders globally in the technology."

Successful niche global players specialize in technologies of interest only to a small firm because the demand has to be created or is limited. Thus, for a long time they have the market virtually to themselves before bigger firms become aware of their products' appeal. By then, however, shrewd niche players will have erected a wall of protective patents, branched into product variations, or obtained private label business of larger companies that want the product fast and without the expense of investing in development and manufacturing.

Besides product uniqueness, successful Canadian global niche players have developed strong management and marketing skills. They persevere despite setbacks, mistakes, and sometimes failure. It can take many trips to clinch a deal and this requires money, stamina, missed anniversaries, and children's birthdays, or quick flights home for them to reduce family strain. Because niche companies usually are small, the president often doubles as export manager and/or does much of the travelling, rather than an international sales team. Thus, the onus for success is on him or her. However, since most are the owner or major shareholder in privately owned enterprises, they do not have to deal with public shareholders critical of expenses, uncertain about the outcome, and eager for instant return on their investment. In fields where technology changes continuously, theoretically a company should update its equipment to keep pace, but that is much easier for large than for small companies. Therefore, niche players must learn to forgo orders to avoid stretching their financial resources precariously.

Caution is best, recommends veteran niche exporter, Joseph Strite, president of Strite Industries of Cambridge, Ontario. Established in 1964, Strite does 80 percent of its $8 million annual volume outside Canada. It makes ultra-precision machined components and assemblies for the aerospace, automotive, nuclear, and medical industries. Twenty years ago, the precision equipment needed to make many of its current products did not exist, and to remain competitive Strite has invested heavily in machinery that enables accuracies within a millionth of an inch. Nevertheless, Strite refused to invest in expensive new lines without guaranteed orders, because to buy on supposition can lead to bankruptcy if expressions of interest are retracted. His yardstick, therefore, is "supplier partnerships in which we are the sole supplier for many parts and for which precision work will be required for many years."

With one exception, the firms described in this chapter were in niches from their outset. The exception is Electrohome of Kitchener, Ontario. It provides a useful study of how deliberate shrinkage of product lines can transform a money-losing domestically oriented firm into a profitable niche world leader. Like many firms, Electrohome diversified into seemingly related areas on a casual rather than a clearly defined basis. It was established in 1907 as a manufacturer of record players by the grandfather of John Pollock, the current chairman and president. Gradually, it "vertically integrated," making motors for the phonograph turntables and furniture as an offshoot of building phonograph cabinets. It also branched into radio and television production and motors for humidifiers, air conditioners, fans, and air purifiers. When FM radio and TV broadcasting developed, Electrohome was an early participant.

By the early 1980s, when North American consumer electronics firms were killed off or adversely damaged by cheaper Asian imports, Electrohome was deeply in debt and in a slew of widely divergent businesses, many of which had little or no future. It was not alone in its dilemma. Most of the big names of the 1970s— Admiral, Clairtone, Philco, General Electric, Sylvania, et cetera— disappeared, were absorbed, or recreated themselves as Electrohome has.

Between 1982 and 1989, Electrohome shed five of its seven businesses, reduced employment from 4,400 to 1,000, and reversed the ratio of salaried to hourly employees from 3:1 to 2:3. Of the two businesses retained, one is internationally oriented, the other domestically. Commercial electronics—data/graphics and video projection systems, display monitors, digital video, and components such as circuit boards—is the global enterprise. Ninety percent of its production is sold outside Canada, and the division accounts for 54 percent of total revenue of nearly $200 million, while employing 31 percent of operating assets. The domestic business is television broadcasting. Electrohome owns two radio stations—one in Kitchener, the other in Edmonton—and CTV affiliates in both cities.

What is significant about Electrohome's divestitures is that several healthy businesses were sold. "We did this because they did not fit our long-term strategy," Pollock explains. "For instance, we sold the furniture business since we did not believe it would do well under free trade with the high Canadian dollar. The new owners went bankrupt in 1990. We also sold our motor business notwithstanding an annual volume of $40 million and market-share leadership in Canada. We realized that what seemed a reasonable size was not, considering that the major American manufacturers have $250 million to $400 million in sales and, therefore, economies of scale that we could not attain."

Commercial electronics, in which Electrohome remained, was a field where it was a technological world pioneer, having been the first to introduce large-screen data/graphics and video projection systems, initially in black and white and subsequently in colour. The commercial systems were an outgrowth of Electrohome's consumer projectors for homes, bars, and clubs. But the evolution was not simple because the commercial line must meet more complex needs. The consumer projectors work on standard electrical frequencies; therefore, considerable research and development were necessary to make the commercial ones "computer friendly" with a wide range of brands and voltages.

Success tends to breed imitation, and Electrohome no longer is alone in its niche. Still, it remains in the top three and is confident that it will stay there. W. Michael Nobbs, group vice-president, electronics, says Electrohome will build on its strength "by continuing to narrow its focus through identifying specific submarkets." Also, Electrohome is being very careful not to regress to former habits. "We are a very different business today," Pollock explains. "Today, we concentrate on marketing, software, and design. The manufacturing side is less important. Instead of being completely vertically integrated, we contract for subassemblies to our design, a procedure followed by many larger companies, too. In electronics, as in many other products, Asia is the world's factory. Considering that Canadian labour costs and benefits are higher and productivity lower, Canadian business cannot succeed if the basis of success is manufacturing effectiveness. Therefore, it must be cleverer in product design and manufacturing. This can be achieved only if the old method of designing products and then identifying markets is reversed."

Electrohome was more than 70 years old and a multimillion dollar firm when it underwent its restructuring. Through its divestitures, it obtained the necessary funding. But what happens to a tiny fledgling company that almost immediately encounters adversity? Med-Eng Systems, the Ottawa manufacturer of $4,000 protective bomb disposal helmets, illustrates how a neophyte niche player can convert seeming catastrophe into opportunity. In 1982, just one year after Richard L'Abbé, an engineering graduate, formed Med-Eng with only $45,000 in startup capital, a recession struck. Like many other undercapitalized businesses, Med-Eng faced potential bankruptcy.

Its problems were compounded by limited Canadian demand for such helmets. Therefore, Med-Eng depended on foreign sales. Like many small firms that lack the resources to mount exporting campaigns, Med-Eng commissioned a trading house for the purpose. Trading houses are companies specializing in exporting and importing on behalf of firms that actually produce the goods. They identify markets and buyers, handle negotiations and shipping, prepare export documents, and provide promotional support abroad. Many small firms are pleased with their trading houses, but Med-Eng was not. According to L'Abbé, "The house led us to believe it had broad contacts, but when interest rates soared in 1982 and Med-Eng, financially strapped like many Canadian firms, asked the house about orders, it replied that it would have liked to have had them lined up but that it hadn't said it definitely would." Med-Eng and the house only had a so-called "gentleman's agreement"; recalling his shock and dismay, L'Abbé dryly comments that "for a gentleman's agreement to be valid, you have to be dealing with gentlemen."

With bankruptcy facing Med-Eng so early in its life, L'Abbé sought ways to save it. A friend suggested he turn to the federal government's trade promotion experts. "They took me by the hand," says L'Abbé, who candidly admits he "knew nothing about exporting." Thus, when he mentioned he was going to Europe to give a technical paper on bomb helmets, his government contact pointed out that L'Abbé himself would be the best person to sell them because he was most familiar with their technology, and potential customers want to be personally convinced about products. "I learned that I had to 'sell' myself first, then the product, and then the company; unless clients trust you, it's difficult to do business," he says.

L'Abbé was made aware of PEMD (Program for Export Market Development), under which the federal government funds up to 50 percent of export development expenses, including visits to potential markets. L'Abbé used the funding to extend his European trip to drum up contacts.

Realizing his speech could easily be made into a sales tool, L'Abbé developed it into a full-scale presentation with field tests. Police and military forces are his target customers, and he now lectures to them in 40 countries. "Demonstrations of sophisticated equipment are the most effective sales method," he says. "Not to give demonstrations would be like hoping people will buy cars without test drives. You can't expect clients to buy safety products like ours from sales brochures."

L'Abbé remains careful to develop worldwide business incrementally because Med-Eng is still small, with limited resources and only 15 employees. At first, he did all the travelling for up to five months a year—"a horrendous commitment that was hard on my family." Now he splits the travel with a staff engineer familiar with the demonstration and sales procedures. Although he has commissioned agents whose performance he checks out onsite once or twice a year, L'Abbé maintains personal contact with customers to get their feedback about the helmets. He appreciates their suggestions for improvements because "if you do this in niche markets, entry is difficult for others."

Today, 90 percent of Med-Eng's sales are to 50 foreign countries, and in 1989 it won the Canada Export Award, a federal government prize for excellence in exporting. L'Abbé has come a long way from the self-described greenhorn on the brink of bankruptcy in 1982. Now he confidently says: "Canadians shouldn't be afraid of export markets. They are there for the taking and if Canadians don't go after them, someone else will."

Nautical Electronic Laboratories (Nautel) of Hacketts Cove near Halifax is another example of a small Canadian firm that went global in order to survive. It did so 20 years ago, long before globalization was fashionable. In its case, the catalyst was diminishing business from its major Canadian customer. Nautel also demonstrates how niche players can do well even in finite markets.

Shortly after its 1969 establishment, Nautel scored a coup when it won a Nova Scotia Ministry of Transportation and Communications tender to make nondirectional radio beacons used in aircraft navigation. Nautel won because the department was impressed by its transistor technology which was longer lasting and, therefore, more cost efficient than conventional solid state vacuum tubes. For the next several years, Nautel did steady business with the government and was lulled into complacency by that steadiness. But then it awoke to reality. As President David Grace recalls: "After a few years, it dawned on us that the ministry was well stocked and, consequently, would not need many more." To reduce its dependency, and because the overall Canadian market is limited, Nautel began to think of itself in broader terms as a North American company, a strategy common to many Canadian firms which find their growth potential hindered by Canada's economic size. Most Canadian companies interested in the U.S. market begin with exports. But Nautel sells its beacons primarily to government agencies which prefer to buy locally to bolster their own economies. Therefore, to meet "Buy America" sentiment, Nautel set up a branch plant in nearby Bangor, Maine. Its role is limited to manufacturing; Nautel continues to conduct all its research and development as well as its design engineering at its Canadian facility. Although Nautel now ships worldwide and does 68 percent of its $14 million business offshore, it has no other foreign plants.

By 1979, five years after it began to go global, Nautel was in a classic good news/bad news situation. On the plus side, it had 70 percent of the world market for nondirectional radio beacons. But on the downside, that was almost the maximum goal achievable because some parts of the world do not yet require such devices or will only buy locally. Moreover, the replacement business is not frequent because the beacons are made to last for 30 or more years. Thus, Nautel was stymied from capturing an additional market share.

In answer to its dilemma, Nautel diversified into a new product in a related field—high-powered, transistor-operated AM radio broadcast transmitters. Its first sale in 1982 was in Nova Scotia; the next five sales were to New Zealand which, as Grace says, was willing to take the risk on new technology made by a small Canadian company halfway around the world. What convinced the New Zealanders was the greater energy-efficient technology and Nautel's track record. By 1990, Nautel had secured half the world market.

Because Nautel makes products for markets in which demand remains relatively static from year to year, it does not follow the conventional marketing wisdom of creating demand through heavy promotion. It does do a little advertising, but mostly it relies on word of mouth and local agents. On the other hand, customer satisfaction is essential for Nautel's continued pre-eminence. Although such satisfaction depends on the equipment remaining in top condition, Nautel cannot afford to station service representatives around the world. Its solution is a detailed technical manual for its agents, round-the-clock telephone advice on technical concerns and, in the worst cases, the dispatch of exchange equipment within 24 hours to the nearest airport. Technology, timely diversification, and customer satisfaction have enabled Nautel to achieve its original lofty goal: to prove that a small company located in Nova Scotia could become a global winner.

Med-Eng's and Nautel's problems were not self-inflicted; those of what is now Recherche et Développement Technologique of Quebec City were. Established in 1983 as Tecrad, the firm, which makes flaw detection equipment for nuclear plants and aircraft, encountered cash flow problems in 1989 and was put into liquidation by its bank. Some employees then purchased the company and renamed it. The firm is now profitable.

Tecrad's first customers were non-Canadian and even today only 10 percent of its business is domestic; 65 percent is offshore, primarily in Europe; and 25 percent, American. Tecrad's mistake was spending too much money on research and too little on development; thus, orders were unfilled, causing the cash flow predicament.

Nevertheless, even during the recovery period, the new owners believed it was essential to have a full-time sales and marketing manager dedicated largely to maintaining and expanding non-Canadian business. Because most of Recherche's customers and competition are in Europe, the manager, Guy Lafontaine, travels to Europe every six weeks to check on distributors and visit possible new ones as well as customers, some of whom recommend sales representatives. In 1990, a full-time European service person was added. Thus, even in its worst days, Recherche spent money to make money—and succeeded. It now does annual business of "a few million dollars" and sells in France, Belgium, the Netherlands, Italy, Germany, and Japan.

Spending money to make money is also the cornerstone of the success of Transformateur Delta of Granby, Quebec. Started in 1983 with eight people in 2,500 square feet, the company, which makes power transformers, now has more than one hundred employees and 45,000 square feet of premises. Despite its youth and the heavy competition in North America, where there are 690 transformer manufacturers, Delta ranks among the top 50 in sales. Approximately three hundred of the firms have revenue of under $2 million; Delta's is somewhat over $7 million.

The founder and president, Roland Pelletier, attributes Delta's fast climb to product uniqueness and rapid customer service. Delta's niche is epoxy vacuum impregnation in which transformers are immersed in epoxy-filled tanks. This process provides greater protection against corrosion and humidity. Delta did not invent the process—it dates back 50 years—but is the only Canadian manufacturer to use it, and one of the very few in North America. Pelletier says others are reluctant to follow suit because the extra cost would necessitate higher prices. Delta's approach is to absorb the expense in order to be price competitive.

So that this cost is not a financial drain, Delta works on a very quick customer-response basis, including custom designed orders. "Our American competitors mass produce and do not stop their lines for special orders. Conversely, we have one line that only does specials. Thus, we can fill such orders in a week, whereas the mass producers would take up to 12 weeks," Pelletier says. "Our philosophy for success is to invest in research and development as well as new fabricating methods and provide fast turnaround orders. By so doing, Canadian firms can overcome the drawbacks of higher wages and social benefits and of lower productivity than in the U.S."

Sometimes global players who sell to niche markets must alter their strategy, refocusing on what seems risky in the short term, but can well mean greater long-term security. This process is highlighted by the experience of Diffracto of Windsor, Ontario, a technological innovator that repositioned itself twice. Diffracto was formed in 1969 by two University of Windsor graduates and their professor. As Windsor is one of Canada's car manufacturing centres and across from Detroit, the U.S. motor capital, the trio naturally settled on an automobile-related product as their original focus. Their first product was electro-optical instrumentation custom-gauging equipment, and Diffracto did well, growing to 160 employees by 1980. Then, an automobile recession occurred, and Diffracto was forced to halve employment. Management also took a hard look at the future and decided that highly competitive custom-gauging was too risky; winning projects depended on engineering skill and the odds were that no firm could always be successful.

At what then seemed fortuitous timing, Diffracto's search for a new niche coincided with a hunt by General Motors for investment opportunities in promising small high-tech firms. Diffracto was the only Canadian firm out of the five in which GM invested. Diffracto's difficulty in selecting a new niche was eliminated by GM, giving it the assignment of making car body sheet-metal gauging equipment. In a rerun of its initial experience, Diffracto had product success but market problems. In this case, the problem was another equally successful company; both had large market shares but were losing money because of their rivalry. A merger or takeover was discussed but proved impossible because of tax difficulties due to Diffracto being Canadian and its competitor American. Finally, in 1990, Diffracto sold this portion of its business to the U.S. firm and restructured its niche strategy once again. The current niche is a machine-based system for measuring automobile surface quality through magnifying dents, waviness wrinkles, blisters, et cetera, that are less than a millimetre high. For this system, Diffracto won a federal government award in 1988 for business excellence in innovation.

In placing its hopes for the future on this niche, Diffracto opted for a newer technology, a business that represented just one-third of its sales, and an employment reduction to 40 people, one-fourth of the peak number in 1980. It did so because it believed there was more potential in this area than from body custom-gauging, from which it had derived two-thirds of its revenue. "We couldn't make a profit in custom-gauging because of the competition, and we expect the market will shrink since one system per auto plant is sufficient," explains President Omer Hageniers. "Conversely, the market for our machine-vision system is potentially much larger; the only competition so far is primarily human visual inspection, and Diffracto has extremely strong patent protection, with more than 80 already and 20 pending. We believe this is a growth market because of the increased demand for and emphasis on better auto-mobile surface quality."

Thus, Diffracto would seem to be ideally positioned: technological leadership in a niche product with a good outlook. But Hageniers says that being first is not necessarily best because it requires mission-ary zeal. "You can distinguish pioneers by the arrows in their backs," he comments. "It's often easier to sell products when there is a competitor also promoting. When you are alone, you have to be a crusader selling the message as well as the product."

As the automobile industry is divided in thirds between North America, Europe, and Japan, and since the small Canadian market yields only 5 percent of Diffracto's sales, the company must be active worldwide. Yet, like Med-Eng, Diffracto has limited re-sources. Its solutions are similar. Like Med-Eng's L'Abbé, Hageniers writes technical papers to educate potential customers and sends engineers to give in-plant demonstrations.

Diffracto exports to the United States, where it had extensive marketing experience. In Europe, it has distributors. In Japan, where the preference is to manufacture and not just distribute foreign equipment, the equipment is made under technology licence, although Diffracto, for intellectual property protection, continues to make some principal components in Canada. Like L'Abbé, Hageniers turned to the federal government for help; Industry, Science and Technology Canada put him in touch with the Japanese firm.

Diffracto voluntarily severed its ties to GM. Hymac of Montreal, a leading supplier of processes and machinery for the pulp and paper industry, demonstrates how a firm cut adrift by its technology supplier can rebound into a world niche player and have the last laugh. Hymac's revenue has zoomed from $15 million to $70 million in the past five years and employment from 180 to 520.

The growth stems from what seemed a crippling blow. In 1983, the Finnish firm which had licensed high-yield technology to Hymac terminated the agreement, having decided to sell directly in North America. Hymac had two choices—to withdraw from this business or develop its own technology. Although there were six well-established competitors, Hymac management was convinced they could succeed through innovation. They designed a machine that refines wood chips into pulp fibre in one step, whereas conventionally two machines are required. While Hymac's machinery was in development, the high-yield industry underwent changes helpful to Hymac. Consolidation halved the number of competitors, and these opted to focus on process, rather than machinery development. As part of the consolidation, Hymac's original Finnish supplier was absorbed in a takeover of its parent by a Swedish firm.

The worldwide market for pulp and paper machinery is substantial, and Hymac already was selling to the United States, Mexico, and Australia. Yet, notwithstanding the uniqueness of its new high-yield equipment, it did not rush to line up a huge international clientele. President Thomas Krieser explains why. "It took Hymac four years after the Finnish withdrawal to gain sufficient credibility as a domestic supplier. If we had tried to globalize before achieving domestic credibility, we would have failed because Canada is a large customer for pulp and paper equipment. Therefore, we didn't look hard at the global marketplace until 1988."

Hymac targeted the Soviet Union instead of a rich nation. There were two attractions. First, pulp and paper consumption is much lower than in Canada; therefore, the growth potential is much larger as the Soviet Union catches up economically. Second, Hymac saw an opportunity to weaken a Swedish competitor that it felt was undermining it in Canada through price cutting.

Krieser realized that Hymac had an uphill struggle against this company due to the deep-rooted economic ties between the Swedes and the Soviets. To succeed would require a different strategy than that of the Swedes. Since the Swedes exported to the Soviets, Krieser proposed a joint venture whereby Hymac would transfer technology, and the machinery would be built in the USSR. This proposal was astute since the Soviets were eagerly seeking Western partners for joint ventures and, indeed, the Soviets liked the idea. However, they wanted help in building the mill. Since Hymac's specialty is process machinery rather than mill construction, it brought in Noranda Forest Sales, a division of Canada's biggest natural resources company, as the expert in mill construction, management, and pulp exports. Half the output is to be exported.

Constant refinement of niche focus is crucial for maximum competitiveness. Its importance is highlighted by the evolution of Milltronics, a Peterborough, Ontario subsidiary of Federal Industries, the Winnipeg conglomerate (see Chapter 5). Milltronics' non-Canadian and U.S. sales have soared from $150,000 in 1977 to more than $14 million in 30 countries, equivalent to 75 percent of total revenue.

Milltronics specializes in ultrasonic instruments that measure inventories of dry and liquid materials ranging from food and beverages to chemicals, sand, and gravel. For some time after its formation in 1954, the company's sole product was an electronic device that determined storage quantities at cement mills. As the company realized the same method was applicable to other materials, it refocused as an industrial-measurement problem-solver rather than a one-function firm.

The next step was a redirection in market strategy. "We decided we wanted to be the best in the world in our industry and that the Canadian market was not large enough for achievement of that goal," says President Alan Gillis. That acknowledgement in the early 1970s was formal recognition of what Milltronics had known for a long time: cement firms were its biggest customers and most are in the United States. Nevertheless, Milltronics had not previously rushed outside Canada because its first priority was to build up its domestic presence.

In 1977, Milltronics opened a plant in Arlington, Texas, a location chosen because it placed the company in the centre of the U.S. and, therefore, in the middle of the then nation-wide cement industry. Also, the Dallas–Fort Worth airport had just opened near Arlington, and direct flights had been introduced from Toronto (about a one-hour drive from Milltronic's headquarters in Peterborough) to Dallas. All the electronics are still made in Peterborough, and Milltronics does its entire business worldwide, in Canadian dollars. It tried doing so in U.S. dollars—as is often done by Canadian companies with substantial foreign business—but found the attendant currency exchange transactions too time consuming.

Simultaneous with its U.S. expansion, Milltronics began to build up a network of overseas distributors. It took almost ten years. "Building representation takes time because at first you tend to get those people not wanted by good companies," Gillis explains. However, Milltronics elected to hire its own salespeople in the United States and the U.K., the company's principal foreign English-speaking customers. It is translating its sales and instructional literature into several other languages.

While steadfastly sticking to its niche, Milltronics, like other global companies, is flexible regarding product design to satisfy differing tastes. As Gillis points out: "North Americans like equipment to be big, easy to connect and to use, and enclosed. By contrast, Europeans prefer the exact opposite, with tiny readouts. For years we resisted accommodating them because we felt we couldn't afford to do both. Finally, we designed a happy medium. The difference is not so much in the technology—although voltages and testing standards vary—as in the packaging. The drawback is that economies of scale through standard worldwide products cannot be achieved. The advantage is that the Europeans face similar problems in North America."

The rewards—both financial and emotional—of global niche success more than offset the challenges, Gillis states. "We are proud that a little company in a relatively little community like Peterborough is known worldwide," he says. "Going global taught us how to be competitive and how to be marketers."

Product uniqueness is insufficient for niche success; receptive markets are crucial, too. How a small, young firm can make this painful discovery and survive is exemplified by Instrumar, the St. John's, Newfoundland manufacturer of scientific instruments for food testing. Instrumar started out in a far different field: sea-measurement instruments for Beaufort Sea oil exploration. For a while, Instrumar, founded by eight people who each invested just one dollar, was the epitome of a shoestring operation with growing success. But its foundation was knocked from under it when Beaufort Sea activity began to collapse.

In anticipation of a complete halt, Instrumar scrambled for another product in order to survive. It settled on a hand-held fish grading instrument for use in the Newfoundland government's planned quality standards program. The purpose of this program was to be the measurement of the texture, colour, and odour of fish. Then, once again, a market vanished for Instrumar. In this case, the government dropped the grading project just as Instrumar neared product development completion. "We were left with a technology of which we were proud and which had sapped our resources, but no apparent market," recalls the founder and chairman, Alastair Allan.

Instrumar decided to make the most of its technology—the world's first hand-held spectrophotometer. (This is a device that determines the relative intensity of two spectra—bands of colour—or of the corresponding bands of colour in two spectra.) Retrospectively, Allan says the setback benefitted Instrumar "because it forced us to look away from our market to the rest of the world and to other product applications."

The conclusion was that Instrumar's Colormet could be used to measure the quality of other foodstuffs; being hand-held, it had an advantage over laboratory devices and the human eye. For example, Colormet enables vegetable and fruit canners to determine if produce is of the same ripeness and colour for processing. Pet food manufacturers use it for gauging the appearance of their products; the animals may not be finicky, but their owners are. Today, Instrumar sells Colormet in 15 countries. "Food is a worldwide commodity; therefore, the need for quality and grading is global," Allan says.

Once it found its niche, Instrumar had yet another lesson to learn: stick to what it does best. This discovery came after it tried to promote Colormet as an all-purpose device suitable also for colour measurement of paints, plastics, textiles, and industrial finishes. Companies expressed considerable interest, but ultimately they decided to rely on laboratory instruments to which they were accustomed. Allan says Instrumar's tight refocus is advantageous "because larger competitors are not in our niche of the food industry."

In commercial and industrial equipment, the prevailing theme is that niche product uniqueness is of little value unless backed by marketing brainpower. What follows are examples of how small niche commercial and industrial Canadian firms have met this challenge. Consumer products are covered in the next chapter.

International Hard Suits of Vancouver is a world innovator in underwater diving gear. It makes the Newtsuit, a lightweight atmospheric diving suit with rotary joints, which enables extensive diver mobility while maintaining one atmosphere internal pressure at depths to 1,000 feet. The one atmosphere system eliminates the need for time-consuming decompression, expensive mixed gases and large support crews and big vessels for diver deployments. Consequently, operating costs are a fraction of those for conventional equipment. Newtsuits can be used for scientific research, deep-water salvage, offshore petroleum support, and defence purposes. Navies buy them for dismantling underwater mines, torpedo recovery, and seaflow surveillance. Although the Cold War is officially over, Phil Nuytten, the subsea technologist who spent from 1979 to 1987 designing the revolutionary suit, points out that "at any given time 35 to 40 wars are brewing in which Newtsuits can be used." Two-thirds of the suits are sold outside Canada.

Demand far exceeds supply and, like other cautious niche executives, Nuytten has no intention of letting the reverse happen. "It takes about a month to build a suit and our method is for each suit's sale to finance the next suit," he says. "The danger in building five or six simultaneously is that the extra machinery and employees could become idle if demand were to slacken. Therefore, we prefer to bootstrap the suits to one another." Although the Newtsuit is patented, Nuytten, like many other investors, says he is "not a great believer in this as long-lasting protection. The chief advantage is that it enables a strong market lead."

Overseas, Nuytten has contrasting distribution policies. In Europe, he picked a large German firm, whereas in Japan he chose a small firm. The German arrangement is a defensive alliance. The German company, which makes competitive equipment, was concerned about potential inroads by the Newtsuit; as its distributor, the firm believes it has ground floor access to it. In turn, International Hard Suits gains entry to the 60 countries where the German company has distributors. As for the Japanese firm, its smallness is offset by connections to a large department store chain and to Sony, the well-known worldwide electronics giant.

Another small niche firm that does most of its business outside Canada is International Road Dynamics of Saskatoon. It was begun in 1984 as a hobby by A.T. Bergen, a University of Saskatchewan transportation professor, now IRD's chairman, and his son, Terry, who is president. Two years later they converted it into a full-time business. Today, the firm has 35 employees.

A.T. Bergen developed remote sensing systems that weigh trucks on high-volume highways. The prescreening reduces the number of trucks that have to stop at roadside weighing stations to only the overweight ones. Bergen decided on this niche based on predictions of increased highway construction and the accompanying need for improved traffic planning to prevent congestion. IRD does the research and development; the manufacturing is subcontracted.

Such a system chiefly appeals to places with heavy traffic. Since this is not true of Saskatchewan, the Bergens had to look elsewhere for much of their business. A.T. Bergen, who is active in Canadian, U.S., and international transportation associations, wrote and delivered papers and designed prototypes. As sales grew, promotion budgets were enlarged. The Bergens attended trade shows and the International Roads Federation and Traffic Engineers Conferences, advertised, and commissioned distributors. Their equipment now is in 26 states and seven provinces.

IRD's first sale was outside Canada—to the Minnesota department of transportation. It is by no means a unique experience for Canadian niche firms and is often a necessity for survival. Controlled Environments (Conviron) of Winnipeg illustrates why. Established in 1964, it makes chambers, insulators, and seed germinators with controlled temperature, humidity, and light for academic and industrial agricultural research in such products as grains, fertilizers, and weed controls.

Conviron's original target market was domestic. The error of this parochialism rapidly became apparent as scarcity of orders caused the company to flounder. To keep going, Conviron looked south to the United States, where agronomists were engaged in research similar to that in Canada. By 1966, when it was just two years old, Conviron had made its first U.S. sale. Today, it sells to 70 countries. As was true 25 years ago, these foreign sales are essential for Conviron's existence. "Conviron is not in high-volume, assembly-line production and already has most of the Canadian market; therefore, it must sell worldwide to have the volume to maintain a viable operation," says Michael Roumi, export sales manager. Two-thirds of Conviron's $12 million revenue comes from international sales.

Because Conviron has only a handful of competitors anywhere in the world, it does not suffer from the many restraints inherent in its product. Inventory for instant shipment is impossible because chambers must be tailor-made to buyers' requirements. Consequently, it takes four months to make a chamber. These logistical problems have their bright side, though, according to Ken MacKenzie, vice-president and general manager. "The lack of manufacturing ease and the fast return on investment makes it a narrow niche that is unattractive to new companies," he explains.

Conviron owes its international success to its willingness to enter markets tried by few others. For instance, its first sale to China was in 1984, well before the rush there by Western investors. For its enterprise, Conviron won a Manitoba Export Award. Its business in Hungary dates back further, again well ahead of Western business interest in Eastern Europe. In the 1960s, shortly after its establishment, Conviron explored opportunities in Hungary. The overtures resulted in the sale of 30 growth chambers in 1972 to a government-sponsored agricultural institute. Although succeeding years brought no follow-up orders, Conviron executives continued to visit the institute. The ongoing contact paid off when Conviron won a contract to update the institute's equipment so that it would be prepared for the next 20 years.

Traditionally, niche companies were founded by entrepreneurs, and their concerns were survival and growth. But a new breed is appearing that will have a major impact on global niche strategy. These are managers who have departed from corporations due to the current trend to reduce costs through downsizing executive ranks, career frustration, or a desire to control one's destiny. Dennis Parass, now in his forties and president of Handling Specialty Manufacturing, a southern Ontario manufacturer of customized handling equipment capable of lifting up to 50 tons, exemplifies this growing group.

Parass has both engineering and MBA degrees and was on the executive fast track at large multinational and Canadian firms. Then he observed that several managers living nearby "had been fired, forced out of their jobs, or failed to get promotions they wanted." He also perceived that publicly owned companies often change executives to pacify shareholders who are upset by poor financial results. Then, too, he wanted independence. He searched newspaper advertisements for opportunities to become a major shareholder in a small company.

Meanwhile, as often happens at entrepreneurial companies, Handling Specialty's founder and chairman was debating whether to sell the company because it was now too large to run it himself; yet it was not large enough to warrant hiring professional managers. This obstacle was overcome when Parass accepted a decrease in salary in return for an equity position. When he joined Handling Specialty in 1983, it was only a $1.6 million business, but it had never suffered a loss in its 20 years. Parass decided his mission was to enlarge the company without deviation from its strengths of specialization, quick reaction, and personalized attention. Today, Handling Specialty's sales exceed $5 million. The company has a plant in North Tonawanda, near Buffalo, as well as at the original Grimsby, Ontario site, and a new head office is located between these at Niagara Falls, Ontario. Its goal is to generate half the revenue in the United States, up from one-third in the last decade.

Parass brought big business organizational techniques to Handling Specialty, starting with drafting a formal mission statement. It defines the company's purpose as the "manufacture of quality-built customized lifting equipment aimed at the professional user." Consequently, Handling is deliberately limited to "customizing" standard equipment to customers' needs. "We couldn't compete with the firms making standard lifts at low prices, nor could we afford the high engineering content of 'specials,' " Parass explains. "Our niche strategy eliminates the issue of size." He also practises big business "presentation power": a glossy brochure that projects strength as well as assurance, and clean, well-organized plants that bear out the image.

To carry out his belief in the virtue of quick reaction and person-alized attention at small businesses and his desire for Handling to grow, Parass is adopting Magna International's concept of many small, separate facilities instead of consolidation. He chose Magna as a role model because he was impressed by the cellular pattern of its rapid growth. As is well known, Magna (described in Chapter 5) has had difficulties recently, but these were not caused by its organizational structure. Parass intends to clone off the North Tonawanda facility when it reaches $5 million in sales. "People are the issue, not geography," he says. In answer to whether the U.S. plant in effect is exporting jobs from Canada, Parass states that the Grimsby factory "is at full capacity and we do not intend to move the business out of Canada. However, having a U.S. plant delivers the message to the U.S. market that we are not merely hanging around the edges of the camp to pick up the scraps."

Successful global niche companies never forget that specialization made them winners. Conversely, they do not allow their niche to become a rut. Thus, few depend solely on one product. But they broaden the applications of existing products to steer clear of avoiding unrelated diversification that might weaken them. The following are some examples of companies that have diversified successfully.

Instrumar, now specializing in instruments that test the quality of fruits and vegetables, has developed a "pork probe." The probe determines whether slaughtered pigs still contain water. Alastair Allan says it could boost port exports to Japan which will not accept "exudative pork" because of the weight loss involved. Already, Instrumar is shipping probes to Parma, Italy for use in the pickling of their famous hams because exudative pork cannot be pickled.

Diffracto believes its surface-flaw detection equipment, now used for cars, is also suitable for pinpointing outer surface delaminations in composite-material fighter planes and foresees potential for the equipment in commercial aircraft corrosion detection. International Road Dynamics, which began by selling its automated weighing system to government highway departments, has expanded its target audience to truckyards, aircraft, and vehicle-carrying ferries. International Hard Suits has developed a one-person, one-atmosphere mini submarine (price, $40,000–$50,000) which it is promoting as an "underwater sports car" for the recreation market, as well as for deep-water marine surveyors and coast guards. Transformateur Delta is doing private label work of some models for multinationals, which President Roland Pelletier says "enhances our buying power of materials" because lower prices per unit are charged for bulk orders.

Niche strategy is essential to the global success of Canadian business. It is particularly suitable for small and medium firms, which are the backbone of much of Canada's economy. Canadian niche firms are global pioneers and/or world leaders. Many niche companies make the bulk of their revenue outside Canada. Their international success cushions domestic downswings, increases their acceptance at home, and can even be the decisive factor in their survival. But as they illustrate, understanding what should not be attempted is as important as knowing what can be accomplished.

CHAPTER

3

More Niche Strategy: Consumer Products

"Going global is good insurance for long-term survival."

David Ganong,
President,
Ganong Bros.

S elling bomb disposal helmets, agricultural controlled environment growth chambers, and other industrial and commercial niche products, in which world competition is limited, certainly might seem easier than going global with consumer products. Yet, some Canadian companies are successful global niche players in such fiercely competitive and crowded consumer industries as clothing, health care, and recreational items. Moreover, they are doing well despite the overall low recognition and often poor perception of Canadian innovation and quality in these fields. These companies took on the world because of the small Canadian market and the erosion of domestic sales that occurred after the lowering or removal of Canada's protective tariffs allowed increased competition from imports.

Their formula for success is basic: specialized or unique product lines, flexibility in design, competitive manufacturing and marketing methods, and quick response to customers. Some see their unique items as door-openers for selling standard ones. Many find it easier to sell offshore than in the United States. Some do all their manufacturing at home, others manufacture abroad, too. Some have strong patent protection and fight against knock-offs by foreign companies, others rely on continued innovation. Some are more than a century old, others less than ten years. What follows are examples of how success can be achieved.

Ganong Bros. typifies the long-established, stay-at-home firm that wakes up to the need to go global. Located in St. Stephen, New Brunswick, almost on the border with Maine, the family-owned candy firm was founded in 1873, just six years after Confederation. For the next century, as President David Ganong says, "It was the perfect depiction of Sir John A. Macdonald's economic thinking." In other words, Ganong flourished thanks largely to high Canadian tariffs that barred outsiders and pursued east-west sales within Canada. Then, suddenly, in the 1980s, continues Ganong, "Our comfortable pew of a country began to change." Large foreign companies began to buy one Canadian candy manufacturer after another, and imports of European boxed chocolates soared. By the late 1980s, one out of every four pounds of boxed chocolates sold in Canada was imported, mostly from Europe. As Ganong saw it, the Canada–U.S. free trade agreement would intensify this trend.

Inasmuch as Ganong has only a "couple percent" of the Canadian candy market, David Ganong concluded that his company's survival in this vastly altered environment depended on its internationalization. "Our firm is just one example of tens of thousands of Canadian companies living in a cocoon," he states. "They don't realize that the competition no longer is the guy next door, but instead companies from Japan, Brazil, or Europe against which they must compete in their own marketplace. Globalization will accelerate during this decade; therefore, Canadian business must develop a global mindset."

To internationalize his company, he launched a three-pronged strategy in 1987: defend Ganong's position in Canada through the construction of modern facilities and the implementation of a new marketing strategy; develop export sales because incoming giants would make growth in Canada tough and nominal; establish an offshore plant where Ganong could continue to make candy that he believed could no longer be economically produced in Canada due to high wage rates, yet that he wanted to retain in Ganong's product lineup.

The marketing strategy was changed from no-name generic

commodities to premium value and priced brand names. The century-old New Brunswick plant was replaced with a state-of-the-art one. Unlike the original facility, it makes only two of Ganong's five lines. The specialization enables longer production runs and the improved equipment makes greater volume possible. Thus, even though fewer types of products are being made, the new plant employs more people than the old one.

Production of labour-intensive items was moved offshore to Thailand. This seemingly innocuous statement masks the many factors involved in shifting production abroad, ranging from convincing the company's board of directors of the wisdom of such an investment to selecting a country and replying to charges that Canada is being hurt through the export of jobs. Ganong says such critics "must understand that there are some things Canadians do well and some they don't. Canadian labour is very highly paid but medium in productivity; therefore, labour-intensive products cannot be made in Canada. The question is whether to make them elsewhere. We would not have been able to produce our labour-intensive products in Canada by the 1990s. We had to decide whether to stop or make them offshore."

He promised Canadian employees that none would lose their jobs because of the transfer of the three product lines overseas and, as it turns out, 17 Canadian jobs are related to these lines. All told, Ganong has 250 employees in Canada; the Thai plant only has 25.

Three years elapsed between the idea for the plant and its July 1989 opening. Such delays are to be expected when precedents are being set. First, Ganong had to convince his board of directors. This was difficult since no other major Western candy firm was doing the same thing in Thailand. "It wasn't a matter of following people, but of wondering why no other foreign candy firms were there," Ganong recalls. "Naturally, it was scary to us." Thus, the plant had low priority, especially as Ganong was busy strengthening its Canadian presence. Often, four months passed before Ganong resumed negotiations and, when he did, they proceeded leisurely because Asians place more importance on relationships than on contracts. Development of rapport is slower than drafting legal documents, and it took time for the Thais and Canadians to understand each other's objectives fully.

Thailand was one of four Asia–Pacific countries considered by Ganong. Thailand offers tax breaks and other economic benefits to attract foreign investment, but Ganong's decision was also influenced by other factors. Thailand has the requisite raw materials (sugar, cocoa, coconut), political stability, and cheap labour (although Ganong pays topscale). Moreover, Thailand has almost no chocolate manufacturing industry, leaving the market wide open for Ganong. Furthermore, it is near Japan, South Korea, and Taiwan, all of which have lowered their tariffs on imports of chocolate products at a time when disposable incomes are rapidly rising. Thus, the Far East is much easier to enter than Western Europe, with its famous confectionery firms, steep tariffs, and already high candy consumption rate.

In addition, a well-established Thai sugar and confectionery company was willing to form a joint venture with Ganong. Ganong believes joint ventures enable medium-sized companies like his to build offshore because they minimize investment and risk. Ganong invested no cash; instead, it supplied the technology and much of the machinery, and made recommendations for the plant layout. Within its first year, the plant broke even financially, justifying Ganong's confidence in it.

The third part of Ganong's internationalization strategy—the development of export markets—has been slower in paying off, but he expected this. His first move was to create the position of export manager, hiring Christopher Wilkinson, who had eight years' experience in the export department of a fairly large Canadian canned food firm. So far, as tends to happen at small and medium-sized companies, Wilkinson is a one-person department. However, as the "champion" of Ganong's internationalization, David Ganong travels extensively to make it work. In a typical year, he spends 150 days in such places as Thailand, the United States, South America, and Turkey, as well as in other parts of Canada.

Inasmuch as Ganong's New Brunswick plant is so near Maine, the United States was expected to account for 70 percent of foreign sales; only 30 percent was anticipated in the Pacific Rim. Contrary to expectations, progress in the United States has been "painfully slow" and 95 percent of Ganong's foreign sales are in the Pacific Rim. Wilkinson explains why: "The U.S. is extremely regional in its market composition, and U.S. retailers and consumers are very conservative, sticking with famous, dominant brands. Thus, it is very difficult getting our product on the shelves." Recently, Ganong hired a U.S. sales manager whose local experience and contacts at drug and candy stores, it believes, will open doors. The emphasis is from New York west to Detroit, because not all the country can be covered initially. Particular attention is on Maine, where the Ganong name is known and where the population is as large as the combined one of the Maritime provinces.

Ganong is happy about its Japanese prospects even though annual Japanese chocolate consumption is merely half a pound, compared to 11 pounds in the United States. As Wilkinson sees it, an increase of just half a pound per person in Japan would double the market. His optimism is warranted because Japan's confectionery imports are ballooning and the Japanese, according to him, "are hungry to try every flavour and product." Also, Japan has two Valentine's Days: February 14 ("Red Day") when men give candy to women, and March 14 ("White Day") when women reciprocate. Then, too, the Japanese buy boxes by the dozen as "obligation gifts" for their hosts at social and business events.

Ganong has also found that Japanese tourists like to buy the company's candy before embarking on overseas travel. The growth potential is big, since Japanese tourist departures, already doubled between 1985 and 1990, are expected to double again by 1995. "The Japanese buy their gifts at tourist shops before leaving Japan and mail them to avoid carrying back presents," Wilkinson explains. "But they like the gifts to appear touristy; thus, we have scenes on our boxes of the Rockies, autumn-coloured maple leaves, and the Golden Gate Bridge."

Not only is Japan a growing market for candy, it also is a competitive arena, with many Western firms pursuing sales. To survive the onslaught, Ganong follows the classic niche strategy of personalized service. "If buyers want brochures, photographs, and samples shipped within a week or so, we do it," Wilkinson says. "Big companies usually don't react as quickly." In the future, David Ganong hopes for sales in Eastern Europe despite low incomes there. "Although East Europeans have less money, they tend to buy soft drinks and processed foods like boxed chocolates," he points out. "They are luxuries for those who live on farms."

In the furniture industry, most Canadian manufacturers are in deep trouble because of imports, especially from the United States, in the wake of the free trade agreement. Even though the phaseout of furniture tariffs will take until 1993, two dozen Canadian furniture makers declared bankruptcy a little more than a year after the agreement came into effect on January 1, 1989. Almost another three dozen halted manufacturing.

Yet in the midst of this gloom, Shermag Furniture of Sherbrooke, Quebec, Canada's largest solid-wood furniture manufacturer, has managed what most of its Canadian counterparts have found impossible—successful penetration of the U.S. market. About 15 percent of Shermag's furniture is sold in the United States; the goal is 50 percent by 1995.

Shermag Furniture's president, Kenneth Herring, attributes Shermag's U.S. success to "a niche approach using existing strengths." Shermag's wedge into the United States is its line of glider rockers. The rockers are not Shermag's top seller, but were regarded as best suited for the United States because they do not have to compete with broad-product, U.S. furniture manufacturers. Moreover, should U.S. firms become interested in this line, Shermag has a strong competitive edge: as Canada's leading solid-wood furniture maker, it can obtain wood more cheaply. Also, brand names play a smaller role in consumer purchase decisions of glider-rockers than other household items, such as appliances and mattresses.

To kick off its now seven-year-old U.S. initiative, Shermag purchased a small, century-old Massachusetts factory, not because it intended to manufacture in the United States, but because it believed a U.S. address would open doors at American retailers. It converted the factory into a warehouse and distribution centre and still does all manufacturing in Canada. In addition, a detailed marketing strategy was developed, reflecting the significant differences between the U.S. and Canadian markets. In the smaller Canadian market, stores carry baby-to-adult furniture, and more independent outlets exist. In the much bigger U.S. market, specialization is common and so are groups of 30 or more retailers that bear the same name and buy in bulk.

Although Sears Canada is a major client, Shermag deals in the United States with J.C. Penney department stores instead of Sears Roebuck, Sears Canada's controlling shareholder. Penney was chosen because its product assortment is in the medium to upper price range, as is Shermag's and Sears Canada's. Herring regards the merchandise at Sears Roebuck as more downscale. At first, Penney carried Shermag gliders on a trial regional basis. Now, Penney sells them nationwide and features several models on its furniture floors as well as in promotional Christmas, Mother's and Father's Day flyers. It also carries them in its growing chain of free-standing furniture stores.

Subsequent to Penney's, Shermag signed up major New York and midwest department store chains. To obtain orders from buying groups representing chain and independent furniture retailers, Shermag offered to produce a different "major collection" for each group. The result is an element of exclusivity that does not preclude sales of different models to other retailers in the same region. Like Ganong, Shermag hired U.S. sales talent familiar with American retailers and tastes, rather than parachuting in Canadians.

Its niche specialization insulates Shermag from the myriad differences in U.S. and Canadian preferences, buying habits, and manufacturing methods in furniture. In dimensions, according to Herring, Canadians like coffee tables that are 24" wide × 48" long × 16" high; Americans, 24" × 52" × 16". Canadians favour 60" × 66" × 68" dressers; Americans, 64" × 66" × 74". As for workmanship, Herring says "Canadian consumers feel finishes and look inside drawers. Therefore, Canadian manufacturers emphasize assembly and sanding, but not the finish, because they do not want to hide their work. By contrast, Americans tend to buy from a distance on the basis of appearance. Thus, U.S. furniture manufacturers pay less attention to joints and sanding and more to the finishing, which can cover shortcomings. In effect, these differences protect markets, more so in expensive than lower-priced items." As Shermag proves, it is possible to survive in the lion's den—the complex U.S. market—if a firm's niche strengths are applicable there.

Shade-O-Matic, which makes window blinds and related components, parlayed technological innovation and a strong marketing background into rapid worldwide expansion. As a result, the Toronto firm has grown from three employees in 2,000 square-foot premises in 1983 to 120 employees in 96,000 square feet, almost half of which has been added recently. The niche product that gained Shade-O-Matic quick attention is a corner hinge for a one-piece angle track for blinds covering bay or bow windows. Previously, bay windows required three separate tracks and controls.

So far the financial impact of the invention has been slight; it accounts for only about 2 percent of sales, the rest being from the manufacture of blinds and other component parts. But Norbert Marocco, its inventor as well as Shade-O-Matic's founder and president, says the hinge catapulted Shade-O-Matic onto the world scene, leading to the sale of other parts.

To protect his invention worldwide, Marocco spent a hefty $200,000 on legal and patent fees. Then he devised separate domestic and international strategies for it. In Canada, where his goal is leadership in finished product sales, he does not sell components to other manufacturers so as "not to compete with ourselves." However, outside Canada, he does license manufacturers for speedy worldwide exposure. He targeted five out of the thousands of firms in the industry because they supply many others. He visited personally "to have a record that they saw me and to get their verbal commitment not to copy my device." This was essential because Shade-O-Matic could not afford to contest these firms in court, should they infringe patents. Marocco also believed his in-person visits would speed up sales. "It's easy to convince marketing people but not engineers because they dislike buying from outside; therefore, I won them over through vigorous onsite testing of my hinge," he says.

To ensure that Shade-O-Matic would gain worldwide credit for the hinge, Marocco insisted that the licensing agreements commit the firms to feature Shade-O-Matic as the designer in advertisements. Most of the licences are for two years with renewal options. But Marocco likely would not be heartbroken at nonrenewal since Shade-O-Matic would be well known by then and could sell directly. The hinge also has made customers receptive to other Shade-O-Matic products that are industry standards. "Our innovative reputation helps in the sale of other parts," comments Donna Battiston, managing director.

Besides knocking on doors, Marocco pursues export business through brochures translated into French, German, and Italian, and participates at major international trade shows. He selects these carefully because of the expense. He calculates that participation in just one trade show can cost at least $30,000. This estimate includes the costs of an exhibit booth, its shipment, promotional literature and video presentations, travel, hotel, meals, and hospitality.

Concern about increased imports, especially from the U.S. due to the free trade agreement, is not confined to Canada's furniture industry. The fashion industry also is vulnerable and scrambling to increase exports to compensate for lost business at home. It has an uphill battle, though, because international recognition of Canadian fashion talent is low and under ten percent of annual production is exported. Two sportswear firms are dramatic exceptions: Tilley Endurables of Toronto, established in 1984 and best known for its premium-priced— more than 40 dollar—all-weather outdoor hat, and Sun Ice of Calgary, established in 1978, and "official clothing supplier" to the 1988 Olympic Winter Games held in Calgary.

Outside Canada, Tilley sells its hats and other outdoor wear by mail order and through retailers in the United States, Japan, and some Western European countries. About three-fourths of the North American stores are in the much larger U.S. market. Tilley also has toll-free Canadian and U.S. numbers for catalogue requests. Building up U.S. sales was tough, says founder and co-owner Alex Tilley, because what worked in Canada often failed in the United States. His painful learning experience is useful for others who blithely regarded the United States and Canadian market as alike.

Lesson No. 1: Shopping habits differ. Tilley erroneously believed that since his flagship Toronto store, located in a suburb, attracted his target audience—middle-aged, well-off, well-read, well-travelled customers—the same out-of-the-city core approach would work in Boston. He chose that city because he thought "Bostonians were like Torontonians," and opened near a highway. He soon discovered his error. Bostonians may share the same income and personality characteristics, but not Torontonians' willingness to drive some distance to Tilley's. After two-and-a-half years, Tilley decided "to beat a retreat." Subsequently, he opened a mail order office in Buffalo, which is near Toronto and where he was able to find "a relatively inexpensive location and staff."

Lesson No. 2: Advertising must be custom-tailored. In Canada, where he is well known to outdoor enthusiasts, Tilley's ads are folksy and personal, often featuring or referring to his family. This approach failed dismally in the United States, where Tilley was unknown. It also stumbled in a narrowly focused campaign geared to the well-to-do. This was a direct mailing to one thousand Neiman Marcus platinum credit card holders. "The response was dreadful, but because we had not tried nationally, the cost was low," Tilley recalls.

Subsequently, he decided he needed expert help and hired an American public relations agency. He also advertises in "Outdoor Retailer," attends sport and boat shows, and seeks celebrity product endorsements. He is emphatic, however, that he will continue to manufacture in Canada, even though labour rates are much lower in southeast Asia. This commitment could conceivably stem in part from his output being far less than that of mass producers, since he is a specialty manufacturer. However, a plaque on his office wall proclaims patriotism as the reason.

> You could make it cheaper offshore, I'm told.
> Perhaps. But I believe it's the patriotic
> thing to do, to make our clothes here.
>
> Honour.
> Patriotism.
> Rare words nowadays.

Sun Ice, Canada's largest outerwear and sportswear manufacturer and winner of several federal government Awards for Business Excellence, is a classic entrepreneurial success story. It began as a hobby of Sylvia Rempel, now president and chief designer of the company. She taught sewing at a Calgary technical school, and one year decided to add skiwear to her course. She studied how to make it in the United States and, on her return, made ski suits for her husband, their four children, and friends. The vibrantly coloured skiwear caught the attention of a local retailer, who offered to sell the clothing. Mrs. Rempel hired one seamstress, now a supervisor at Sun Ice, and then many more, for whom she rented and converted a pool hall. Her husband, Victor, now executive vice-president, was then a principal at a junior highschool. He went on the road part time to sell and their children modelled, did office chores, and helped on the production line. He retained his school position for seven years, and the six Rempels ran Sun Ice. But in 1985, when it reached $9 million in sales, they made it a full-time enterprise. Today, Sun Ice's sales exceed $30 million and the company has a 110,000 square-foot plant as well as subsidiaries in Seattle and Hong Kong. Its styles have grown from ten to three hundred and fifty.

The secrets of success that have made Sun Ice North America's fastest-growing outerwear and sportswear manufacturer are dynamic design, substantial promotion, state-of-the-art manufacturing, controlled growth, and extensive in-house training of production workers. Also, the firm's success shows what a family can do, starting on the homefront. The Sun Ice label is prominently displayed on the outside of the clothing, serving as a constant advertisement. In addition, Sun Ice sponsors high-profile skiing events, sports stars, and national teams. As "official clothing supplier" to the 1988 Winter Olympics, the company received national and international television attention. Victor Rempel says ten cents of every dollar of revenue is dedicated to promotion.

The Rempels invested $2 million in computer-aided design and manufacturing to shorten their manufacturing cycle, reduce costs, and improve quality. Robotic cutting, for example, is 15 times faster than manual. According to the Rempels, their system is one of the most advanced in Canada. Additionally, they made their premises attractive to counter the traditional sweatshop image of fashion factories and developed in-house production training. Nevertheless, as is true of the entire industry, the staff is comprised primarily of immigrants.

Rempel maintains that the future of Canada's fashion industry depends on getting young people to realize its career potential. "Canada is four years behind the United States in technology implementation in the garment industry," he comments. "In our province of Alberta, there is little manufacturing tradition and, therefore, it is difficult to get people to work in factories. We must convince Canadian youth that they can earn good wages on sewing machines and even better money as cutters, supervisors, and production engineers."

In addition to its Calgary factory, Sun Ice subcontracts in Winnipeg, Seattle, Portland, and Hong Kong. The work in Hong Kong is done by a dozen factories. Hong Kong was chosen because it is the Far Eastern garment centre and, consequently, has all the requisite resources from skilled labour to threads and zippers. It is expected to remain the hub even after 1997, when the British will hand it over to the Chinese. Lack of co-ordination and monitoring at Sun Ice's Hong Kong suppliers in 1989 led to late deliveries and, as a result, depressed profits. "It's difficult to get reliable quality and timely production; unless you are there supervising, factories change their commitments for a nickel," Rempel says. To overcome the fickleness, one of the Rempels' daughters, who was vice-president of merchandising and product development, and her husband, formerly sales manager, moved to Hong Kong in 1990 to supervise production, quality, and delivery. The Rempels may establish their own Far East plant, possibly in China where sewing is very skilful.

Despite its marketing savvy, Sun Ice initially had sales problems in the United States. It began there in 1986 with an agent, but dropped him because "In effect, he gave away the product by promises of major discounts for volume buying and of substantial co-operative marketing efforts," Rempel says. Subsequently, Sun Ice set up its own sales force. Since the United States has more retail chains and fewer independents than Canada, Rempel points out profit margins are lower due to buying groups demanding discounts. However, this factor is counterbalanced by the greater sales volume. The United States accounts for 24 percent of Sun Ice's revenue. In 1990–91, European and Japanese ski and sporting goods retailers began to sell clothing made by Sun Ice.

The Rempels believe the key to continued success is controlled growth. They still consider Canada their prime market, followed by the United States as free trade evolves, and by other countries as opportunities occur, as they did with Europe and Japan. Mrs. Rempel maintains her custom of "almost sitting on each stage of a garment's development."

The consumer product manufacturers knew outright what niche interested them. The experience of Medionics of Markham, Ontario, established in 1976 and the first Canadian manufacturer of kidney dialysis machines, is heartening for prospective niche entrepreneurs casting about for product ideas. Before health care, Medionics's founder, Mahesh Agarwal, considered the diametrically opposite field of entertainment. Then Agarwal and his partner, who was a dialysis technician at a Toronto hospital, decided they could, in their view, make better kidney dialysis equipment than that which existed. They worked to reduce operating expenses for dialysis users and to increase their comfort with temperature controls and information displays.

Because the Canadian market is small, Agarwal realized the bulk of Medionics's sales would have to be international. He attended big trade shows in the United States in the hope of obtaining an American distributor "since the market is too big for us to go in on our own." He correctly reasoned that a U.S. firm would rather pay for exclusive distribution rights than spend on research and development for a product for which the need is limited. The U.S. company does distribute internationally, but due to apprehensions that the Americans would devote most of their attention to their large home market, Medionics decided to handle global sales itself.

Repeat business in dialysis machines is minute, as they are designed for long use. Thus, Medionics cannot exist solely on the machines. However, sales had to be good to enable Medionics to lessen its dependence on them through related diversification: the production of disposable tubing. Such tubes must be made in bacteria-free "clean rooms" and even small ones cost several hundred thousand dollars. It took Medionics until its eighth year to afford the investment. Henceforth, sales snowballed, and recently Medionics moved into much larger premises with a clean room five times larger.

To offset steep research and development costs, Agarwal installed computerized accounting that keeps administrative staff to a minimum. As a newcomer to the hospital market, Medionics must work at overcoming entrenched business relationships. Agarwal's solutions are to persuade hospitals to try as few as two machines and to reach patients directly through advertisements in dialysis magazines.

In the service sector, fast-growing Molly Maid International of Oakville, Ontario, established in 1978 and now Canada's largest franchise house-cleaning service, is also in the United States, Europe, and Asia. By 1992, it expects half of its revenue to come from non-Canadian franchises. Molly Maid's international strategy is in stark contrast to that of most firms with global ambitions: it waits for the business to come to it.

President James MacKenzie deliberately expresses disinterest to determine how sincere inquirers are. Those who persevere convince him that they have the tenacity to succeed as Molly Maid franchisees. "I don't want to waste my time or that of my staff on fishing expeditions," he explains. "Businesses aren't successful; people are."

Also, he wants to be certain that international expansion does not "jeopardize our Canadian operations through tying up money and management time, because there are two main reasons businesses succeed or fail—capital and management." A believer in lean, efficient management, MacKenzie has only two people at head office to oversee international activity. His caution stems from a deterioration in Canadian profit margins in 1988, just when the company had plans for generating 75 percent of its revenue from outside the country by 1992. Simultaneously, a recently granted franchise in Norway failed, and MacKenzie believed the cause was the failure of the master franchisor there "to listen to Molly Maid" experts in Canada. Moreover, Molly Maid had had to defend itself against trademark infringement in the United States. It won, but its legal costs were steep.

MacKenzie decided to concentrate on improvement in Canada, especially as demand is high for house-cleaning services. According to him, the total market equals $620 million, of which 75 percent is earned by independent cleaning women and the rest by "professional" franchise operations like Molly Maid. As he sees it, gaining just a portion of that independent share enriches Molly Maid.

Still, he did agree to Molly Maid franchises on a gradual basis in the United States, England, Germany, Japan, and Taiwan. Molly Maid receives at least ten letters a month asking for a franchise in a foreign country, but MacKenzie's policy is master franchises covering an entire country. The master franchisor then parcels out single-unit franchises. Molly Maid master franchises cost an average of $500,000.

MacKenzie points out that Molly Maid offers no global marketing advantage, as does an international consumer products franchisor like McDonald's. But it does offer useful detailed performance measurement analyses. These cover the number of houses cleaned, the number of people on each cleaning team, the number of temporary and permanent cancellations, and the quantity purchased of Molly Maid supplies. Also, it conducts extensive pool-financed market research.

Molly Maid's chief attraction is that the climate is ripe worldwide for its concept. "Housework is common throughout the world, and increased standards of living and time pressures are intensifying the demand for home-cleaning services," MacKenzie explains. "Organized services are growing in popularity because householders are afraid to criticize cleaning people for fear they will quit. Moreover, many are absent when the cleaning is done. In effect, we take over the management and supervisory functions from them."

Molly Maid differs from franchises like McDonald's which can transplant its North American standards worldwide. Standardization is far more difficult to achieve in housecleaning, especially as cleanliness is not considered as important in some countries as it is in Canada. Then, too, stronger pollution and humidity impair even the best of efforts. Thus, Molly Maid sets basic standards but allows indigenous differences.

In the recreational sector, Atlantis Submarines International of Vancouver introduced the world to an imaginative new concept—tourist submarines. Its 65-foot-long submarines can carry up to 48 passengers and dive to 150 feet. Atlantis had an intriguing idea when it began in 1983, but also some unique challenges. Foremost, the product was new and of a nature requiring that all sales be to offshore tourist sites. Initially, Atlantis targeted the Caribbean and Hawaii. Mass production is impossible and Atlantis generally builds just one submarine a year. Therefore, supplementary income sources had to be found. These difficulties slowed the raising of startup money; eventually 160 private Canadian shareholders invested $12 million.

Having devoted considerable time and money to product development, Atlantis wanted to stave off competitors in the industry it had created. Its solution was unusual and clever. Vessels operating in American waters must meet U.S. Coast Guard standards, regarded as the world's most rigorous. Atlantis obligingly assisted the agency in developing extremely tough safety standards. So strict are they that they acted as a protective barrier against less quality-minded, price-cutting competitors. Nevertheless, when the first sub, designated for the Cayman Islands, was ready, Atlantis was still awaiting approval from local authorities. Because financial constraints made Atlantis vulnerable to continued delays, it sent the submarine during the deliberations. The pressure tactic prompted quick approval.

As a novel niche item, the submarines required thousands of dollars in promotion at international trade shows of travel agents, hotels, and amusement parks. Market surveys to identify potential sites also had to be conducted. These expenses were the main reason Atlantis was unprofitable in its first three years. Promotion will always consume 20 to 30 percent of revenue, President Dennis Hurd says.

Because the tourist subs were a world first, Atlantis had to develop a customer base; to do this, it had to be willing to structure each deal to suit the investors. The result is a mixture of joint ventures, wholly owned subsidiaries, and royalty arrangements. Licensees and wholly owned operations pay 2 percent of gross ticket sales to a group marketing fund. Atlantis arranges for reduced flat rates for insurance. To reach a broader audience than it could on its own, Atlantis has marketing agreements with 16 cruise lines, plus several large tour wholesalers. Money also had to be provided early in the company's development for facilities in Washington State to comply with U.S. regulations that boats for the American market be manufactured in the United States. The other subs are made in Canada.

Atlantis receives about ten inquiries monthly from potential licensees, enabling it to be selective. It has learned when to cut losses; it closed its European office in 1990 since the cost proved to be unwarranted. In addition, it does not want to overextend; mass production would entail big outlays on facilities and workers both at the plants and onsite. Moreover, it takes a year to train pilots. Supplementary revenue is derived from the sale of spare parts and tools, as well as from consultant fees for site surveys and assistance in construction of dock facilities, power sources, and warehouse premises. The careful gradualism has paid off: $15 million in annual sales from carving out a unique global niche.

Canadian companies selling consumer products or services can succeed globally, provided they are in a well-defined, carefully promoted niche and take into account different buying habits. At the same time, wise ones do not neglect their home market, especially since competition from foreign invaders is intensifying.

CHAPTER

4

High Technology

"When a company thinks of where it can sell, it should think of the entire Planet Earth, not just New York City."
Eugene Joseph,
President,
Virtual Prototypes

Canada's high-tech industry is a vivid microcosm of the motivations, methods, stresses, and ramifications of the globalization of Canadian business. For Canada finally to shed its traditional image as a hewer of wood and drawer of water, its high-tech industry must make its mark worldwide, as world trade in sophisticated technology goods is growing about twice as fast as general trade. By 1995, trade in computers, aerospace equipment, electronics, chemicals (including pharmaceuticals), and telecommunications will represent one-fourth of all goods traded in the world, according to the Organisation for Economic Co-operation and Development.

Canadians have shown repeatedly that they can excel in technology. But to become a world high-tech leader, Canada will have to invest far more in research and development, and high-tech companies will have to overcome a troublesome penchant for runaway expansion, which time and again has led to heavy financial losses. Also, an increasing number of high-tech firms are coming to the painful conclusion that to obtain the resources to compete globally, they must give up their independence and become controlled by bigger Canadian companies or by foreign enterprises.

For years, Canada's imports of advanced technology products have far surpassed exports, and this deficit likely will continue as total Canadian research and development spending by governments, businesses, universities, and nonprofit organizations is abysmally small. At just over 1 percent of gross domestic product (the value of all goods and services produced within Canada), it is way behind the level of most industrialized countries. Moreover, its projected increases between 1990 and 1995 rank a lowly 19th out of 23 industrial countries surveyed in 1990 by the Swiss-based World Economic Forum. Canadian businesses account for the lion's share—56 percent—of the nation's R&D spending, but their expenditures, in terms of gross domestic product, substantially trail those in the United States, Germany, Japan, Sweden, France, and the Netherlands, and are only a tiny fraction ahead of Italy's.

Moreover, save for one exception, Canadian-owned high-tech firms are dwarfed by foreign competitors. The exception is Northern Telecom, with 1990 sales of $6.8 billion (U.S.).* No other Canadian high-tech firm has revenue that surpasses $1 billion. The ten largest foreign-owned computer hardware firms sell more than ten times the amount sold by the ten leading Canadian-owned ones. Although sales at Ottawa-based Gandalf Technologies, the biggest Canadian-owned firm, were $162 million in 1990, they were only 3.5 percent of that of IBM Canada.

In the United States, 50 computer software manufacturers have sales surpassing $25 million; in Canada, just Ottawa-based Cognos has; it had 1990 revenue of $141 million. Further, the growth rate among Canadian software producers is only about one-third of that in the United States. This is in an industry about which it is said, "There are no winners, only those who live to fight the next battle."

The chief motivations for the globalization of Canadian high-tech firms are the small domestic market and the general reluctance of Canadian firms to invest in state-of-the-art equipment. Also, increased revenues from going global enable greater amortization of R&D and large investments in marketing and after-sales service. In addition, a bigger in-place customer base enhances repeat busi-

---

The company, which derives the bulk of its revenue from the United States, reports its results in U.S. dollars.

TECHNOLOGY INFLOW PROGRAM
(TIP)

The Technology Inflow Program helps Canadian businesses acquire foreign technology to develop new Canadian products, processes, or services. The program is open to all companies, but is intended especially for small and medium-sized firms. It helps Canadian companies to identify sources for obtaining the technology they need to improve productivity and to take advantage of opportunities to collaborate with foreign companies.

Financial assistance is available for technology transfer projects, such as:

■ Exploratory or longer-term working visits abroad by individual Canadian companies
■ Industry-oriented group technology awareness missions abroad organized by Canadian professional or trade associations
■ Visits by foreign technical experts to companies in Canada

For more information contact:

Science and Technology Division (TDS),
External Affairs and International Trade Canada,
125 Sussex Drive,
Ottawa, Canada K1A 0G2
Telephone (613) 996-0971

ness and the sale of add-ons to the original products. But paramount is access to far more people. As Michael Potter, president and chief executive officer of Cognos, says: "To realize the growth potential from their technology, Canadian firms must go global. Companies near Los Angeles with one million dollars a year in revenue can grow more rapidly to $10 million or even $100 million, because 12 million people are within a one-hour drive. By contrast, the Canadian market is small; therefore, there is no choice but to become export oriented."

Canadian high-tech firms also bemoan a lack of venture capital backing in Canada. Therefore, those that obtain stock exchange listings do not confine themselves to Canada. They list as well on Nasdaq (the National Association of Securities Dealers Automated Quotation System), the fast-growing floorless electronic U.S. exchange that specializes in high-tech listings. In the first quarter of 1990, just after its Nasdaq listing, Intera Information Technologies of Calgary, the world's leader in remote-sensing airborne data collection, had the distinction of being the best-performing new stock issue in the United States.

For Canadian high-tech firms to grow to $100 million and beyond and to withstand international competitors like IBM, Siemens, Philips, Hewlett-Packard, and so on, requires the global mindset that underlines the strategies of these world-famous companies. In brief, they go after the market rather than wait for customers to come to them. Companies that are serious about doing well globally must sometimes place competitiveness ahead of nationalism. Specifically, they perform R&D and manufacturing outside, as well as within their home country, so as to be welcome in foreign lands.

Also, sophisticated, aggressive marketing is essential. Since the large U.S. market is the principal target of Canadian high-tech firms, more and more are opening U.S. regional offices. Some are even shifting worldwide marketing management to the United States. Further, the importation of American and overseas experts, already on the rise, will accelerate because high-tech industry suffers from a chronic shortage of skilled managers. This shortage is blamed for the recent financial woes of several Canadian firms in their metamorphoses from entrepreneurial to big corporation status. Most are recovering, thanks to more stringent controls.

Cognos is a good example of the restructuring process. From March through October, 1989, it suffered significant losses. It pinpointed the cause as internal operational weaknesses, rather than external factors like market conditions and product competitiveness. Subsequently, it undertook a series of corrective measures, including the elimination of 16 percent of its workforce through layoffs, attrition, and the sale of a small division. It also split operational responsibilities between the United States and Canada. R&D, administration, and finance remain headquartered in Canada. Worldwide sales and field marketing are now in Boston, reflecting the fact that the United States accounts for 41 percent of Cognos's revenue and total non-Canadian sales contribute 82 percent.

"We are in a highly competitive industry and virtually all our competition is American; therefore, we felt we would not be able to compete effectively unless we were closer to our customers and had access to more experienced managers in sales and marketing," Michael Potter explains. "In general, there is not enough experienced talent in Canada for a firm to become a world-class player." Since Boston is a high-tech centre, Cognos has ready access to a big talent pool at firms comparable in size to it. In Ottawa, the next largest software company is one-twelfth of Cognos's size.

The internationalization and decentralization such as occurred at Cognos do not have to shortchange Canada. For example, half of Cognos's staff is in Canada, even though it accounts for under one-fifth of total revenue. "We feed five hundred families directly through employee paycheques and another fifteen hundred to two thousand through payments to suppliers," Potter says. "But some jobs had to be moved out for the company's best interest. Between 8:00 A.M. and 6:00 P.M., I only care about making Cognos hum, so if it's important to do something that may not seem to be in Canada's best interest, it's my job to do it. I believe Canada needs lots of billion-dollar technology companies. That revenue cannot be achieved without being a major international player." Inasmuch as Cognos became profitable after its restructuring as "a stronger, leaner, more competitive company," Potter's actions appear to have been effective.

Another fact of life that Canadians will have to accept is a likely increase in foreign ownership of Canadian high-tech firms. Canadian nationalists abhor such takeovers, maintaining that Canada is losing control over a vital economic sector. But the acquired companies say gratitude should be the reaction, because the infusion of foreign money makes it possible for them to become world-class, worldscale global companies. They also point out that either Canadian companies did not make counter offers or those that were made were too low.

Certainly, enthusiasm is the reaction at Ottawa-based Lumonics, the world's leading supplier of laser-based product-identification coding systems. Its acquisition in 1989 by Sumitomo Heavy Industries of Japan touched off an alarmed outcry by opponents of foreign takeovers. But Lumonics regards its acquisition as the formation of a "winning combination" rather than a takeover. Established in 1970, Lumonics is now one of the world's five leading companies in laser technology. At the time of its sale to Sumitomo, its revenues topped $87 million. Its future is bright, since only 10 percent of business in laser technology has yet been tapped.

Nevertheless, it needed outside help because technological progress is shortening product life cycles and, hence, requiring heavy investment in R&D so as to stay in the top tier. Considering that Lumonics had losses in 1986, 1987, and 1988 before the sale of a software division, the amount of money it required to remain worldclass in R&D would have been a severe drain had it remained independent. Moreover, it was at a marked disadvantage in funding laser programs against global companies like Toshiba and NEC of Japan, General Electric of the United States, and Siemens of Germany, which all earn billions of dollars in revenue. Further, U.S. government funding for lasers nearly equals the total value of worldwide laser sales. Much of the U.S. money is from the Defense Department for the "Star Wars" program, but large chunks are also awarded by the Department of Energy and the National Science Foundation.

Most laser companies sell regionally rather than worldwide. As a major component of the worldwide Sumitomo Group ($2 billion in sales when Lumonics was acquired), Sumitomo Heavy Industries has the money and the scope to permit Lumonics to achieve its goal of becoming the first truly global laser company. The Sumitomo connection gives Lumonics easy entrée to the Japanese and other Far Eastern markets. Previously, Lumonics concentrated on North America and Europe. "Sumitomo's purchase of Lumonics doesn't speed up the process of globalization; it makes it possible," Lumonics's president and chief executive officer, J. Hugh MacDiarmid, states firmly. "It is now realistic for Lumonics to set its sights on being a long-term major international player in lasers." Also, now that Lumonics is part of Sumitomo, it no longer is publicly traded and, therefore, not subject to shareholder criticism if earnings dip from time to time. This allows Lumonics to plan in three-, five-, and seven-year cycles, compared to the old quarterly and annual pattern. With its money worries a thing of the past, Lumonics has the reverse problem of not wildly overspending. MacDiarmid says the watchword is "prudence" to avoid "irresponsible goldplating."

In allowing the purchase of Lumonics by a foreign buyer, the federal government mandated that Lumonics remain a separate legal entity. It also has considerable autonomy. Lumonics's nominated directors outnumber Sumitomo's on its board, and MacDiarmid is not besieged with daily telexes, facsimile messages, or telephone calls. The Japanese wait for his monthly reports. In other words, he has more independence than many subsidiaries of Canadian companies.

To MacDiarmid, controversy over foreign ownership is a "red herring. If foreign ownership is the demon that critics claim it is, then it's 'game over' for Canada, because Canadian high technology is substantially foreign-owned by IBM, Xerox, Digital Equipment, Control Data, and so on," he says. Adds Desmond Cunningham (19 percent shareholder) of Canadian-owned Gandalf: "Canadians generally don't mind if one Canadian company takes over another. For some Canadian high-tech firms to succeed internationally, they must be associated with a player already on the international market. The Canadian domestic market is such a small percentage of the world market that the Canadian tail can't be expected to wag the rest of the dog."

Two other well-known Canadian high-tech firms that became foreign-controlled are Ottawa-based Mitel (telecommunications), which is 51 percent owned by British Telecommunications of the U.K., and Vancouver-based Mobile Data International (mobile data communications), wholly owned since 1988 by Motorola of the United States. Both praise the results. When British Telecom paid $222 million in 1985 for its stake in Mitel, "the infusion of money was absolutely necessary" for Mitel's growth, says F. Robert Dyer, executive vice-president, marketing, at Mitel. The investment reflected British Telecom's desire at the time to be a telephone equipment manufacturer as well as a supplier of telephone service. Mitel supplies 25 percent of Canadian PBXs (private branch exchange) and is the fourth largest supplier in the United States. PBX systems are designed for businesses, hotels, and other customers who need a private telephone network.

When British Telecom announced its intention to pull out of Mitel in early 1990, it said it preferred to concentrate on telephone service, rather than do everything. Financial analysts, however, blamed Mitel's heavy losses, caused largely by intense competition in the United States, the world's biggest telecommunications market. But weight must be given to British Telecom's explanation because Mitel had suffered losses in the two years before the British takeover, and in its fiscal year ended March 31, 1989 recorded its first profit since its acquisition. Although some of that profit was due to a British Telecom R&D contract, that contract was two years old in 1989 and was not in itself enough to save Mitel from losses in 1987 and 1988. Mitel also had a profit in fiscal 1990 but reverted to losses in 1991, which executives attributed to promotion expenses designed to benefit the company over the long term.

Established in 1978, Mobile Data did not seek a stock exchange listing until 1986. The timing proved bad since the stock market declined in 1987 and high-tech stocks were particularly hard hit. Like other underpriced companies, Mobile Data became a takeover target. BCE, the controlling shareholder of Northern Telecom, made what Mobile considered too low a bid; it chose a much higher offer from Motorola. Mobile also was pleased with Motorola's decision to fold its worldwide mobile-data activities into the Canadian firm's, instead of following the usual procedure whereby the acquired company is reduced to a satellite. Mobile Data now ranks first worldwide in its field.

"Motorola provides us with worldclass technological, financial, and distribution resources to which we did not have access as a small company," says David Sutcliffe, vice-president, marketing. "Admittedly, that could have happened with any multinational company, including Canadian ones, but there were no Canadian bids other than BCE's. Moreover, high technology is very much an international business in which there aren't boundaries from an investment and ownership view."

The key to global success for high-tech firms is the selection of niches below the size that would attract the attention of giant firms. That way, fatal confrontations are avoided. In addition, it is imperative to steer clear of products that are too far ahead of customers' needs. Young companies also face another dilemma: diversification is essential to make up for declining sales in older products, yet there is a limit to what a small firm can do. Thus, the usual growth strategy is add-ons, which can be marketed and distributed in the same way as the original.

What follows are the strategies of a cross-section of Canadian global high-tech firms:

Computer Hardware

As mentioned earlier, Gandalf Technologies is the foremost Canadian-owned computer hardware firm. Established in 1971, Gandalf makes data switches, transmission devices, and application servers; it also develops software. Its sales doubled between 1985 and 1990. Besides its Canadian facilities, it develops technology as well as manufacturers in England and has numerous foreign field services offices—two dozen in the United States, seven in the United Kingdom, two in continental Europe, and two in Australia. It derives 70 percent of its revenue from outside Canada. Its success is in sharp contrast to Canada's overall trade deficit in computer hardware, one of the worst among industrialized countries.

Gandalf has done well globally because, as chairman and founder Desmond Cunningham says, it realized "from day one that it had to export. Canadian business is trivial in size compared to the global market." Cunningham also was certain that the large U.S. market was the first outside Canada that Gandalf should tackle "because to be successful in exports, you have to succeed in the U.S." Another reason for his decision is that "it is easier and less expensive from Gandalf's Ottawa headquarters to cross the border than to go west of Ontario."

Therefore, Gandalf entered the United States in 1974, just three years after its formation. Four years later, it moved into Europe. Manufacturing is assigned to Canada or to England, depending on where the products' designers are located and on which country has the best tariff relationship with the countries for which the products are destined. A computerized system analyzing the availability of finished products and parts as well as order volume also determines which country gets the nod. "When you are exporting to 30 countries, it's irrelevant where the products are made," Cunningham says.

Today, about one-third of Gandalf's sales are in the United States, 19 percent in England, 18 percent in continental Europe, and about 7 percent in the Pacific Rim. It is the U.S. operation, where Gandalf has been the longest outside of Canada, that caused headaches in the late 1980s. Why and how they were solved is indicative of the surprises that the U.S. market can hold for Canadian firms. Cunningham readily admits that the fault lay with Gandalf, not with any external factors. He says the firm's principal error was that it "globalized so fast, it failed to pay due regard to the differences in the U.S. market." Too late, Gandalf discovered that "U.S. buyers are more pragmatic and concerned with today's imminent problems, prices, performance, and delivery than longer-term solutions, the chief interest of Canadians and Europeans."

Because it was blind to the differences, Gandalf made what turned out to be unwarranted investments in the United States. A printed circuitboard assembly plant was opened, the U.S. head office staff in Chicago greatly expanded, and strategies devised for selling value-added services, in which, as it happened, the Americans had no interest since their principal concern was basic equipment. In short, as Cunningham ruefully recalls, "Gandalf pushed ahead too quickly." No wonder he says that the lesson Gandalf learned was "to do business the way your customers want, not the way you want."

When 1989 U.S. profits dropped by 51 percent on top of a 30-percent decline in 1988, Cunningham took swift, sharp action. He closed the U.S. plant, consolidated circuitboard assembly at the Canadian factory, sold a Washington, D.C. information systems office, pared U.S. head office staff so that there were no longer "lots of frills," and returned responsibility for sales to the regional offices. Further, he revised the marketing style to match U.S. tastes. Subsequently, in May 1991 Gandalf acted to increase its international competitiveness through a merger with Infotron Systems of New Jersey that expands its product line and customer potential. Both firms are about the same age, but Gandalf's revenue was somewhat larger at the time of the merger. Gandalf specializes in local area network equipment that enables computers to communicate within buildings and Infotron in wide-area equipment that transmits data across cities and countries. The two firms believe that through merging they can now afford the type of research and development necessary to be globally competitive that neither could have done on its own. The merger was by a share exchange with two shares of Infotron to one share of Gandalf.

Computer Software

Although Canada has a computer software trade deficit, Canadian ownership in this industry is four times greater than in computer hardware. The number of firms in this field is rapidly increasing with, all told, an estimated two hundred across Canada. The largest, Cognos, was described earlier in this chapter. Here are the diverse global strategies of three more software firms: Eicon Technology, Empress Software, and Virtual Prototypes, including how they corrected their errors.

Within five years of its 1984 establishment, Eicon Technology of Montreal, which now exports to 40 countries, won the federal government's Canada Export Award. From the outset, Eicon concentrated on foreign sales. The result is that it is much better known abroad than at home. An Eicon employee who told an acquaintance in the Quebec government civil service, "I work for Eicon," received the response, "Is that an American company?" When the employee reported the comment to Maks Wulkan, Eicon's executive vice-president, Wulkan "considered it a compliment because there is a stigma associated with Canadian companies that they are unsuccessful in high technology." He was less pleased, however, by his own encounter with this lack of familiarity. When he attempted to interest a reporter at a U.S. trade show in Eicon's products, the journalist replied that he was only writing about Canadian companies since he was from a Canadian newspaper.

Eicon specializes in high-speed, multiple-function data communications systems for personal computers. For example, its plug-in "script card" provides a wide variety of typefaces and makes possible multiple-page printing in the background while the user goes on to edit or perform the next job. It also makes products that electronically connect personal computers with IBM mainframes. Two years after it was founded, the company won its first international contract: the connection of 650 Bank of Finland branches to IBM computers by means of Eicon's "gateway" circuit board communication cards. Subsequently, it went on to sell to such prominent customers as Telecom Australia, American Airlines, United Parcel Service, the Union Bank of Switzerland, and the Vancouver Stock Exchange.

The principal reason for Eicon's success is conservatism. Its policy is not to spread itself too thin by trying to do everything. Therefore, rather than borrow, it self-finances, and rather than spend on manufacturing, it invests in R&D and subcontracts production. Also, it sacrifices potential growth in revenue if such growth could endanger profitability. This strategy has saved Eicon from two fates common to young high-tech companies—failure or takeover.

The caution is rooted in the background of Eicon's founders and the company's penny-watching fledgling years. Peter Brojde, Eicon's president, and Wulkan previously worked at a word-processor company. It poured millions of dollars into a rapid buildup of a large direct sales force and then suffered huge losses due to high staff turnover and failure to capture much of the marketplace.

To Brojde, who oversees finance and administration at Eicon, the lesson was clear: a big company could afford to lose millions of dollars but such losses would instantly kill a startup one like Eicon. Therefore, he imposed strict financial controls from which Eicon has not deviated, even as its revenue has swelled. "We base our spending on what has been earned, not on projections," he states. In Eicon's difficult first two years, when its capitalization was low and only $400,000 could be raised from outside sources, Brojde encouraged employees to become shareholders to help finance the company. As Eicon is privately owned, how well these initial investors have done is not public knowledge. But its growth to 150 employees in just six years, its low staff turnover, and its selection in 1989 as one of Canada's 50 best-managed private companies in a survey by chartered accountants Arthur Andersen & Company are favourable indicators.

By opting not to manufacture in-house, Eicon can devote its money to R&D, so essential for high-tech firms, and to marketing. Out of Eicon's 150 employees, only one person has manufacturing responsibilities. He checks that Eicon's contractors meet its quality assurance procedures. The firms are all located in Eicon's home province of Quebec, enabling easy supervision. According to Brojde, the production failure rate averages 2 percent or less, lower than at many larger companies that manufacture in-house. Sixty of Eicon's employees are engaged in R&D. Here again, the company is pragmatic, constantly querying customers' needs so that new products will meet their expectations.

From the outset, Wulkan, who oversees product development and marketing, followed what he calls an "unorthodox approach for a Canadian company." Because the Canadian market is small, he decided to "pretend it did not exist" and went after business elsewhere. He ignored the conventional wisdom that the United States should top the list of Canadian exporters. Instead, he first courted Europe, as European buying habits seemed more compatible with the sales strategy and budget of a young, unknown company that was solely reliant on its product to open doors of potential customers. Wulkan explains: "In Europe, distributors invest more in technical know-how, have lower turnover in sales personnel, and are service oriented. They have an established end-user base or can establish one quickly. By contrast, American distributors operate on lower margins, lack time for end-users because they sell lots of products which sometimes compete, and are not interested in long-term selling cycles. They tend just to be box movers." Consequently, Eicon has 80 distributors across the United States compared to only three in France. Of course, France is considerably smaller and its population less, but the ratio is still extremely disproportionate.

Also, Europe's economic concentration simplified Eicon's sales drive. In Europe, most telephone companies are government-run monopolies; in the United States, many independents exist, thanks to the deregulation of American Telephone & Telegraph (AT&T). In Europe, just a few banks covering an entire country have most of the business; in the United States, nationwide banks do not exist. Also, most European countries are easier to tackle since there is far less territory to cover than in the United States. Finally, in Europe, according to Wulkan, buying decisions are reached faster, as they are made by lower management and not referred upwards through the hierarchy, as in North America. As a result, Europe now accounts for 45 percent of Eicon's sales. Its objective is an even one-third split between Europe, the United States, and the rest of the world, including Canada.

Reflecting Eicon's credo of temperate, well-managed growth, Wulkan waits until sales volume justifies establishing regional marketing offices, instead of opening them in anticipation of sales. For example, opening the London-based European office was preceded by a year of developing a network of British distributors on the premise that if the U.K. tryout were to fail, it would only be a local setback, from which the rest of Eicon's European program would be immune. A similar go-slow approach characterizes Eicon's Pacific Rim expansion. Rather than tackle all the countries, it followed a two-phase approach, starting with Australia, New Zealand, and Hong Kong, and then moving on to Japan, South Korea, and Taiwan, where English is spoken less.

How Wulkan built Eicon's European distribution network is illustrative of his methods worldwide and a useful illustration for other companies starting cold in foreign countries. He consulted Canadian government overseas trade commissioners and read trade journal articles and advertisements on leading distributors. From these sources, he distilled a list of distributors of interest to him. Then he invited them to Montreal, but in keeping with Eicon's tight-fisted policy, informed them that they would have to pay their own way. He figured Eicon's technology was a drawing card and his confidence proved warranted.

Subsequently, as Eicon developed worldwide ambitions, Wulkan hired local public relations agencies to promote the company. Eicon does not advertise; it believes newspaper articles generated by public relations firms deliver the message more convincingly. The stories, along with customer referrals, smoothed Eicon's entry into the fiercely competitive U.S. market. Consequently, the U.S. vice-president of operations has yet to make unsolicited "cold" sales calls; instead, his pleasant task is to respond to inquiries. Because account management and personnel hiring are handled by the distributors, Eicon can devote the substantial funds that would have to be set aside for such functions to marketing and R&D.

Eicon is sufficiently successful for Brojde and Wulkan to admit their record is not flawless. For example, at times they waited too long to replace distributors whose sales were disappointing. They also sometimes misjudged sales targets, with the result that their salespeople concentrated too much on small customers. But these are not organizational weaknesses; rather, they are the regular ups and downs of any sales effort. Wulkan says the plan for Eicon's future is "maximum growth at a rate that will not destroy the infrastructure. After all, it is more fun when a company is profitable."

Toronto-based Empress Software, founded in 1981 by John Kornatowski immediately after he graduated from the University of Toronto, is regarded as a world leader in advanced relational database management systems. The Flexible software can be used for casual queries, quick prototyping, and complex application development. These applications including mapping, voice messaging, simulator design, image processing, and computer-aided design and manufacturing.

Like Brojde and Wulkan at Eicon, Kornatowski concentrated from the start on international sales. In his case, the chief reason was that "it was difficult to sell our leading edge technology in a conservative business climate like Canada's." How he refined his marketing strategy is a useful study for this decade's global novices. Initially, when his financial resources were very limited, he telephoned prospective customers, starting with high-tech contacts he had made while working on a research project at the University of Toronto. When revenue increased, Kornatowski hired a Canadian advertising and public relations agency. This proved to be a mistake because Empress was targetting an international audience, starting with the large U.S. market. Kornatowski soon realized he should have hired an agency that was well known in the United States. "A typical magazine throws out most of the press releases it receives and only pays attention to those about companies with track records or with well-regarded PR representatives," he comments.

Therefore, Kornatowski switched to an American public relations agency in 1988, the same year he opened a sales and marketing office in Greenbelt, Maryland, a suburb of Washington, D.C. The office was opened to underscore Empress's commitment to U.S. sales. "Our American customers told us that to show we were truly serious, we should establish a major U.S. presence," he says. His choice of location reflects the predilection of small niche firms to steer clear of head-on conflicts with larger rivals. In the case of Empress, its primary U.S. competition is in California's high-tech Silicon Valley near San Francisco. Kornatowski selected Greenbelt, all the way across the country. It places him near two desired customer groups: the U.S. federal government and East Coast computer hardware and software firms.

Today, 93 percent of Empress's sales are outside Canada, including in East Germany, where Empress set up a representative office in July 1990. The opening was timed to coincide with the establishment of a common "hard" (foreign exchange convertible) currency by East and West Germany in advance of their October 1990 reunification.

International business is usually developed by the firm seeking it. But as Empress's experience in Japan demonstrates, foreign companies will sometimes pursue suppliers, sparked by their needs and/or word of mouth. Empress has much-praised technology and is one of the more than twenty-four thousand Canadian companies registered at no charge in the Canadian government's WIN Exports (World Information Network for Exports) computerized international sourcing directory.* Canada's trade promotion officers around the world use the directory to bring together foreign customers and Canadian firms. In Empress's case, a small Japanese software consulting firm requested the name of a Canadian database firm. Because database expansion is still in its early stages in Japan, the Japanese suitor believed an alliance with a well-established firm would give it a commanding lead.

Virtual Prototypes of Montreal designs software for complex control and display systems used in aircraft cockpits, car dashboards, and in monitoring workstations. Its evolution typifies the global entrepreneurial route. Founder and president Eugene Joseph, formerly an aerospace software manager at a multinational company, had the idea for Virtual Prototypes in 1980. He obtained his initial outside funding in 1984, hired his first employees in 1985, and got fully underway in 1987 with the introduction of his breakthrough technology. Using graphic visualization, the technology simultaneously addresses three basic functions: rapid prototyping of operator interfaces, real-time simulation, and automatic

---

This program is outlined on page 245 in "Appendix A: Federal Government Assistance."

software generation for operational systems. One year after its launch, the technology won a federal government Award for Business Excellence for innovation. Today, Virtual Prototypes employs more than 70 people and does 95 percent of its business outside Canada, selling to foreign government defence agencies, aircraft builders, and car manufacturers.

The first people Joseph hired were engineers. For some time he performed all other functions including sales, marketing, finance, accounting, and even coffee making. As sales increased, he hired salespeople and, later, professional financial managers to oversee budgets "like a hawk." Five vice-presidents now cover overall marketing, North American sales, offshore sales, engineering, and finance.

Joseph's international background prepared him for going global. Romanian born and later an Israeli resident, he moved to Canada in 1979. He speaks several languages and regards himself as "mentally attuned to thinking globally." What he says about himself also applies to thousands of other immigrants to Canada who share his competitive edge in taking a business global. But Joseph says unilingual Canadians can do well abroad, too, "if they have the flexibility of mind to understand other people and their customs." Of course, some mastery of one or more foreign languages helps, too.

At the inception of Virtual Prototypes, Joseph was in the position of most high-tech entrepreneurs: he had a unique but unknown product, the value of which he had to prove. Therefore, instead of the usual aggressive sales pitch, he sounded out how receptive a government agency or company would be to a system like his. Nor did he necessarily start with the purchasing department. On his first trip to the United States Air Force, he demonstrated his technology to its human factor psychologists, who are consulted about the design of equipment from the user's point of view. This tactic ultimately served as an introduction to other U.S. government defence agencies. When sales were made to these agencies, word of mouth led to other countries as well as aerospace companies throughout the world, giving Joseph a receptive hearing.

Virtual Prototypes sells directly in North America, where it is familiar with the market. To avoid missteps overseas where customs and cultures are considerably different, the company works through distributors. At first, it turned to a European firm of management consultants that specializes in distributor recruitment, but subsequent displeasure with their recommendations forced Virtual

Prototypes to conduct the hunt on its own. Joseph looks for people attuned to local buying habits. "The French, Swedes, and Japanese are very technically oriented," he says. "The Italians want exceptional design, and the Americans focus on management and financial benefits." Besides sales calls, Joseph relies on brochures, videotapes, and trade shows to promote Virtual Prototypes. He waited to hire a public relations agency "because agencies do not regard under $150,000 to $200,000 a year in business as worthwhile, and that was above our means at first." For the future, Joseph plans "more of the same," but he points out that planning is only part of the process. Opportunity-based growth is also important. "People who say they plan everything are lying," he maintains.

Engineering, Medical, and Scientific Instrumentation

Intera Information Technologies of Calgary, as already mentioned, is the world's leader in remote-sensing airborne data collection. Its imaging radar technology penetrates clouds and haze, which hamper optical mapping techniques. Intera does 80 percent of its business in 85 foreign countries and won the federal government's Canada Export Award in 1988. Due to the large gains in its international business, Intera's revenue jumped from $12 million (U.S.) in 1985 to $57 million (U.S.) in its fiscal year ended September 30, 1990. It predicts fiscal 1991 revenue of $75 million (U.S.). The company is 30.6 percent owned by Trimac, also of Calgary; its revenue is well over $300 million. In addition to bulk highway transportation, Trimac drills gas and oil fields and constructs oil fields and pipelines, and these activities are the link with Intera's specialty. Sixty percent of Intera's work is for petroleum and mining companies. The rest is for the governments of such countries as Canada, the United States, the United Kingdom, Greece, Pakistan, India, and Indonesia, and for international funding agencies like the World Bank, the United Nations Development Program, and the Canadian International Development Agency.

Brian Bullock, Intera's founder and president, attributes Intera's success to pinpointing a niche where it could attain and maintain world leadership. "Canadian firms considering going international should pick a niche in which they estimate their credentials are the best," he says. In addition, Intera demonstrates that a small Canadian firm which is a newcomer to a field can sweep ahead of a much bigger rival. When Bullock decided Intera's mission was to be the market leader in remote-sensing airborne data collection, he knew he faced competition from a subsidiary of Litton Industries, a prominent U.S.-based manufacturer of aerospace and defence equipment, including airborne radar. Nevertheless, Bullock proceeded because airborne radar was not Litton's main line. "If you seek the nooks and crannies around mainline businesses and then pick your corner well, new market possibilities can be created," Bullock explains.

When Intera introduced new technology in 1983, Litton chose not to counterattack through updating its system. Instead, it raised nontariff barriers by urging the U.S. government to "buy American." Bullock realized Intera could only overcome these barriers by devising technology so good that the U.S. government would have to buy outside the country. In 1989, the breakthrough was achieved with "Star-Map," which enables airborne radar to be used for the production of three-dimensional digital terrain models. "Star-Map" received rave reviews in the reconnaissance community and quickly gained the attention of the U.S. Defense Mapping Agency. Within months, it awarded Intera a $7.9 million contract. At that time, it was Intera's largest terrain mapping project in its history. Shortly afterwards, in what could be classified as a sweet victory, Intera purchased the Litton subsidiary.

That purchase reflects Bullock's penchant to expand outside Canada through the acquisition of troubled companies with turnaround potential. They give Intera an instant presence, saving it the hardship of starting from scratch. Their bargain prices are also easy on budgets. For example, within two years the profits from an Intera-acquired financially strapped U.K. company paid for its purchase. Europe accounts for the largest portion—34 percent—of Intera's foreign sales, prompting Bullock to form a remote-sensing joint venture with a Spanish mapping firm. He chose Spain because it receives sizable technological development funding from European Community programs aimed at encouragement of local high technology. Intera is the majority owner and manager of the venture.

Although his goal is continued expansion, Bullock rejects opportunities in countries where the terms offered are so poor that Intera would lose money. But his chief concern echoes that of all burgeoning high-tech companies: how to control growth rather than be controlled by it. In Intera's first five years, Bullock sought to attract young talent by giving them enough stock at dirt cheap prices that they would become millionaires if the company did well. He calculated this would encourage dedication, loyalty, and commitment. His calculation proved correct, since the stock's value did appreciate considerably.

Subsequently, in 1981 Bullock set up a deferred profit-sharing plan. The company contributes 7.5 percent of full-time employee's annual salaries (to a maximum of $3,500) and 3.5 percent of contract employee's earnings for their first five years of employment and 7.5 percent thereafter. Five years later in 1986, employee stock option purchase programs were introduced, as well as an annual bonus pool based on profitability and payable in cash, shares, or a combination.

Intera's initial employees were technicians, who learned how to manage as the business grew. But the recent rapid growth prompted Bullock to hire outside management consultants to provide in-house training and to employ professional managers whom Intera instructs in its technology. Bullock believes the "mix of the two backgrounds helps each group." Originally, Intera's global marketing was run on a functional product line basis with sales-forces assigned separately to the business units for petroleum and resource management, and for mapping and reconnaissance. This made possible easy detection of whether profit centres had deteriorated into cost centres. However, the advantage was offset by a lack of geographic co-ordination. To overcome this drawback, in 1991 Bullock appointed area co-ordinators for both project and marketing activities on a one-year trial basis. The co-ordinators scout sales opportunities and then turn over their prospects to the relevant product line. Bullock says the benefit is that regional product representatives "now go to see live prospects, rather than spend time on cold calls."

A substantial portion of Intera's in-house training deals with the importance of improved timeliness in delivery to customers. Such responsiveness is essential in high-technology industries where new products are in development before the ones they are designed to make obsolescent are even on the market. Also, customers' expectations often outpace technology's capabilities. Intera conducted customer surveys to determine where it fell short, and found that despite its speed, clients still wanted faster service. "Even when we cut our delivery time by a factor of ten, we receive no praise," Bullock says. Nevertheless, repeat orders are a very gratifying form of praise.

Nordion International of Ottawa, a Crown-run business recently privatized, specializes in nuclear medicine products. It is the world's major supplier of cobalt 60, the radioisotope most commonly used as an energy source in cancer therapy and commercial radiation processing. Nordion also produces most other nuclear reactor-produced isotopes used worldwide for medical diagnosis, sterilization of surgical and medical supplies, protection of agricultural crops and livestock, and waste disinfection. Close to 95 percent of its products are exported. In addition, Nordion engineers have designed and installed more than half of the world's commercial, research, and clinical irradiators. In short, this high-technology niche is another in which a Canadian firm is paramount. Nordion's president and chief executive officer, W. Paul O'Neill, attributes the supremacy to Canada "being in the forefront in the development of peaceful uses of atomic energy."

His remark sums up Nordion's history. It began modestly in 1946 as a three-person commercial products division of the federal government-owned Eldorado Mining and Refining. Its mission was to market radium, a radioactive element found in uranium ore and widely used at the time to treat cancer. Shortly afterward, the division embarked on a more ambitious quest: to develop beneficial new uses and markets for radioisotopes produced in the National Research Council's reactor at Chalk River, Ontario. Within two years, Eldorado began to export radioisotope products to the United States, and three years later it installed the world's first cobalt 60 cancer therapy machine at the Victoria Hospital in London, Ontario. In 1952, the commercial products division was transferred to a new Crown corporation, Atomic Energy of Canada. It continued to develop medical uses for radioisotopes that furthered its competitive position in world markets. In 1988, the division was spun off on its own under the name Nordion International. It remained in its Kanata, Ontario facilities just west of Ottawa. Its move there in the early 1960s played an important role in the establishment of Kanata as a Canadian high-tech centre. In 1987, Nordion's breakthrough technology for the production of a low-cost, high-purity iodine radioisotope used in brain, heart, kidney, and thyroid studies won the federal government's Business Excellence Award for innovation.

Nordion differs from the other companies in this book in that its initial purpose was not to make money, but rather to give away its technology. Thus, when the government declared its intention in 1985 to privatize it as part of the sell-off of several Crown corporations, Nordion had to plan how it would survive without the prop of government support. "For Nordion to be a leader in the year 2010, it had to begin doing things differently than in its preceding 30 years," O'Neill says. His first step was to include "International" in the firm's name to emphasize that the bulk of its business is outside Canada. A company slogan "Towards a better world" was devised and is used in all of Nordion's promotional literature.

Nordion had the advantage of an existing global customer base and an extensive distribution network, but O'Neill was not content with a simple continuation of the status quo. His goal is reduction of Nordion's dependence on the United States, now Nordion's largest export customer. Thus, in 1990, he opened a Hong Kong office to be closer to Nordion's agents in the Pacific Rim, which he regards as a market with big growth potential for nuclear medicine products. "The onsite supervision enables better management of the agents and closer contacts with customers," he states.

Across the world in Europe, Nordion acquired a Belgian company in 1990, well in advance of the 1992 unification of the European Community markets and close to Eastern Europe, as well Unlike companies in most industries, Nordion's list of acquisition candidates was limited because the world does not contain many firms making nuclear products of a peaceful nature. Indeed, the only similar European company up for sale was a Belgian government-owned one that had been recently privatized. It was available for a reason—it was losing money. Nevertheless, O'Neill elected to overlook the red ink because the firm was licensed to manufacture nuclear-related products on a regulated site and such licences not only are expensive, but also very difficult to obtain, owing to the opposition of antinuclear activists.

While Nordion's acquisition hunt had its unique characteristics, a complication arose that is a hazard that many companies going global could face: a lawsuit to stop the sale by an irate distributor. It was upset by Nordion's desire to replace it with an in-house sales force; Nordion counter-argued that coverage by a full-time team would substantially boost sales. Only after the Belgian government agreed to indemnify Nordion should the distributor's litigation succeed, did Nordion proceed with the final negotiations.

Health care is one of today's fastest growing industries, but the market for nuclear medicine products is increasing at a slower pace. Thus, international expansion will continue to have priority at Nordion.

Newtech Instruments of St. John's, Newfoundland has followed a novel strategy that might appeal to other small companies. It has diversified domestically in sectors with steady business in order to earn the money to maintain its world lead in its unique marine technology, called the "hydroball," for which demand is limited. Priced at $35,000, it is a tracking device that profiles the depth, speed, direction, and temperature of ocean currents. From this information, fishing and naval vessels, as well as offshore oil and gas rigs, can calculate weeks in advance whether icebergs will drift into their paths. Advance knowledge that no collision will occur eliminates unnecessary removals of equipment. Consequently, hundreds of thousands of dollars are saved.

Newtech was formed as a joint partnership in 1986 by the hydroball's inventor, William Russell, and NewTel Enterprises, which owns Newfoundland Telephone. In turn, NewTel is 56.2 percent owned by BCE (Bell Canada Enterprises). Russell sold his share to NewTel in 1989. Newtech's president, Donald Nickerson, was formerly vice-president, network services, and chief engineer at Newfoundland Telephone. He is responsible for Newtech's ingenious diversification. He decided that Newtech "required more arrows to its bow because the marketplace is such that it is impossible to sell a hydroball every month. Therefore, hydroballs cannot be expected to provide a stable revenue base."

Nickerson believed more general appeal manufacturing would provide stability. For contracts, he went both outside and within Newfoundland Telephone. As a source of outside revenue, he moved Newtech into the production of instrument panels for military vehicles. Newtech's first bid was submitted to General Motors' military vehicle plant at London, Ontario. At stake was a $500,000 contract, and General Motors was dubious about Newtech's capability, although impressed by its product and price. What finally gave Newtech the winning edge was the credibility provided by Newfoundland Telephone which owned it. Since then, Newtech has pursued business with other foreign defence manufacturers that produce military vehicles in Canada. However, their activity has been weakened by government cutbacks in defence budgets. Newtech's third activity is repair work on telephone electronic circuit cards for its parent company. NewTel decided it was faster to farm out the work than do it itself. For Newtech, it provides the security of around $100,000 in annual business.

The revenue obtained through the diversification has enabled research and development on add-on products for the hydroball. The first one developed is a salinity sensor for such diverse purposes as the detection of river pollution and of ocean plankton, the sea's basic food source. Ever on the search for new global niches,

Newtech's latest product is a protective antisplice moulding for telephone cables. It deliberately was designed for heavily populated countries with cheap labour where, as Nickerson comments, "governments love to have something that is labour intensive, yet easy to install."

Although Newtech is small, with only 16 employees, it devotes considerable effort to international expansion. One of the two marketing people goes on twice-a-year worldwide prospecting trips, partly on federal government export market development grants for business. Most of his activity is for the hydroball, which Nickerson says "has to sell worldwide to be successful" because of limited demand in Canada. Because Newtech could not afford to hire its own global sales force, it relies on distributors as well as advertisements in internationally read oceanography magazines.

Telecommunications

More than any other industry, telecommunications is responsible for growing worldwide recognition of Canadian excellence in high technology. Moreover, the industry's dynamic growth provides substantial opportunities for further gains by Canadian companies. Within this decade alone, the total global telecommunications equipment market is expected to triple from $120 billion to $360 billion.

Canadian firms excel internationally in telecommunications primarily because they patiently and aggressively earned their reputations. Significantly, telecommunications firms are Canada's largest corporate spenders on research and development, accounting for 14 percent of the total. Annually, Northern Telecom, the biggest Canadian telecommunications firm, spends 12 percent of its revenue on R&D. In 1990, that amounted to $773.7 million U.S.* ($902.7 million Canadian). That percentage far surpasses the just overall 1 percent average spent on research and development by the entire country. The enormity of Northern Telecom's R&D outlay can further be appreciated when compared to the revenues of Canada's top 500 industrial companies. In 1990, all but 125 earned less in sales than Nortel spent on R&D.

In addition to gaining international respect for their technical creativity, Canadian telecommunications manufacturers are well regarded for "their high degree of integrity," according to F. Robert

---

As mentioned earlier, Northern Telecom does its accounts in U.S. dollars.

Dyer of Mitel. As a 24-year industry employee, he worked at Bell Canada and Northern Telecom before coming to Mitel. He says he is well acquainted with Canadians' good international reputation. "It is a tremendous asset in foreign countries where the concept that 'my word is my bond' is valued highly," he adds.

Another reason for the global success of Canadian telecommunications companies is that they offer a choice between American Telephone & Telegraph (AT&T) of the United States and European giants like Philips of the Netherlands, Siemens of Germany, and Ericsson of Sweden. Finally, Canadian competitiveness in this industry is not harmed by high wages and poor productivity since the labour content is low. In some products, it accounts for as little as 10 percent of the selling price. For example, the labour content in a telephone has declined from a not very time-consuming 25 minutes in the 1970s to just 8 minutes today, and work is underway to reduce it even further.

What follows are the stories of five telecommunications firms active globally: Mitel and Newbridge Networks of Ottawa; Novatel of Calgary; Mobile Data International of Vancouver; and Positron of Montreal. Northern Telecom, Canada's largest telecommunications firm, is profiled in Chapter 5 on large Canadian companies that have gone global.

Mitel, Newbridge, and Novatel have all suffered the common high-tech ailment of out-of-control growth culminating in losses. They are at various stages of trying to recover. The Alberta government, owner of Novatel since January 1991, has warned it might shut down the company if it fails to put its finances in order.

Following its 1971 establishment, Mitel enjoyed a dozen good years. But then in its fiscal year 1983 it plunged into many years of losses due to the conjunction of an industry-wide decline in the sale of private branch exchange equipment, one of Mitel's main products, and rising administration costs from a too rapid growth in head count.

The stagnation in PBX sales was particularly pronounced in the United States, which is Mitel's principal source of revenue. The situation was made worse by a letter that AT&T sent to Mitel's U.S. customers suggesting that they should be concerned about Mitel's future and, therefore, should consider switching to AT&T equipment. In response, Mitel sued AT&T, alleging that the U.S. telecommunications giant had deliberately damaged its reputation.

Despite its setbacks, Mitel is still Canada's largest telecommunications equipment manufacturer after Northern Telecom. Its revenue now exceeds $400 million. To strengthen its U.S position, Mitel bought one of its largest U.S. dealers in 1990 to have more control over much of the U.S. distribution of its equipment. Coradian, the distributor acquired by Mitel, was in the red at the time of Mitel's purchase offer; nevertheless, Mitel went ahead. "It was quick and more efficient than starting from scratch and, moreover, Coradian's problems were a temporary aberration due to price pressures affecting the entire industry," explains Robert Dyer.

In addition, Mitel is broadening its product base in order to be less vulnerable to downturns in one line, as happened with the PBX equipment. It is developing a range of value-added sophisticated applications such as telemessaging, telemarketing, and inventory control systems as well as licensing its technology. Also, it supplies semiconductor "chips" to telephone answering machine manufacturers and security inscription products to security enforcement agencies.

Furthermore, it has invested heavily in the development of ISDN (integrated services digital network) capability, the hot new area in telecommunications. Whereas traditional telephone networks are voice-only carriers, ISDN has the capacity to transport and provide access to information in all its forms: voice, data, graphics, still and full-motion video, telemetry, and facsimile. However, competition in this field is intense.

Mitel learned the hard way about the pitfalls of overexuberant growth. Most of the managers were replaced, and substantial reductions had to be undertaken in employees, sales costs, and inventories. Other high-tech companies, in danger of falling into this all too common trap, should bear in mind Mitel's unpleasant experience.

Newbridge Networks was established in 1986 by Terry Matthews, Mitel's co-founder. Newbridge specializes in integrated service digital networking products. It has customers in 35 countries and makes 94 percent of its revenue outside Canada. The youthful company grew extremely fast—too fast, as it turned out. Newbridge's fiscal year ends April 30; its sales leapfrogged from $1.7 million in the period covering May 1, 1986 to April 30, 1987, to $121 million in the 12 months ended April 30, 1990. Employment soared from one hundred to more than twelve hundred.

As is common at fledgling companies, Newbridge was unprofitable during its first two years. What was discouraging was fiscal 1990's two-thirds decline in profit from the previous 12 months, culminating in a heavy fourth quarter loss for February through

April, 1990. Much of the slump was traceable to an enormous 129-percent increase throughout fiscal 1990 in selling, technical support, and general administrative expenses due to Newbridge's budgets being based on forecasted rather than actual results.

The danger in this prevalent practice is that it fails to take into account the lag between the hiring of personnel and resultant sales. "It's difficult to manage from the bottom line upwards when a company is growing quickly," explains F. Michael Pascoe, vice-president and general manager for Canada, Asia/Pacific, and Latin America. "Now that this mindset is in place, it will pay off." In the interim, however, Newbridge implemented draconian measures to prevent further slippage, including layoffs, a hiring freeze, a 10 percent cut in managers' salaries, and smaller advertising and trade show budgets.

Still, Newbridge has several factors in its favour. First, its technology is well regarded. Second, some solid, well-known firms, including E.I. du Pont de Nemours and New York Life Insurance, are investors in it. Third, it has strong international distribution. For example, a branch of Sumitomo Corporation, the large Japanese trading company, is Newbridge's major Japanese distributor. As mentioned earlier, Sumitomo Heavy Industries, a different division than Newbridge's representative, now owns Lumonics, the Ottawa laser producer.

Novatel was founded in 1983 as a 50:50 partnership between Alberta Government Telephones (AGT) and Calgary-based Nova Corporation (petrochemicals and plastics). They wanted to prove that a high-tech company can flourish in Western Canada, traditionally known for oil and agriculture, as well as become prominent worldwide.

Novatel's sales did indeed thrive, rising a spectacular twentyfold between 1983 and 1989, but it was only nominally a Western Canadian high-tech company, since it farmed out 80 percent of production, primarily to low-cost manufacturers in the Pacific Rim. Not until 1990 did it begin to repatriate most of the production to Alberta, investing $37 million in state-of-the-art machinery at plants in Calgary and Lethbridge.

Unhappily, Novatel's dramatic gains in revenues were made at the expense of profitability. It committed three errors common to young high-tech companies that tend to be more skilled and interested in technology than in financial forecasting and accounting.

First, like many newcomers, Novatel was so eager for business that it chased every lead in order to swell sales volume. Its sales representatives spent 75 percent of their time on airplanes, travelling around the world in pursuit of potential customers. It was not until five years had elapsed that Novatel cut back on the globe-trotting to concentrate on such major markets as the United States, the United Kingdom, and Australia. It also acquired a small Norwegian company to have an onsite presence in the fast-growing European market, but steered clear of Japan, a tough market to crack, as it is the home of such electronics giants as Toshiba, Matsushita, and NEC.

Second, Novatel continued to project enormous year-to-year sales growth, even though industry-wide price-cutting caused by intensifying competition made such increases impossible to achieve. Its sales in 1990 increased by only 1.9 percent over 1989, a vast decline from the big gains in its first six years.

Third, at a time when it should have been carefully monitoring expenses in view of the impact of the price wars, Novatel instead was spending a great deal of money on worldwide recruitment expeditions. The company maintained these jaunts were essential in order to obtain the best talent, but it would have been less of a financial drain to recruit closer to home.

By letting its expenses mount too quickly in its pursuit of growth, Novatel failed to make a profit, and as its losses accumulated, its owners backed out. In 1989, saying it wanted to concentrate on its core business, Nova sold its share in Novatel to AGT. In November 1990, Novatel's ongoing red ink resulted in the firing of its chairman, president, and group controller, and at the end of December, Telus Corporation, the parent of both Novatel and AGT, sold Novatel to the Alberta government. Then, in March, 1991, Novatel reported a 1990 loss of $203.9 million, contrary to its predictions during 1990 that the year would be its first profitable one since its formation. In May, it said that it would no longer manufacture in Calgary, and laid off 387 workers, primarily in that city. However, Novatel will continue research and development there.

With the Alberta government's guarantee to take Novatel off Telus's hands due to expire at the end of 1991, Novatel is under great pressure to meet the government's demand that it improve dramatically. The company's dilemma, therefore, is a strong reminder that global expansion must be governed by financial realities rather than visions of grandeur.

Mobile Data International supplies computer hardware and software to businesses on the move: taxi and courier companies, utilities' field-service representatives, and police and fire departments. It demonstrates how an unknown, fledgling company can achieve international recognition through riding the coat-tails of a major customer. When it was established in 1978, mobile data was an infant industry. What transformed Mobile Data almost overnight from a thinly financed, modest success into a secure firm was a contract it obtained in its third year from Federal Express, the giant U.S.-based courier company. "Mobile Data greatly needed a lead client that had significant volume yet wanted product innovation, and found it in Federal Express," remarks David Sutcliffe, Mobile Data's vice-president, marketing. "Federal Express took a calculated risk, and it paid off for both companies." Today, Mobile's lobby walls are lined with testimonial letters from Federal Express. Word of mouth about the Federal Express deal sparked international demand for Mobile's equipment, and now 90 percent of its business is international (60 percent in the United States and 30 percent offshore).

Annual 50-percent compound increases and sales now over $100 million have made Mobile's biggest challenge the management of its growth. That challenge will intensify, since Mobile is the world leader in an industry that is expected to jump from $500 million in annual sales today to around $3 billion by 1995—a sixfold increase in fewer than five years. Mobile's answer is substantial investment in training and heavy emphasis on customer service. In this regard, Sutcliffe stresses that Mobile makes a sharp distinction between marketing and sales. The marketing department identifies market segments, and subsequently profiles the needs of these markets and how to meet them. The sales force deals with specific customers. Sutcliffe says Motorola's ownership of Mobile since 1986 gives Mobile opportunities to grow that it would not likely have achieved on its own. Mobile has access to much more money for R&D; on its own, its ability to finance R&D was limited. Also, it is plugged into Motorola's vast worldwide regional distribution network; it could not have reached such international exposure on its own.

Positron was started in 1970 on the grand sum of $20 by Reginald Weiser. It now has 380 employees and annual sales of more than $35 million. As an engineer, Weiser had a wide range of business sector choices. He gravitated to telecommunications because he regarded it as "dynamic and rapidly evolving." Also, its broad scope enabled him to concentrate on fringe areas in which he could achieve economies of scale in the same way that large companies can spread their costs over their mass-produced items.

In effect, his goal was to make Positron a big fish in a small pond. Moreover, he calculated that even when the pond became bigger, it still would be too small to attract huge fish like AT&T, Northern Telecom, or Japan's NEC, which could overpower Positron. "Small firms can be more nimble and adroit in discovering and developing niches," Weiser points out. "While they should diversify so as not to be weakened if the market for one product sours, they must resist the temptation to take on the giants in large, glamorous markets. Such arrogance can lead to major expenditures from which recovery is impossible. It is far better to stick to one's niche."

At the same time, Weiser wanted a niche from which he could not be knocked out quickly by newer technology and which would lend itself to rapid production. Fast turnover tides over companies in their early thinly financed days. Weiser started with PHREND (short for Positron's High Reliability Emergency Number), computer programming that identifies the name, telephone number, and address of callers to 911, the North American emergency number. People in distress often forget or fail to give this basic information which is essential for the rapid dispatch of assistance.

To check out Positron's chances in the United States, his foremost sales target, Weiser attended American trade shows. He gave the United States priority since its marketplace is more open to independents. In Canada, the telephone system is primarily dominated by Bell Canada, and it buys principally from Northern Telecom, its equipment subsidiary. In the United States, the deregulation of AT&T resulted in the creation of many "Baby Bells," independent telephone companies that buy separately from one another. This independence creates dual opportunities for suppliers like Positron. Not only do the Baby Bells buy from it, but they are also willing to pass on information about its product to one another because they do not compete.

Positron's U.S. sales also have been boosted by federal and state legislation requiring enhanced 911 service; such regulations are not widespread in Canada. Weiser recalls with relish that Pacific Bell replaced AT&T's 911 enhanced technology with Positron's and then successfully sued AT&T on antitrust grounds when AT&T refused to permit the interconnection of Positron's system to other AT&T equipment installed at Pacific Bell. "We penetrated the U.S. market by encouraging end-users to push for our products," Weiser states. "This is not as possible in Canada where there is less user push." Seventy-five percent of all Positron's sales are in the United States.

To avoid being "knocked off the merry-go-round," Weiser deliberately operates Positron at lower than usual profit margins. Fifteen percent of revenue is ploughed back into R&D, which he feels is essential to maintain a competitive edge. As Positron is privately owned, Weiser does not have public shareholders clamouring for a higher return on their investments. He directs Positron's R&D to add-on products and new items to avoid "saturation in our market spheres." For example, he first sold 911 systems to large communities; now, he is pursuing medium and smaller ones. In addition, he has added computer-aided dispatch to the system's capabilities.

To expand his product line, Weiser branched into telephones for the disabled and programming that protects lineworkers and equipment in high voltage power networks from the effects of severe overloads and faults. As anticipated, the diversification cushions downturns. For instance, at the same time that Positron's sales of trading telephones (turrets) sagged in the wake of Wall Street's troubles, its sales of 911 systems doubled, more than compensating for the telephones' decline.

Canadian high-tech firms have proved they are of world-class calibre. Indeed, they have to be because the Canadian market is too small to provide a return commensurate with the necessary substantial investment in R&D, talent, and equipment. But they are in an industry undergoing considerable stress and upheaval. The high costs are forcing even large companies to form partnerships and joint ventures, or undertake mergers or takeovers. For Canadian high-tech firms, most of which are not world-scale, to survive requires careful selection of niches, ongoing research and development, and aggressive promotion. More may opt for foreign ownership to tap into the financial, technological, and marketing skills of larger companies. An increasing number will establish foreign branch operations, rather than merely export, as they transform themselves from domestic to international companies. Considering the big growth predicted for the high-tech industry, how well Canada's participants do will have a tremendous impact on the country's economic destiny.

CHAPTER

5

Big Canadian Companies

"Business people must look into the future as to what paths they must take, rather than expect to be able to run their companies based on past patterns."

William Deeks,
President,
Noranda Sales

The misunderstanding between a large Tokyo department store and Northern Telecom, widely regarded in Canada's business community as the quintessential model for how Canadian companies should go global, was genuine. When the store signed Nortel as its telephone equipment supplier, it asked Nortel to play music while customers were "on hold." Nortel interpreted this request as applying to the period between when the main switchboard answered and relayed calls to departments. But what the store really wanted was music to be played whenever calls were transferred, including within departments. The Japanese are accustomed to these musical interludes and when they did not hear them on Nortel's system, they hung up, believing they had been disconnected. Irate at a potential big business loss, the store threatened to remove Nortel's system. "Either we had to retrain Japan's total population of 130 million or modify our system; so, of course, we did the latter," recalls Hugh Hamilton, president of Nortel's Pacific operations from 1984 to 1988.

The moral of this story is that no matter what their size, companies can suffer setbacks, learn from them, and consequently improve their international competitiveness. This chapter describes the global production, planning, marketing strategies, role of management, setbacks, and successes of a cross-section of Canada's largest businesses: Alcan Aluminium, Bombardier, Dominion Textile (Domtex), Federal Industries, Magna International, Molson Companies, Noranda, Northern Telecom (Nortel), and Nova.

Although they tower over most Canadian companies, their experiences and strategies are readily applicable across the board. Some took the initiative to go global; others were forced into it. But all are firmly dedicated to staying global. Albeit on a much larger scale, they demonstrate the importance of top executives' commitment to international growth, as well as to innovation, flexibility in planning, intense marketing analysis, targeted geographic expansion, customer satisfaction, and lean management to prevent expenses from becoming uncontrollable.

Moreover, the global performance of these firms affects tens of thousands of Canadian employees and shareholders. Alcan, Nova, and Domtex are widely held stocks. In the case of Bombardier (the Bombardier family), Molson (the Molson family), Magna (the chairman and the president), and Noranda (Peter and Edward Bronfman), and Northern Telecom (BCE—Bell Canada Enterprises), large individual shareholdings exist, but a substantial portion is still widely traded.

All of these huge corporations owe much of their growth to globalization. However, there is a downside to their success. Most laid off many workers during the 1980s as they "restructured" and "rationalized" to be more competitive. Noranda, for example, reduced its workforce by twenty thousand, Alcan by fourteen thousand. Together, these figures represent considerably more people than the Ford Motor Company of Canada employs and is equivalent to the combined workforces of Imperial Oil and Chrysler Canada. While it was devastating to those who lost their jobs, the companies' desire to be strong at home as well as internationally prompted the layoffs.

Here is a company by company description of the global evolution of these big Canadian corporations.

Northern Telecom

The winner of a 1990 Canada Export Award, Northern Telecom epitomizes how far Canadian firms have travelled, as well as the distance they have yet to go in their globalization drive. Northern Telecom has made big gains in North America since the 1970s. In addition to being Canada's leading telecommunications equipment manufacturer, it now ranks second in the United States, close on the heels of American Telephone & Telegraph from which it licensed technology until 1956. The bulk of Nortel's revenue—58 percent in 1990—is derived from the United States, compared to 18 percent in the late 1970s.

But worldwide, Nortel faces much more intense competition than in North America. Today, Nortel ranks fifth among the 15 major telecommunications equipment manufacturers. But their rivalry is so ferocious that analysts expect only five, or perhaps six, still to exist in the fast-approaching year 2000, with their survival dependent on the extent of their global-spanning business.

For Nortel to be one of these, company executives say it will have to increase its offshore revenue from 6 percent of total sales in 1990 to 25 percent during this decade. Should it succeed, Nortel's entire revenue will soar to around $30 billion, making for a fivefold increase during the 1990s, compared to a threefold climb in the 1980s. To put this goal into perspective, as of 1990 no Canadian company had sales exceeding $20 billion.

Nortel intends to expand internationally both on its own and through acquisitions. Its sales outside of North America are growing at a much faster rate than those in the United States and Canada, and in 1990 Nortel took over STC, a leading English manufacturer of telephone equipment, thereby enhancing its European presence. All told, Nortel conducts business in more than 70 countries, and five of its 40 plants are outside North America—Australia, China, France, Malaysia, and the Republic of Ireland. Moreover, Nortel is listed on the New York, London, and Tokyo stock exchanges, further increasing its international profile.

Those Canadian companies eager to emulate Nortel's success would do well to study its early weaknesses as well as its later strengths, and the evolution of the management structure of its international operations. First, Nortel's road to the top proves that while Canadians possess the brainpower to become world pioneers and leaders in technological innovation, they need more willpower. It was not until a decade after a 1956 U.S. antitrust judgment severed the design links between AT&T and Nortel that Nortel's engineers began to develop its own technology.

The company set aside a substantial 5 percent of revenue for research and development, well ahead of the lowly national average of 1 to 2 percent. This risk-taking paid off handsomely, as the international recognition that Nortel garnered for its technical expertise swiftly led to multimillion-dollar sales.

Having learned its lesson, the company proceeded to increase its R&D expenditures to the point where, as mentioned earlier, it now yearly invests 12 percent of its revenue, making it Canada's largest corporate spender on R&D. Thanks to this commitment, Nortel is the world's leading supplier of fully digital telecommunications switching equipment and the first global telecommunications manufacturer of a complete family of switching and transmission products for the construction, operation, and service of fibre optic networks. Its technology can handle text, image, and full-motion video, as well as voice. It introduced its digital system in 1976, and 13 years later launched its fibre optic line. The company estimates that by 1992 it will have invested approximately $1 billion on the development of its advanced fibre optic products.

Digital switches simultaneously transmit voice and data signals, whereas older electromechanical switches can only handle voice. Optical fibre carries far more messages in much thinner strands than traditional copper wire. Through its trend-setting digital system, Nortel made swift and enormous inroads in the United States, and it has high hopes that on a global scale history will repeat itself with its optical fibre products.

Besides demonstrating how technological skill can propel a relatively unknown Canadian firm into worldwide prominence, Nortel makes it crystal clear that because of the small domestic market, large firms cannot rely on Canadian sales alone, even when they have the lion's share. When Nortel began its U.S. push, it had 70 percent of Canadian telecommunications equipment sales; yet the California market alone was bigger than all of Canada's. Nortel also owes its success to its pragmatic attitude about the visible and invisible barriers that protect local telecommunications firms, which are government-owned in much of the world. Instead of complaining bitterly, as do some of its counterparts, particularly its U.S. ones, Nortel adapts to the situation.

To be welcome in foreign lands, it conducts research and manufacturing outside Canada and engages in joint ventures or licensee relationships. As Hugh Hamilton explains: "It is pointless to argue that a country's trade practices are unfair, because nobody said they are supposed to be fair. After all, it is the customer's playing field and he may like it to be full of bumps and holes, rather than level. Therefore, incoming firms must learn how to run around on his field." Nortel first zeroed in on Japan and the United Kingdom because they privatized their telephone networks around the time Nortel accelerated its global endeavours. Nortel benefitted from the desire of domestic customers in both these countries for a choice of suppliers.

Another lesson that can be gleaned from Nortel's success will not be palatable to independent-minded businesspeople. It is that outside ownership may be essential to make the leap from the Canadian to the world stage. Nortel's expansion would not have been possible without its parent company, BCE, serving as both backer and major customer.

Nortel's international management structure has changed four times since its global push began in the late 1970s, veering twice from a centralized office overseeing field operations to decentralization into two geographic divisions: Europe and Asia–Pacific.

The most recent switch began in 1988 when the company decided that sales volume was insufficient to justify the overhead cost, and closed its European office in Zurich and its Asian–Pacific one in Tokyo. In their place it established Northern Telecom World Trade, a 40-person centralized accounting and marketing group based in Toronto, which it said would provide a sharper focus on non-North American business.

But since World Trade President Desmond Hudson flew overseas on average six times a month and had offices in six places around the world, in practice the head office was wherever he was. Additionally, Nortel's executives came to believe even more fervently that much of its growth during the 1990s and subsequently must come from offshore, and that to attain that goal the company must be nearer existing and potential customers.

Thus, in 1991, the World Trade office was dissolved and Nortel reverted to Europe and Asia–Pacific geographic divisions, with Hudson in charge of Europe, including recently acquired STC, and with John MacDonald, a career Nortel employee, president of Northern Telecom Asia–Pacific. As of now, Nortel's Far East business exceeds its European sales volume; thus, Hudson's goal will be to expand the European side and MacDonald's aim to maintain the pace of growth in his part of the world. Nortel has found that in the Far East in particular customers want to deal with the top people as suppliers.

Nortel's non-North American operations continue to be regionally divided—the United Kingdom, France, Germany (newly formed), Turkey, the rest of Europe plus the Middle East, Japan, China, and the rest of the Pacific Rim. Each has its own president, and they now report to the European head office located in Maidenhead, England, or to the Asia–Pacific headquarters in Tokyo. Previously, they reported to Northern Telecom World Trade in Toronto. While both Hudson and MacDonald are Canadian, most of the senior people under them are local nationals and the regional presidents are natives, or Nortel plans that they eventually will be.

It remains to be seen whether the alteration in corporate structure will be followed by a consolidation of similar Canadian and U.S. manufacturing operations and/or there will be a shift of some North American production overseas, in both cases at the expense of Canadian jobs. Company executives say Canada will not be affected because plants in Canada and the United States making the same product supply different parts of the world. Also, Nortel regards its non-North American plants largely as marketing tools that help obtain orders because their onsite presence gives them a native flavour.

Furthermore, Nortel maintains that its internationalization actually creates jobs for Canadians. "The company employs more people in Canada today than 15 years ago," Hamilton says. "Although it manufactures offshore, it has not deprived Canadians of work. For example, four hundred people in our Bramalea, Ontario plant owe their jobs to Nortel's Turkish joint venture, as they are responsible for supplying parts to it. Also, Nortel contributes both directly and indirectly to Canada's R&D through the Bell–Northern Research (BNR) laboratory in Ottawa, which is the largest in the country's private sector. The lab employs most of BNR's six thousand employees, and at least 35 high-tech companies in Ottawa alone were started by former BNR employees." Nortel owns 70 percent of BNR and BCE owns 30 percent. It has facilities in the United States and England, as well as in Canada.

Awareness of the political repercussions that would erupt if Nortel, BCE's principal supplier, were to move its headquarters to the United States serves to prevent a pullout. However, corresponding to the bulk of Nortel's money being made in the United States, that is where the majority of its employees are now located. The current chairman, like his predecessor, is American. Thus, although executives say its Canadian operations will not be adversely affected as Nortel increases its international presence, it is probable that what will actually happen is that the status quo will be maintained in Canada, with the result that the proportion of Nortel's workforce that is Canadian will continue to decline.

Significantly, Nortel has steered clear of its rivals' globalization difficulties. AT&T has had problems adjusting its self-sufficient corporate culture to Europe and Asia where joint ventures are popular, and European manufacturers of telecommunications equipment are making little headway in North America against AT&T and Nortel. Nortel has done well because, as Hugh Hamilton says, it accepts market conditions rather than wastes time trying to overturn them. It should be emphasized, though, that unacceptable business practices are forbidden. Senior Nortel executives are required to sign affidavits that no bribery has been involved in deals. Entertainment and the presentation of mementos such as Eskimo carvings are permitted since such gestures are common courtesy in the business world.

Nortel's patient plodding for international deals is exemplified by its strategy in Japan where it is now the leading non-Japanese supplier of telecommunications equipment. Its initial contract, a $250 million, seven-year deal signed in 1986 with Nippon Tele-graph & Telephone, was NTT's first major purchase from a foreign manufacturer. It was the culmination of a four-year multilayered campaign by Nortel. To underline its commitment, it opened a permanent office in Tokyo. Then, at a time when AT&T, like many U.S. corporations, was attacking Japanese protectionism, Nortel's chairman told U.S. congressional committees that the way to do business in Japan was to play by its rules.

But in one of the strange contradictions that characterize trade relations, Nortel's sales to Japan are handled by its American, rather than Canadian, operations. The reason is that Japan favours U.S. over Canadian companies due to the politically sensitive U.S.–Japanese trade gap. Since it is dealing with a culture where loss of face is the ultimate disgrace, Nortel is careful not to offend Japanese pride in their technology. Moreover, it was content to start with the sale of smaller equipment to rural and semi-rural communities, to avoid stepping on the toes of major Japanese suppliers.

The credo that underlies Nortel's globalization should be taken to heart by companies of all sizes: listen to the customer. In this regard, Hamilton relates a striking analogy: "I remember when my university professor put a chalk mark on the blackboard and said, 'That's an atom. Let's listen to what it tells us about itself.' We sat silently for five minutes and then he began to speak about the properties of atoms. The same approach is effective in international marketing. Listen to the market—government, suppliers, and clients—to realize what it is possible to do."

Bombardier

Like Northern Telecom, Bombardier expects much of its growth during this decade and beyond to come from international sales. It does 85 percent of its business outside Canada and expects 1995 revenue of $4 billion, which is double 1989's. Similar in some areas, widely divergent in others, the international strategies of Nortel and Bombardier amply prove that there are many formulas for global success.

The similarities between these firms begin with their being newcomers to offshore countries. Bombardier did not place vigorous offshore expansion high on its agenda until 1985; Nortel waited until 1987. Previously, consolidation of their North American growth had priority. Also, neither intends to let its North American business slide as it pushes overseas. They also concentrate on what they regard as the most promising markets, rather than fritter away their resources through heading to every part of the globe at once. Bombardier elected to make its first offshore move into Europe. "Its markets are more accessible than Asia's, since Europe's culture is closer to Canada's," explains President Raymond Royer. Bombardier landed in Europe well in advance of the 1992 economic unification of the European Community.

Both companies take risks if there is the promise of a good payoff. Nortel gambled millions of dollars on the development of innovative technology, calculating that its merits would persuade subscribers to switch from conventional equipment with which they were comfortable. In 1985, although Bombardier was eager to widen its product line from snowmobiles and subway cars, it chose to put this plan on hold. Instead, it acquired BN Constructions Férroviaires et Métalliques of Belgium, a mass transit manufacturer with a strong European presence and worldwide customers. The following year, Bombardier did diversify through the purchase of Canadair, an aerospace and defence manufacturer which had been a federal Crown corporation.

In addition, both Nortel and Bombardier are listed on foreign as well as domestic stock exchanges, have offshore as well as North American factories, and more employees outside than within Canada. Like Nortel, Bombardier maintains that its international thrust does not deprive Canadians of employment, but instead creates new opportunities at home. As substantiation, Royer points to a $650 million order for shuttle cars that will carry automobiles and buses through the English Channel tunnel. "That contract will bring $225 million worth of work into Canada," he says. "All the engineering, plus the construction of the frames, will be done at our Quebec plant." The rest of the work will be divided between two European subsidiaries: BN and ANF-Industrie, a French railcar manufacturer acquired in 1989. BN will assemble the cars, and ANF will supply the interiors. Consequently, Bombardier can say it is a good corporate citizen in three countries.

While these similarities between Nortel and Bombardier are notable, they are opposite in many other strategic areas. Nortel invests heavily in R&D; Bombardier prefers to acquire proven technologies. These include the acclaimed people mover and monorail systems developed by Walt Disney Productions and the world-renowned Budd and Pullman railcar designs. Also, Bombardier holds the North American rights for the marketing and manufacture of France's popular *train à grande vitesse* (high-speed train). Bombardier's policy to buy rather than develop is cheaper and less time consuming than the arduous, trial and error process of in-house research. Its own technological performance is sometimes spotty. For example, the LRC (light-rapid-comfortable) train it supplied to Via Rail compiled one of the worst defect records of Canadian passenger trains.

Bombardier intends to remain in the niche of transportation products in which it has enjoyed considerable success: snowmobiles, railcars, small personal motorized watercraft, mass transit, and smaller aircraft. Canadair is developing the Regional Jet, a 50-seat plane targeted at lightly travelled routes that are too long for turbo-prop travel. In 1990, Bombardier bought Learjet, a leading U.S. builder of small business jets. Bombardier's stress on niche products reflects its belief that a mid-sized company like itself should aim at the possible instead of the impossible. It would be futile for it to tackle transportation giants like General Motors or Boeing, but it can achieve success in specialized lines through concentration of its resources on these less competitive areas.

On the other hand, Nortel has no choice but a wide range of products that enable it to compete head-on worldwide against firms that are up to twice its size. It has expanded internationally primarily through direct sales, joint ventures, and licensing agreements. So far, it has made only one major acquisition, STC of

England. By contrast, Bombardier has extended its global stretch principally through acquisitions, and whereas STC was healthy when Nortel bought it, Bombardier prefers troubled companies available at bargain prices because of their sagging condition.

Neither Nortel nor Bombardier could have managed to fund their growth independently. They raised their money in considerably different ways. Nortel relied on the private sector through its own resources and those of BCE, its parent, whereas Bombardier has received substantial assistance from Canadian and foreign governments in gratitude for its taking money-losers off their hands. For example, Bombardier had to pay only $120 million for Canadair; the Canadian government, its previous owner, absorbed Canadair's $2.2 billion debt and development expenses. Canadair also receives generous funding from the federal government's Defence Industry Productivity Program, designed to help Canadian-owned companies and foreign subsidiaries compete in defence-related products.

Overseas, Bombardier paid the British government a rock-bottom $60 million in 1989 for Short Brothers (Shorts), the world's oldest aircraft maker and Northern Ireland's largest industrial employer. Relieved to find a buyer, since Shorts was losing money, the Thatcher government sweetened the deal by awarding Bombardier $1.5 billion in subsidies.

Bombardier has a good reputation for its ability to resurrect moribund companies. "The main question we ask ourselves in considering takeovers is whether the bottom line results will improve if we manage the companies differently," Royer says. Bombardier does not belong to the school of thought that foists all the blame for an acquired company's woes on its managers and resorts to firing them as the best cure. It believes in redemption rather than damnation and, therefore, retains employees. A side benefit is management continuity.

Bombardier chiefly concentrates on improvement of the managers' planning and communications methods because, given the nature of their businesses, they tend to be more adept at technological than interpersonal skills. Bombardier's orientation program covers the factory floor as well as the executive suite. For instance, besides meeting in Northern Ireland with the leaders of seven different unions in Shorts, Bombardier executives invited representatives of the workers to visit Canadair's Montreal factory for three days to discuss labour-management relations with their counterparts. They returned home with a favourable report card.

Although Bombardier's and Nortel's global strategies are not identical, both have been successful. The message to be gained is that while companies should not be too proud to learn from the examples of others, they should also be prepared to be original.

Noranda

Noranda, Canada's largest and most diversified natural-resource company, is also the nation's biggest exporter next to the automobile industry. Noranda derives 70 percent of its sales from exports. A typical pound of Noranda copper or zinc travels an average of five thousand miles from where it is mined to its point of purchase.

Besides minerals, Noranda's activities include pulp and paper, oil and gas, wire cable, and aluminum sheet and foil. Forty-five percent owned by Brascan, a widely diversified holding company controlled by Peter and Edward Bronfman, Noranda is itself a major or controlling shareholder of MacMillan Bloedel, Falconbridge, Norcen Energy Resources, Canada Wire and Cable, and Canadian Hunter (oil and gas).

While they do not have the retailers' chore of catering to ever-changing consumer tastes, natural resource firms like Noranda have their share of quandaries. With consumer products, manufacturers can create a loyal following and spurts in demand through design changes and price wars. But in natural resources, where one company's products are much the same as another's, purchases are made only when customers need them, and demand is not affected by short-term price changes. Therefore, to be internationally competitive, Noranda has concluded it must be innovative and responsive to change, invest substantially in recruitment and ongoing training, focus on profitability, and concentrate on customer satisfaction.

Noranda has separate sales organizations for its forest products and for its metals and minerals. However, neither oversees all the business within its orbit. MacMillan Bloedel handles its sales independently since it largely sells to different markets. Falconbridge, 50 percent acquired in 1989 in a joint takeover with a Swedish firm, acts on its own in nickel sales because of its longtime track record. Of the two marketing divisions, the forestry one concentrates primarily on North America, whereas Noranda Sales, the minerals and metals sales department, has customers in 65 countries. Furthermore, while prices of the forest products are determined by market forces, those of metals and minerals are set by trading on the London Metal Exchange.

Since 1980, transactions by Noranda Sales have doubled to more than $4 billion, comparable to the revenue of such giants as Dofasco (steel), Air Canada, and Canada Safeway (supermarkets). Noranda Sales has three hundred employees; 110 are at the Toronto head office, and the rest are stationed worldwide. It also is one of the few minerals organizations anywhere in the world to own a London Metal Exchange commodity broker and, thereby, indirectly sets prices for its products.

President William Deeks is a fervent believer in concentration on the future for international competitiveness in this era of constant change. "A year or two ago, managers tended to say that what was done a year earlier was no longer relevant; nowadays, the pace of change has accelerated so much that what happened as recently as a month ago is irrelevant today," he says. "Companies cannot expect to be successful if they pattern their planning on the past." As a cautionary example, he points to the fate of the Swiss watch industry which failed to recognize that battery-operated watches made by American and Japanese electronics firms would virtually eliminate manually wound timepieces. However, he believes that change challenges natural resource companies far more than high-tech ones. "Natural resource companies face a variety of issues worldwide—environmental, health, safety, and energy conservation—and can no longer reply, as they did in the past, 'Get off my back,' " he explains.

How Noranda Sales recruits and trains staff reflects its emphasis on the future. Rather than number crunchers, Deeks seeks people who understand different cultures and political systems, as well as communicate well. Therefore, graduates in English, History, Political Science, and Languages are as welcome as those in Business Administration. What they must have in common is the capacity to exhibit "neither a sense of superiority nor inferiority" to another country's customs, art, and culture. In line with this thinking, Noranda's two-year apprenticeship program encompasses personal as well as business skills. Trainees study letter writing, interviewing, and public speaking; crisis management; export terms, practices, and analysis; transportation and distribution methods; accounting; and health, environmental, and safety regulations. In the search for the best recruits, Deeks sometimes puts candidates through ten interviews. One of those rejected after this gruelling process got Deeks to reverse his decision by saying Deeks had made a mistake. He went on to become a manager.

As a supplement to the in-house courses, Deeks steeps himself and his employees in books and videos that focus on the future and exhort managers to be motivators in the style of inspiring football coaches, rather than seek personal acclaim. Recently, Deeks implemented job assignment rotations; this had been suggested by the staff who felt it would expand knowledge and inspire fresh thinking. The rotations occur every 18 months, since on average in business it takes about six months to become fully at ease in new postings. All told, Noranda Sales spans 25 metal and mineral products divided into ten departments run as separate profit centres. Deeks believes decentralization enhances cost control conscientiousness, and he believes the benefits extend to business trip planning. "Noranda gets maximum value from sales representatives drawing up very full schedules," he comments with a smile.

Noranda's 1970 purchase of Rudolf Wolff, its London Metal Exchange commodity broker, was a calculated risk. While Wolff, established in 1866 and a founding member 11 years later of the Exchange, was a pillar of the commodity establishment, it was a shaky pillar. Like many other family partnerships, Wolff was on the brink of collapse owing to its inability to compete against global trading companies. Many of these giants already had swallowed struggling small London Metal Exchange firms; Wolff was one of the few well-known names still available. Noranda believed ownership of Wolff would provide it with a source of information about the market trends of metals and minerals, and thereby contribute to its advance planning. When Noranda acquired Wolff, the broker's capitalization was just £500,000; today, it exceeds £28 million. Noranda maintains strict confidentiality between its brokerage and marketing activities.

In many businesses, customer loyalty can be courted through price discounts. But metals and minerals companies cannot engage in this practice because the prices of metals and minerals are determined on an industry-wide basis by the London Metal Exchange, rather than by individual firms. Therefore, for competitive advantage, Noranda has only the option of building customer satisfaction through product knowledge, information exchange, and speedy response. Deeks calls the relationship which Noranda seeks to create "non-equity partnerships" in which Noranda and its customers remain independent but work together "to do a superior job for end-use buyers. We want the issue between Noranda and its customers to be 'How will we do business this month?' rather than 'Will we do business this month?' "

Noranda Sales can pursue this strategy, since with one thousand global customers, it has far fewer to keep happy than the millions which a soap manufacturer, for example, must satisfy. Nevertheless, Noranda grades its customers according to the amount of attention it elects to give them. Of the seven hundred "regulars," just 30 are "core" buyers, without which Noranda could not get along. This core group gets constant stroking from Noranda's operational and executive ranks. "A customer relationship team" consisting of technical, administrative, and distribution employees is responsible for the development of linkages with customers, so that they can work together to short-circuit problems. The team is supplemented by "Executive Customer Appreciation Meetings" at which approximately five senior Noranda managers, including those from its mines, meet with customers for candid appraisals of how well Noranda rates as a supplier. "In today's highly competitive world, sellers must be highly responsive in offering value and full service to customers in order to defend their relationship against other potential sellers," Deeks stresses.

Thus, although Noranda has total sales exceeding $9 billion and is Canada's eighth largest industrial company in revenue, it is well aware that the only way for it to grow even bigger is to continue its global thrust. Moreover, its strategy illustrates that no matter how large, a company is not destined to stay on top: it must constantly respond positively to change and give priority to customer satisfaction.

Alcan

Alcan Aluminium, the country's most profitable corporation in 1988 and 1989,* is also one of Canada's most globally active companies with operations on six continents. In addition, in terms of revenue it is the world's second largest aluminum company after the Aluminum Company of America (Alcoa). Alcoa owned Alcan until 1928, when a U.S. antitrust decision forced it to sell its foreign holdings.

Unlike Noranda, which has most of its natural resources at its fingertips in Canada, no supply of Alcan's base material—bauxite—is found at home. Instead, it is located primarily in tropical areas.

In 1990, Alcan ranked third, after BCE and Seagram.

Although Alcan does have smelters in the southern hemisphere as well as in the United States and United Kingdom, Canada is where it does the bulk of its aluminum smelting because of the country's abundant hydroelectric power. Aluminum is produced by an electrolytic process, which uses large quantities of electrical energy to separate aluminum from oxygen in alumina extracted by a chemical process from bauxite. Since it takes between 13,000 and 17,600 kilowatt hours of electricity to produce just one tonne of aluminum and Alcan produces 1.6 million tonnes annually, its access to inexpensive power in Canada is a distinct advantage. As a result, it is one of the world's lowest-cost primary aluminum producers and has better profit margins than Alcoa.

Alcan's international thrust dates back to its earliest days of independence from Alcoa. With a small market in Canada, close to 85 percent of its Canadian smelter output had to be exported. Overseas fabricating plants were built as outlets for the Canadian output, and an international sales office chain was established to develop a worldwide customer base. Today, more of Alcan's revenue (86 percent), profit (57 percent), and employees (68 percent) are without than within Canada. It should benefit from its strong presence in Europe and Asia because consumption in these markets is expected to surpass that in North America in this decade. Alcan was a pioneer among Canadian firms in forming joint ventures in Japan. The first was established as far back as 1931 and the second in 1939.

Alcan's global strength today stems from a rude awakening it had in 1982 when it lost $45 million (U.S.)*, its first red ink in 50 years and a grim way to mark its eightieth birthday. In the rigorous self-examination that followed, Alcan faced the harsh fact that although depressed aluminum prices were partly to blame, the loss was largely self-inflicted due to unproductive assets and a bloated bureaucracy. To turn the company around, it sold less profitable ventures and laid off redundant employees, including 25 percent of its managers. "I disagree with those who say big business cannot act entrepreneurially," chairman and CEO, David Morton, says. "Fewer management layers, combined with a clear, strategic intent, enable quick, correct decisions. Admittedly, speed can cause mistakes, but so far no serious errors have occurred. My position is that I tolerate errors arising from well-meant intentions—once."

Alcan declares its results in U.S. dollars.

As a natural resource firm, Alcan cannot escape constant swings in demand and prices. It is lessening its vulnerability through increased emphasis on manufactured goods that are less subject to cyclicality. These include beverage cans, homebuilding products, aluminum freight railcars, and automotive aluminum structures—the part under the skin—for sportscars.

The lesson other firms can derive from Alcan's recovery strategy is that, in the worst of times, companies must pinpoint which markets will be the most lucrative, not just in the present but also in the future. It is Alcan's forward thinking that has preserved its strong global presence. In its darkest days in 1982, Alcan picked beverage can recycling and transportation as markets of the future because the demand of both for aluminum was forecast to outpace the overall demand for aluminum. To Alcan's intense satisfaction, this prediction is coming true. In 1989, Alcan opened the world's largest beverage can recycling plant, located in Kentucky, and in 1991 it opened a similar sized plant in England, the first in that country. Since European consumption of aluminum beverage cans is far less than in North America, the English factory is an expression of faith in the future. However, European consumption is expected to expand due to both the single post-1992 market and widening public support for recycling. It is easier to recycle aluminum than steel.

It was also in 1982 that Alcan gave the go-ahead for the development of aluminum automotive structures, again to position itself for the future. Mass production of aluminum cars is not expected until 15 years from now because aluminum is considerably more expensive than steel. However, a smaller quantity is needed than with steel. Aluminum is also corrosion-resistant and lighter, making possible improved fuel economy, fewer emissions, and rapid acceleration. For example, the new Jaguar XJ220 (price $500,000), for which Alcan provided the aluminum structure, accelerates from zero to 124 miles per hour in just 12 seconds. Its top speed is 220 miles per hour.

Another lesson from Alcan's strategy is that glamorous new products should not cause neglect of bread-and-butter business. Alcan's core activity is still primary aluminum production, and investors buy or sell its stock based principally on the near-term outlook and not in response to plans for the future. Moreover, its competitors are investing millions on modernization. To avoid falling behind, Alcan is spending $5 billion on a five-year expansion and upgrading program, including the installation of more productive high-speed machinery. It also has instituted cost-cutting waste control measures. Thus, Alcan shows that for a business to do well abroad, it must first be strong internally.

Nova

The internationalization of Novacor Chemicals, the recently spun off petrochemicals and plastics division of Nova, Alberta's largest industrial company*, is comparable to the age-old riddle: Which came first—the chicken or the egg? With Novacor, the query is: Did Novacor go international because it built a world-scale petrochemicals plant, or did it gamble on the multimillion dollar plant because of its international potential? The answer to both parts of this question is yes and has to do with Nova's evolution.

For 20 years after its 1954 establishment, under the name of Alberta Gas Trunk Line Company, Nova's sole activity was gas transmission. Beginning in the 1970s, it became part of the overall diversification trend in Alberta to petrochemical derivatives of natural gas. Today, Novacor produces 85 percent of Canada's ethylene, a plastic feedstock, and ranks tenth amongst worldwide petrochemical firms.

It was a 1.5 billion pounds a year, world-scale, state-of-the-art ethylene plant, opened in 1984 at Joffre, near Red Deer, Alberta, that catapulted Novacor onto the worldwide scene. For the plant to be internationally competitive, it had to be capable of enormous output; conversely, for the size and cost to be justified, the plant had to sell globally. Nova's decision to proceed was a bold wager on the future, since it was uncertain whether it would have enough customers. It knew it could not rely solely on Canadian orders because it had built the plant to world-scale capacity. On the other hand, it had no assurance of international business. First, it faced considerable competition from oil-rich Arab nations building similar projects with the same type of technology in order to diversify their economies. Second, many of the potential end-users were developing nations that could not afford the modern machinery necessary for conversion of the petrochemicals into finished products. Third, while prices were good when construction began,

---

*1990 Revenue: $4.7 billion.

warranting faith in the project, they nosedived around the time it opened.

Novacor had signed a long-term supply contract with Union Carbide's U.S. operations, somewhat minimizing its risk. But it concluded that for its purposes, the United States was part of an overall North American market and that its real export market was offshore. Therefore, in a step by step program, Novacor developed an international marketing department and a country by country strategy. The department, opened in 1986 with two employees, grew to three in 1988, four in 1989, and five in 1990. Only two of the five are fluent in a language other than English, one in French, the other in Mandarin.

Most had little or no international sales experience; instead, they learned on the job. Their principal guidelines, according to George Pan, one of the group, "are to keep an observant, open mind, be 200 percent polite, develop friendships, and provide customer satisfaction." They are given considerable autonomy in decision making because buyers expect deals to be closed during their talks. However, thanks to today's modern communications, overseas calls can be placed from a dinner table in Hong Kong, Beijing, or Taipei, for example, to senior management in Calgary for approval of items added at negotiations.

"Our cardinal rule is to hang onto customers," Pan continues. "Thus, we never ignore an inquiry. If we don't have a product available, we explain why and ask whether the customer would consider doing business in another area. Our theory is that even if we don't make a sale, salesmanship still is important. It also pays off because the goodwill built in upcycles tends to keep customers loyal in downcycles. Thus, we do the unconventional—such as shipping orders that are smaller than the standard container size— to keep customers happy."

To a company the size of Nova, with total operating expenses of more than $3.6 billion in 1989, the establishment of Novacor's international department is a minuscule investment. Richard Kendon, senior international marketing analyst, likes to point out that "Our department's costs are negligible compared to those for a network of Canadian and American sales offices." In order to cover several countries, each of the five sales representatives makes about five overseas trips per year at approximately $10,000 per trip. Their total travel budget is a mere fraction of what Nova earns in revenue in just one day. Even so, the international group scrutinizes its expenses closely. For instance, it has no overseas representative offices, having calculated that on average it takes six months of sales to pay the rent. It considers such an outlay unwarranted for its type of product.

Novacor was equally cautious in not throwing its money in useless directions when it developed its market selection campaign. Thus, it rejected Europe as an initial target, even though it is the largest market for petrochemicals after North America. Instead, it zeroed in on Asia–Pacific, where the growth rate in demand is much larger. Because Alberta is relatively near the Pacific Rim, Novacor's plants can ship at rates competitive with those of its Middle East rivals. There is one major exception to Nova's Asian coverage. So far, it has avoided Japan due to its steep import duties and long-deferred payment terms. "We just do business where it makes sense," Pan comments.

One of Novacor's first international sales, though, was to China in 1986, well before the Western rush into that country. As is customary in initial contacts between Westerners and the Chinese, Nova's negotiators found they were drinking toasts more than hammering out a deal. "By North American standards, we seemed to be accomplishing nothing. However, in reality, we were patiently building the contacts that led to the contract," Pan says. What also contributed to Novacor's success was its policy of treating each country as a series of different markets instead of as one solid mass. "Some parts of China are proactive, such as the special economic zones which are designed to encourage foreign investment, and others are reactive," Pan continues.

Now that Novacor has steady business in most of the Pacific Rim as well as in Latin, Central, and South America, and the Caribbean, it believes it has a good foundation on which to launch its drive into Europe and is in the process of doing so. With its export effort less than a decade old, Novacor can already say that being forced to sell internationally has turned out to be a blessing. In 1985, it sold a few hundred tonnes offshore; by 1989, the amount had grown to 50,000 and the quantity now exceeds 140,000, equivalent to 314 million pounds, or between 20 and 25 percent of total production of the Joffre facility.

Molson Companies

The joint beer venture created in 1989 by Molson Companies, Canada's oldest brewer, and the five times larger Elders IXL of

Australia was a milestone in Canadian corporate history. The venture combined Molson's North American brewing operations with Carling O'Keefe Breweries of Canada, controlled by Elders, in a 50:50 Canadian partnership named Molson Breweries. Intended to provide the fighting strength necessary to withstand competition at home and increase market share internationally, the alliance has rapidly proved its worth. Despite its short history, the combined Molson Breweries has supplanted Labatt as Canada's biggest brewer, and its products have moved from third to second place among U.S. imports.

The formation of Molson Breweries is a landmark for Canadian business as a whole. For the first time, a major Canadian company reached thousands of miles across the world to establish a strategic alliance with a competitor rather than buy it out. Such transnational relationships between strong corporations are becoming the norm as they seek to increase their survival capacity, yet still retain their overall independence in this era of globalization. More will likely occur between Canadian and foreign companies, because even though some Canadian firms are multibillion dollar enterprises, they are only a fraction of the size of the world's largest firms. Transnational alliances provide the economies of scale and a collection of popular brand names that better equip companies to compete on the world stage, especially if consumer demand declines, as it has for beer. Beer consumption is down due to a greater emphasis on fitness and an increased concern about drinking and driving.

While such partnerships have much in their favour, there is a significant drawback that should be weighed. The human toll is steep, even in a friendly merger like Molson Breweries. Its shockwaves were vividly and semi-humorously described in a speech a year afterward to the University of Western Ontario Business School Club by Ed Prévost, a former senior Molson's executive. Prévost was president of Quebec Carling O'Keefe and then of the merged Quebec operations. He is now president of Montreal-based Sico, a major paint manufacturer.

Prefacing his remarks with a description of the merger as a "bold and brilliant deal," Prévost continued: "There was a lot of mutual respect at senior management levels. In the trenches, however, people were trained to hate the competition and, over time, actually believed the opponent was inferior, crass, and unworthy. Overnight, a merger imposes on you the prospect of actually having to work with those useless twits. To complicate matters, mergers only make sense because of synergies and rationalization. Rationalization is a dignified word for cutbacks. Consequently, employees must not only adapt to the idea of working with people they have grown to dislike, but also face the uncertainty of whether they will still have a job. The prospect of losing a job to someone inferior is the ultimate insult." As it turned out, the creation of Molson Breweries caused the elimination of fourteen hundred out of seven thousand jobs.

Other firms that are subject to similar pressures will find Molson's reasons for proceeding instructive. In brief, Molson wanted to position itself against growing international competition, a threat common to every company, no matter in what industry it is. When Molson Breweries was created, the Canadian beer industry still was highly protected from outside invaders. (It was the only industry excluded form the free trade agreement with the United States.) Moreover, provincial regulations requiring brewers to operate a brewery in each province where they wish to sell serve as a further barrier. The Molson Breweries merger resulted in the closure of underutilized Molson and O'Keefe plants located in the same province. On average, Molson was only at 75 percent of capacity and O'Keefe at just 50 percent.

Furthermore, Molson wanted to become stronger domestically before competition from foreign beers increased. Since foreign beers made under licence by Canadian brewers, including Molson, already were selling well, Molson was concerned that licensing arrangements would end and foreign beer shipments into Canada would multiply once Canada's barriers against beer imports come down in response to a ruling by the General Agreement on Tariffs and Trade (GATT). Although the ruling only applies to European beers, it could make it possible for U.S. brewers to ship to Canada, notwithstanding their being shut out under the free trade agreement, because the United States is a member of GATT.

In addition, the competitiveness of Canada's beer industry, like that of the economy as a whole, is hampered by higher raw material and production costs, as well as lower productivity than in most industrialized countries. Canada's relatively small plants cannot match the efficiencies possible at larger American and overseas breweries. Moslon Breweries believes its combined effort provides the concentration of power necessary both to withstand and compete against the international giants, 19 of which are still bigger than it is.

Like breweries worldwide, Molson is much more than a beer

company. On the consumer side, it owns Beaver Lumber, Canada's foremost home improvement/do-it-yourself supplier. On the commercial-industrial side, it owns Diversey Corporation, one of the world's leading suppliers of cleaning and sanitation systems such as institutional kitchen dishwashing operations. Each division has distinct marketing strategies. Because of worldwide differences in consumers' home improvement buying habits, Beaver is content to remain domestic. Mindful of the failure of Canadian Tire in the United States and the many problems there of Dylex, Molson regards itself as astute rather than weak in acknowledging that it cannot necessarily transplant Beaver's formula for success elsewhere in the world.

Conversely, 85 percent of Diversey's sales are outside Canada, and it manufactures in more than 30 countries. "Diversey is a transportable business whose products can readily be transferred from Canada to as near as the United States or as distant as Kuala Lumpur," says Kim Robinson, vice-president, corporate development at Molson. Because Diversey sells worldwide, Molson revised its organization in 1988 to reflect that globalization. Hitherto, each of Diversey's 51 operating divisions did its own R&D. Under the new system, R&D is conducted by geographic region. "By keeping it regional, rather than completely centralizing it, Diversey remains close to local markets while at the same time the regionalization provides the wherewithal for quick product development and introduction," Robinson adds. By eliminating the previous duplication, Diversey makes optimum use of its resources and has improved its chances for beating competitors to the marketplace. Thus, Molson highlights why even a well-entrenched Canadian business must go on the offensive to withstand increasing international competition on its home turf as well as abroad.

Federal Industries

Ten years ago, when Federal's corporate planners crystal ball-gazed into the future, they decided that going global would have to figure prominently in their strategy. They further determined that Federal would first have to build a sizable foundation at home to have the resources to go farther afield. This approach, they reckoned, would prevent Federal from being caught unawares by the inescapable process of globalization. "We wanted to manage change, rather than have it forced upon us," explains Roy Cook, senior vice-president, planning.

Therefore, during the 1980s Federal assiduously transformed itself, largely through acquisitions, from a regional to a national operation in a cross-section of industries. The Federal potpourri now includes Cashway Building Centres, W.H. Smith Canada (the country's largest bookstore chain), Jelinek Sports, Willson Stationers, Milltronics (weighing and measurement devices), Kingsway Transport, and Consolidated Fastfrate. All told, it has two dozen operating divisions. Within just nine years, Federal transformed itself from a medium-sized company with $160 million in sales in 1980 to a $2 billion giant in 1989 that ranked forty-ninth in revenue among Canada's top 500 industrial companies.

Although most of Federal's growth was within Canada, some of the companies that it acquired already were active outside the country. In 1989, Federal derived 15 percent of its revenue from outside Canada, principally from the United States. A year earlier, as Federal neared the size it deemed necessary to launch stepped-up internationalization, its corporate planners began to develop a long-range strategy. After 30 months of microscopic examination, they settled on four corporate goals for the 1990s and beyond: emphasis on profit performance over rapid growth: increased attention to customer satisfaction; increased opportunities for employees; and "looking beyond Canada to become globally competitive in everything we do." The reference to profit reflects the erosion in Federal's gross margin ratio since 1982 due to both heavy outlay on acquisitions and to Canada's economic strains. The stipulation of global competitiveness marked the first time Federal formally assigned this goal top priority. "Previously, it was well down on the list and done only if we had been able to do everything else," Cook says.

Federal's strategy sharply differentiates between international competitiveness—its principal aim—and international expansion. The distinction arises from Federal's conclusion that clear cut demarcations between Western Canada, national, and world markets no longer exist. Instead, domestic markets are evolving into global ones as tariff walls tumble. "As a company, we remain proudly Canadian, but we are under no delusions about the rapidly disappearing importance of nationality as a variable in the international business equation," says John Fraser, chairman and chief executive officer. "Borders are now little more than dotted lines on a map, not protective barriers behind which the weak or poorly managed can hide. Our goal is to ensure that we are worldclass competitors in domestic markets. And to truly become more competitive, we will be much more global in our orientation and our thinking in order to protect—and wherever possible expand—our markets in North America and around the world."

To achieve this competitiveness, Federal is evaluating its strengths and weaknesses, placing more emphasis on foreign experience in recruitment and training, enhancing its international profile, and compiling a global database on companies and firms. It analyzed each division to identify the clear winners, the borderline, and the seriously weak, and thereby determine whether the feeble ones could be strengthened or would have to be discarded. In this diagnosis, it was careful to delineate between those not ready to expand internationally and those incapable of withstanding competition from incoming companies. It is only the latter debility that concerns Federal. The first category, in its estimation, can do perfectly well for the time being in Canada through further geographic and market share expansion.

However, with the emphasis on international opportunities, those Federal divisions with international plans receive the most favourable allocation of financial resources. "Before we were equally open to opportunities in Canada, the U.S., and outside North America, but now those in Canada rank last," says Gary Goertz, senior vice-president and chief financial officer. However, he adds that Federal has no set goal or timetable regarding how much revenue it earns outside Canada. What is certain, though, is that over time Federal will make more money outside than within Canada.

To equip management with the right attitude and skills, Federal has begun paying for the cost of learning a second language or participating in international management exchange programs and sabbaticals to learn about other cultures and business customs. The thrust of executives' reading has changed from an emphasis on Canadian publications to a concentration on international ones. To enhance its international profile, Federal plans to list its stock on the New York Stock Exchange within three to five years. Also, Goertz is developing a network of contacts at American merger and acquisition firms, as well as in the U.S. financial community.

Furthermore, Federal restructured its corporate planning department into two functions—research and planning—to sharpen its global readiness. R.J. Vahsholtz, an American, is responsible as senior vice-president, research, for the study of global trends and issues and for the identification of industries and industry segments that would fit into Federal's strategy. His decision to relocate from Winnipeg to California to conduct his research resulted in some good-natured jokes from his colleagues about his flight from Winnipeg's cold winters. Since he is a one-man investigative unit who works from his home and since Federal sees its immediate opportunities as being in the United States, his relocation is described by the Winnipeg office as providing "greater objectivity because he is removed from the conventional wisdom of group thinking." Roy Cook, senior vice-president, planning, is based in Winnipeg and focuses on the strategy side.

Federal's initial international thrust will be in its industrial products, since they do not require the expensive mass marketing that consumer merchandise must receive in order to build buyer awareness. However, its consumer products—books, stationery, greeting cards, sporting goods, do-it-yourself building supplies—are not fashion items and, therefore, are less vulnerable to consumer taste variations from country to country.

In its evolution from a regional to a national to an international enterprise, Federal demonstrates that a company at Portage and Main in Winnipeg should be as committed to global planning as one at King and Bay in Toronto, Canada's financial hub. "There are some minuses in that there are fewer international flights from Winnipeg, but there is the plus of being midway in North American time zones," Cook says.

Magna International

Contrary to its name, Magna International, the largest Canadian-owned auto parts manufacturer, is only on the threshold of going global—largely due to its own mistakes. How it stumbled is a cautionary tale for other Canadian companies. But its ability to recognize its errors provides a useful object lesson, because despite the relative weakness of its international thrust, it is still one of the few Canadian-owned auto parts firms to penetrate global markets.

As a victim of both circumstances and misjudgment, Magna is likely to remain on the fringe internationally for some time. The circumstances is a severe slowdown in the North American automobile industry, Magna's foremost customer. The misjudgment stems from a misreading of the market outlook. Since North American automakers have been losing their market share to the Japanese for a decade, Magna should have realized in the late 1980s that it needed to trim its expansion plans. But Magna believed in growth for growth's sake, especially since that theory had worked well during its first 30 years. Founded in 1957, Magna had become North America's fastest-growing auto parts company by the 1980s. Its revenue soared from $153 million in 1980 to $1.9 billion in its fiscal year ended July 31, 1989. Such results would tend to make even the most prosaic company feel invincible. Thus, Magna proceeded at full throttle, with the unhappy result that the completion of its additional capacity coincided with the onset of the worst slump in the North American auto industry since the early 1980s.

Moreover, like all car parts manufacturers, Magna's financial resources are under pressure because automakers are now demanding that suppliers assume much of the cost of R&D. Its internal failings and the external factors led to Magna recording its first-ever loss in the 12 months ended July 31, 1990. The loss of $224 million was greater than the combined profit in the previous seven years. In addition, doubling of its debt load in 1989–90 to more than $1 billion forced Magna to sell several operations. With one exception, none were core businesses. The exception was its electric motors division which it sold to Siemens of Germany.

Magna is convinced it must go global, even though the automobile industry is Canada's leading manufacturing sector, and Canada is the world's sixth largest assembler of cars and trucks. Its reason is rooted in simple economics: only 30 percent of world car production is in North America; the rest is evenly divided between Europe and the Pacific Rim. It was not until 1984 that Magna ventured outside North America, when it began to build a plant in West Germany, and it was as late as 1989 when it made its first major sale to a European carmaker—Volkswagen. Magna has no presence in the Asia–Pacific region, the world's fastest growing area for automobile production. As part of its retrenchment program, it reluctantly closed its representative office in Tokyo in 1990 after just one year's operation.

"The cost of maintaining an office, representative, and secretary in Japan is extremely high, and Magna's financial situation necessitated cutting overhead," explains Patrick Lavelle, vice-president, corporate development. "It's impossible to do everything at once." Nevertheless, Magna has only postponed its Asia–Pacific plans, not shelved them. "We hope to return because it is a dynamic market with millions of people," Lavelle continues. Magna already has some joint ventures with Japanese parts manufacturers and is a minor supplier to Japanese transplants in North America. But with

Japanese and South Korean carmakers increasing their proportion of world sales, enlarging its Pacific Rim connections is important for Magna's future.

Conversely, Magna's Western European foothold was established eight years in advance of the region's 1992 economic unification. The company now has two plants in Austria and two in Germany. It has high hopes for purchases from European carmakers, as well as from North American and Japanese transplants. If its expectations are realized, Magna will not be as dependent on the North American market. It projects $100 million in European sales in 1992, about 5 percent of current total revenue. Magna also has a small joint venture in the Soviet Union.

In Magna's favour in its international endeavours are its unstinting expenditures on R&D, and its decentralized, profit-sharing structure. Magna's charter calls for it to spend 7 percent of pretax profits annually on R&D. "Unlike many companies, Magna does not reduce R&D when times get tough," Lavelle points out. Technological innovation also is encouraged by Magna's organizational methods. Frank Stronach, Magna's founder, chairman, and 53.9 percent shareholder, is a proponent of numerous small factories to spark entrepreneurship, enhance quality, and keep out unions. Furthermore, the system minimizes head office bureaucracy and overhead. Today, Magna has 17,500 employees at 130 factories.

However, as years passed and sales skyrocketed, Magna veered from its successful strategy by interposing an intervening management layer to which the plants reported. This stifled the entrepreneurship that the multiplicity of factories was intended to nurture. Magna's 1990 problems forced it to realize its error, and many middle managers were scrapped. A return to the original system should help Magna internationally because it fosters swift on-the-spot adaptation to market forces.

Dominion Textile

Although much of global business expansion tends to be opportunity-based, Dominion Textile, Canada's largest textile manufacturer and the world's leading supplier of denim, demonstrates how an opportunity is not an opportunity until it is recognized as one. For its first 70 years, Domtex, established in 1905, confined itself almost entirely to Canada and had a limited product lineup. Like many industry leaders, it was content—indeed, almost smugly so— with its pre-eminence on its home turf.

Not until some time after Domtex acquired a large, innovative but money-losing American supplier in 1975 did it realize the firm was a springboard to world markets. On the other hand, Domtex did not then fully appreciate the upheaval to its management structure that going global would entail. But if it had, it would not have desisted, because its architect, Thomas Bell, like Noranda's William Deeks, strongly believes in constructive change. As president and then chairman, Bell shepherded Domtex's transformation from a national to an international company throughout the 1970s and 1980s. He retired in 1990 after 50 years with Domtex. "While corporations generally acknowledge the wisdom of keeping pace with change, they often find it hard to apply it to themselves," he observes.

Certainly, Domtex has altered considerably since the early 1970s when its sales were under $300 million and only about 7 percent were derived from exports. Today, 20 years later, its sales have more than quadrupled and 60 percent of its revenue comes from outside Canada. Twenty-eight of its 42 plants are in the United States and overseas, and it is broadening its network even farther through joint ventures with customers such as jeans manufacturers. Its global presence lessens Domtex's vulnerability to the intense pressures eroding the competitiveness of Canada's textile manufacturers. Foremost, the liberalization of trade, including the free trade agreement with the United States, has ripped away the industry's protective cocoon of steep tariff walls, leaving the Canadian market wide open for low-cost imports. In the past, the industry believed the installation of state-of-the-art robotics and other high-speed equipment would offset the cheap labour of lesser developed countries. But now, these places are acquiring similar technology, doubling their advantage. Simultaneously, textile makers in industrialized nations no longer have the cushion of large orders from regular customers year after year; they have stopped buying in depth due to the increased unpredictability of consumer tastes.

About 1970, Domtex began to consider widening its scope from Canada for a reason common among Canadian firms: its dominance at home restricted its prospects for future domestic growth. In deciding where to expand, it selected the United States, the conventional first choice among Canadians. "We believed then, and still do today, that if we could succeed in the U.S., we could anywhere," Bell says. In those days, as Domtex searched for the most suitable way to enter the United States, such jargon as strategic alliances and joint ventures did not yet exist. So Domtex hunted for "opportunities."

Opportunity was found on its doorstep: DHJ Industries, a New York supplier of interlinings, interfacings, denims, and doubleknits. In 1974, the two formed a joint marketing company. A year later the turning point arose for Domtex when DHJ went into bankruptcy. As a creditor, Domtex could have sat on the sidelines waiting to be repaid, since DHJ did ultimately reimburse all its creditors. Instead, Domtex decided the time was opportune for making a takeover bid because the offer could be low.

In addition, Domtex believed it had much to learn from DHJ's business style. Whereas Domtex was making $300 million with thirteen thousand employees, DHJ had revenue of close to $200 million with just one-fourth the number of workers. It avoided high labour content through manufacturing partnerships with factories in low-cost countries in Africa, Asia, and South America. In addition, its denims and doubleknits would broaden Domtex's product lineup without plunging it into the unknown, since it already had apparel makers as end-use customers. In short, as Bell happily realized, DHJ was a "feeding ground for Domtex eventually to become involved in globalized trading." Moreover, the move into the United States toughened its competitive spirit, which was necessary for, as Bell puts it, Domtex had a "jam-like" life in Canada as the market leader. "Having to contend every day with the Americans was like a cold shower and equipped us to be more aggressive in quality and service," he comments.

Subsequently, Domtex looked for an overseas feeding ground, bearing in mind that its relationship with DHJ blossomed from a non-equity basis to outright ownership. Since this gradualism had worked well once, it decided to repeat it in Tunisia, beginning as a supplier of technical assistance to a denim manufacturer there. When the Tunisian company decided to go public, Domtex acquired a 36-percent interest (later increased to 44 percent). As an opportunity, the factory turned out to be a mixed blessing in that it lagged far behind world standards and paid little heed to the work ethic. "Many of the employees had been hired off the streets and had never been in a factory before," Bell recalls. "Little attention was paid to detail, and there was no management follow-up." Also, the number of employees was far greater than the factory's capacity, but they could not be laid off due to Tunisian labour protection laws. Boxed in by these rules, Domtex solved the surplus problem by creating another shift to get extra output. Still, ten years passed before Domtex was satisfied with the quality of the goods and reaped profits rather than sustained losses from the factory.

As Bell readily admits, "Globalization sneaked up on us," thanks to DHJ and the Tunisian plant. By the 1980s, however, Domtex had acquired sufficient expertise to embark on the second stage of its globalization: an extensive program of acquisitions and modernization of equipment to enhance productivity and, thereby, competitiveness. In 1988 alone, Domtex spent $565 million on acquisitions. Throughout the 1980s, it invested $540 million in robotics, sophisticated numerical controls, and a direct computer link with customers to facilitate production planning and deliveries. It retained its commitment to both strategies even during unprofitable years to ensure it would be a major international force by the time Canada's protective textile tariffs were swept away.

Furthermore, since demand for fashion in one part of the world tends to remain strong while that in another part falters, Domtex is cushioned against cyclical geographic downturns by its worldwide presence. Thus, by the end of the 1980s, Domtex was prepared for the third phase of its internationalization—re-evaluation of itself. From this self-analysis, it pinpointed what no longer was of strategic value in the 1990s and beyond and undertook a major rationalization of its facilities.

When companies go global, their thoughts can be so concentrated on growth that they overlook the management ramifications. As Domtex's experience illustrates, these ramifications can be of an unexpected magnitude. Domtex moved all the way from a centralized to a decentralized structure which, as Bell notes, is easier said than done. When Domtex was a $300 million, primarily Canadian-based business, he was director of marketing, and all the product lines—sheets, towels, sleepwear, lingerie, tire cords, conveyor belts, knitting yarn—reported to him. "I never had sufficient time, in the right order, to spend with each area," he recalls. The obvious solution was a marketing manager for each line, but accomplishing the obvious took several years. Subsequently, similar reorganization in manufacturing and administration was undertaken. "We should have been bolder and done it all at once, because our method was extremely time-consuming," Bell says with 20:20 hindsight. It also created internal friction, as existing fiefdoms were dismembered and new empires created.

Today, Domtex is divided into six different "businesses," each with its own president as well as manufacturing, marketing, personnel, planning, and finance executives. Not all are at Domtex's Montreal headquarters. Instead, Domtex locates its divisional offices wherever the president of that division lives or wherever he or she believes is the best place.

Due to the globalization of business, Canada's largest firms are threatened by much bigger giants from south of the border and across the world. Thus, increasing international competitiveness is as crucial to the future of our country's big corporations as it is to its smaller businesses.

C H A P T E R

6

The Role of Foreign-Owned Subsidiaries

"Foreign investment, like marriage, requires patience to make it work. It is not a weapon, but an important and routine part of doing business."

Hiroyoshi (Mike) Tsuchiya,
Executive Vice-President,
Mitsubishi Canada

The global success or failure of Canadian-based businesses is, to a large extent, in the hands of foreign owners. According to the most recent Statistics Canada figures (for 1989), nonresidents control almost one-fifth of Canadian industry—17.5 percent of the financial, insurance, and real estate sector, and close to 27 percent of nonfinancial industries: manufacturing, oil and gas, mining and smelting, forestry, merchandising, agriculture, and utilities. But in some sectors, the percentage far exceeds that average. It is most pronounced in manufacturing, which is almost 50 percent foreign-owned. What makes this proportion even more significant is that one out of every five employed Canadians works in manufacturing.

The strategies of these foreign owners not only affect their Canadian subsidiaries, but also serve as guideposts for Canadian companies establishing operations throughout the world. Therefore, both this chapter and the next deal with this topic. This chapter describes foreign corporations' contributions to the economy and the advantages and drawbacks for a Canadian subsidiary as just one component in a worldwide web. It also discusses Japanese investment in Canada, since Japan is Canada's largest trading partner after the United States. The following chapter deals with how many Canadian subsidiaries are becoming multinationals in their own right. They have fought hard to earn mandates (or "missions" as some prefer to say) to develop, manufacture, and market a product or several products worldwide for their corporations.

Combined, the chapters describe the strategies of the subsidiaries of such well-known foreign firms as IBM, General Electric, Du Pont, Honeywell, Allied-Signal, General Signal, Pratt & Whitney, Upjohn, and Rockwell International of the United States; Mitsubishi of Japan and several leading Asian carmakers; Siemens and Daimler-Benz of Germany; and Pirelli of Italy. Other lesser-known European names that are a major presence in Canada are also covered. So, too, are subsidiaries that were established by their foreign parents and those that were previously independent Canadian companies.

The advantages of being a subsidiary are access to the parent's money, technology, well-known products, worldwide intelligence, and farflung connections. In addition, the world product mandates that are becoming the key to the globalization of corporations yield economies of scale that make the entire company more price competitive. Also, as a member of the family, subsidiaries are generally assured that their parents will not overcharge them for in-house equipment and that it will be of good quality, as well as delivered on time.

When foreign companies wisely allow their subsidiaries to be autonomous and self-reliant, the relationship benefits both sides and each, therefore, is happy. But when subsidiaries are treated as mere puppets, they can almost come to hate their parent companies. The main sources of this discontent are managers parachuted in for short periods of duty who dread making decisions that might forestall promotions. Their reluctance stifles aspirations and initiative at the subsidiary.

However, many foreign companies with Canadian subsidiaries have come to realize that to succeed in Canada, as elsewhere in the world, they must think global and act local. "They have learned they must be indigenous players with full-scale operations encompassing research and development, manufacturing, and marketing and not just carpetbagger sales operations," says

William Hetherington, president and CEO of Allen-Bradley Canada, a division of Rockwell International, the U.S. firm perhaps best known for its work on U.S. space exploration missions. "The same conditions exist in Canada as in the European Community, where foreign firms fear the development of a Fortress Europe, with invisible trade barriers, following the 1992 removal of actual tariffs. There, the entry ticket appears to be full-scale facilities and the same issue prevails in Canada."

Certainly, in many vital Canadian industries, foreigners will have all or most of the say over their future. Automobile production, Canada's largest manufacturing sector in dollar value and employees, is 100 percent foreign-owned. Foreign ownership also dominates the tobacco industry (99.8 percent), rubber products (89.2 percent), chemicals and chemical products (71.8 percent), and petroleum and coal products (67.7 percent). (See Table on page 136.)

Foreign-owned firms are leaders in several other fields, too. The three top computer and office equipment suppliers are subsidiaries of U.S.-based IBM, Xerox, and Digital Equipment. Sears Canada, the country's largest department store chain next to the Hudson's Bay Company, is owned by Sears Roebuck of the United States. The two largest oil and gas companies are foreign-controlled: Imperial Oil by U.S.-based Exxon and Shell Canada by Shell Petroleum of the Netherlands, which, in turn, is controlled by Royal Dutch Shell of the Netherlands and the United Kingdom; Japanese-owned Mitsui & Co. (Canada) is the third-biggest wholesaler of consumer products. Philips Canada, owned by N.V. Philips of the Netherlands, is the second largest electronics firm after CAE Industries, in which the Caisse de dépôt et placement du Québec is the biggest single shareholder.

Moreover, that foreign control of Canada's economy will increase is highly probable due to the efforts of the Mulroney government to attract more outside money. Investment Canada, established in 1985 by Mulroney, has yet to reject a foreign takeover although it is charged with monitoring foreign investment. That it has not ruled negatively is not surprising, considering its other role is to promote investment in Canada. The agency has defended itself time and again by maintaining that such investment provides jobs and makes Canada more competitive globally through the importation of new technologies.

Foreign takeovers of Canadian businesses have increased significantly since the Mulroney-generated free trade deal began with

FOREIGN DIRECT INVESTMENT IN CANADA AND CANADIAN DIRECT INVESTMENT ABROAD

(By Area)
($ Billion)

1989 AND 1990

FOREIGN DIRECT INVESTMENT IN CANADA	1989	1990
Total	118.4	126.6
United States	75.8	79.1
United Kingdom	15.9	17.1
Japan	4.7	5.2
Other EEC countries (excluding U.K.)	10.8	13.1
Other OECD countries (including European countries not part of EEC plus Australia and New Zealand)	7.7	8.1
All other countries	3.5	4.0

CANADIAN DIRECT INVESTMENT ABROAD	1989	1990
Total	80.0	84.8
United States	50.1	51.6
United Kingdom	9.5	11.8
Japan	0.4	0.4
Other EEC countries (excluding U.K.)	5.2	6.0
Other OECD countries (including European countries not part of EEC plus Australia and New Zealand)	3.2	3.7
All other countries	11.6	11.3

Source: Statistics Canada, "Canada's International Investment Position" Catalogue #67-202.

FOREIGN DIRECT INVESTMENT IN CANADA AND CANADIAN DIRECT INVESTMENT ABROAD

(Ranked by Top Ten Countries)
($ Million)

1989
(MOST RECENT AVAILABLE YEAR)

FOREIGN DIRECT INVESTMENT IN CANADA

Country	Amount
United States	75,825
United Kingdom	15,945
Japan	4,681
West Germany	3,724
Netherlands	3,247
France	2,611
Switzerland	2,321
Bermuda	1,231
Australia	1,055
Hong Kong	1,043

CANADIAN DIRECT INVESTMENT ABROAD

Country	Amount
United States	50,122
United Kingdom	9,488
Australia	2,116
Bermuda	1,847
Brazil	1,543
Bahamas	1,488
France	1,405
Singapore	1,290
Netherlands	957
Indonesia	921

Source: Statistics Canada, "Canada's International Investment Position" Catalogue #67-202.

THIRTY LARGEST FOREIGN-OWNED COMPANIES IN CANADA

(Ranked by Sales)

1989

Company	Sales ($000)	Industry	Owned	Parent	Rank in Sales in Top 500 Companies in Canada
General Motors of Canada	19,668,377	Motor Vehicles	100	General Motors (U.S.)	1
Ford Motor Company	15,311,800	Motor Vehicles	97	Ford Motor (U.S.)	3
Imperial Oil	10,007,000	Oil	69.6	Exxon (U.S.)	7
Chrysler Canada	8,167,400	Motor Vehicles	100	Chrysler (U.S.)	9
Shell Canada	4,917,000	Oil	78	Shell (Netherlands)	17
Sears Canada	4,562,300	Retailing	61.4	Sears, Roebuck (U.S.)	22
Canada Safeway	4,198,581	Food	100	Safeway (U.S.)	27
IBM Canada	4,188,000	Computers, Office equipment	100	IBM (U.S.)	28

Company	Sales ($000)	Industry	Owned	Parent	Rank in Sales in Top 500 Companies in Canada
Mitsui & Co. (Canada)	2,833,401	Consumer products wholesaler	100	Mitsui (Japan)	39
United Westburne	2,654,790	Transportation	79	Dumez (France)	44
Total Petroleum (North America)	2,570,425	Oil	51	Total Petroles (France)	45
Falconbridge	2,436,765	Metals and mining	50	Trelleborg (Sweden)	47
Great Atlantic and Pacific	2,258,803	Food	100	Great Atlantic and Pacific (U.S.)	50
F.W. Woolworth	2,257,546	Retailing	100	Woolworth World Trade (U.S.)	51
Honda Canada	2,171,786	Motor Vehicles	100	Honda Motor (Japan) 50.2% American Honda (U.S.) 49.8%	53
Dow Chemical Canada	2,033,822	Industrial Products	100	Dow Chemicals (U.S.)	59
Rio Algom	1,711,910	Metals and Mining	59	RTZ (U.K.)	66
C. Itoh & Co. (Canada)	1,654,638	Consumer products wholesaler	100	C. Itoh (Japan)	70

(cont'd)

Company	Sales ($000)	Industry	Owned	Parent	Rank in Sales in Top 500 Companies in Canada
K-Mart Canada	1,601,187	Retailing	100	K-Mart (U.S.)	71
General Electric Canada	1,583,521	Industrial Products	100	General Electric (U.S.)	75
Canadian Ultramar	1,542,848	Industrial Products	100	Ultramar (U.K.)	76
Toyota Canada	1,498,035	Motor vehicles	100	Toyota Motor (Japan) 50% Mitsui (Japan) 50%	77
Cargill	1,463,392	Agriculture	100	Cargill (U.S.)	80
Mobil Canada	1,436,961	Oil	100	Mobil (U.S.)	81
Du Pont Canada	1,416,873	Industrial Products	77.8	E.I. du Pont de Nemours (U.S.)	83
Fletcher Challenge Canada	1,402,793	Forest Products	71.8	Fletcher Challenge (New Zealand)	85
McDonald's Restaurants of Canada	1,377,912	Food retailer	100	McDonald's (U.S.)	87
Pratt & Whitney Canada	1,355,676	Industrial Products	98	United Technologies (U.S.)	90
Marubeni Canada	1,330,000	Consumer products wholesaler	100	Marubeni (Japan)	92
Suncor	1,215,000	Oil	75	Sun Company (U.S.) 75%	95

FOREIGN CONTROL OF CANADIAN MANUFACTURING

(By Percentage)
As of 1987
(Latest Available Figures)

Automobile	100
Tobacco products	99.8
Rubber products	89.2
Transportation equipment	75.6
Chemical and chemical products	71.8
Petroleum and coal products	67.7
Nonmetallic mineral products	66.9
Machinery	51.9
Electrical products	46.1
Textile mills	44.2
Food	37.2
Beverages	27.5
Wood industries	26.1
Metal fabricating	25.3
Paper products	21.9
Primary metal and metals	19.0
Leather products	17.4
Furnishings (including furniture)	13.5
Clothing industries	12.2
Printing and publishing	9.2
Knitting mills	7.8

Source: Canadian Manufacturers' Association.

the United States. In 1989, the agreement's first year, a record 691 Canadian companies were acquired by foreign firms, primarily in the United States, according to the federal Bureau of Competition Policy.

Naturally, many Canadians are extremely concerned about the growing foreign infiltration. But their concern is somewhat hypocritical in view of substantial Canadian investment abroad. In 1990, according to Statistics Canada, it was $84.8 billion, a 294 percent increase from 1980, much greater than the 105 percent rise in foreign investment in Canada during the same period. Just as U.S. firms are the biggest investors in Canada (62.5 percent of the total as of 1990), the United States is the foremost destination of Canadian foreign investment (60.8 percent of the total in 1990).

Foreign-owned companies are indeed important to Canada in terms of jobs, technological innovation, exports, domestic purchases, and charitable donations. Pratt & Whitney Canada and IBM Canada have the second and third largest corporate research and development laboratories in Canada after Bell-Northern Research. IBM Canada's software applications lab is the second largest in the IBM worldwide web.

Certainly, IBM provides a good example of a subsidiary out to prove that it is a worthy Canadian corporate citizen. In its 80 years in Canada it has never had layoffs, preferring to retrain and redeploy workers when necessary. It purchases many of its supplies in Canada. For example, in 1989, the company's manufacturing procurement totalled $202 million. Based on its estimate that $75,000 worth of component purchases supports one job, IBM's 1989 shopping list supported close to 2,700 Canadian jobs at suppliers. (The company has 12,370 employees.) All told, IBM annually buys about $500 million worth of supplies and services from several thousand Canadian firms.

The company's international procurement office also assists Canadian suppliers in exporting products and services to IBM plants and laboratories worldwide. In 1989, this amount came to $43 million, and the quantity should rise as IBM Canada's exports are growing at a faster pace than its domestic revenue. Between 1985 and 1989 (latest available figures), export sales rose by 13 percent, more than four times the domestic increase, and exports now account for 38 percent of total sales.

According to the company, its $848 million expenditure on R&D throughout the 1980s made its laboratory the fastest growing in Canada. The lab employs five times as many people as it did in

1980. During the 1980s, IBM Canada also spent $402 million on upgrading employees' and customers' skills, and it maintains that its annual education budget equals that of a medium-sized Canadian university. Moreover, IBM is a major corporate donor, giving $10 million between 1987 and 1989 alone to educational, health, welfare, cultural, and civic projects.

In the automobile industry, Canada's biggest manufacturing sector, four major Asian carmakers—three from Japan and one from South Korea—have recently opened Canadian plants. They join the U.S. Big Three—General Motors, Ford, and Chrysler—which have been here for years. While solidifying the foreign grip on carmaking in Canada, they also contribute to the country's industrial development. Combined, the Asian transplants have created five thousand jobs.* The Japanese firms, all located in Ontario, have fortified Ontario's position in North America as an automobile production centre. They are: Toyota in Cambridge, Honda in Alliston, and Suzuki, in a joint venture with General Motors in Ingersoll. South Korea's Hyundai introduced car manufacturing to Quebec by locating in Bromont, 50 miles south of Montreal. Further, Canada benefits from the transfer of these firms' internationally renowned training and workplace methods (described in Chapter 9) and technology. For example, Hyundai's plant contains 35 percent of the total number of automated manufacturing robots in Quebec.

Whereas Toyota and Honda built plants in the United States before doing so in Canada, Hyundai chose Canada as its first foreign site. It did so for a mixture of emotional and economic reasons. It first decided to enter the North American market via imports to Canada in 1983 because Canada granted it duty-free access. The low prices it could consequently charge quickly made its cars the best-selling automobile import. This rapid success caused consternation at General Motors and Ford. They lodged dumping complaints with the federal government, which responded by levying import taxes on Hyundai.

This change of policy by the government, along with its sales volume, put Hyundai under intense pressure to invest and not merely sell in Canada. Having decided to do so, its chief dilemma was whether to settle in Ontario or Quebec, according to Seung-

---

*At full employment, the Big Three U.S. carmakers employ eighty-six thousand people in Canada.

Bok Lee, executive vice-president of Hyundai Auto Canada and plant manager at Bromont. He was placed in charge of the project on account of his more than 20 years with Hyundai, culminating in his appointment as a board director, as well as head of passenger vehicle manufacturing.

To shift some of the responsibility onto Canadian shoulders, he hired a Montreal consulting engineering firm to suggest potential locations. It drew up a list of 43 sites across Canada, with most in Ontario and Quebec. These were shortlisted to seven in the two provinces and subsequently to one each. What tipped the balance in favour of Quebec was its more generous incentive package, as well as the fact that all other car plants are in Ontario, including the Japanese plants. "Sometimes when you take a risk, you make more profit," Lee explains regarding his decision.

The Quebec and federal governments agreed to pay up to $10 million annually for five years on the interest charged on loans obtained by Hyundai to finance the project, which cost $444 million. Both governments also helped fund employee training programs. Ontario was providing assistance to the Toyota, Honda, and GM/Suzuki projects, and therefore could not match Quebec's offer to Hyundai.

Despite the aid, the plant was a gamble for Hyundai in that during its construction, from 1986 through 1988, massive overcapacity began to develop in the car industry, especially in North America. Consequently, when Hyundai's plant opened in December 1988, it was not at full capacity of 100,000, and it is not expected to reach that point until 1994. Thus, employment is only at two-thirds of the objective. Moreover, financially, it won't reach its breakeven point of producing 80,000 cars until 1993. To make extra money, it is selling some cars to Taiwan as a way for the parent company to circumvent Taiwanese quotas on imports; Hyundai Korea is at the maximum allowable. However, as only about 5,000 Hyundai Canada cars were exported in 1990 to Taiwan, the slack in North American sales was not offset.

Although all foreign-owned subsidiaries in Canada are alike in that they are just one member in a worldwide family, they are very different in their characteristics in this era of business globalization. Hence, their dissimilarities contain helpful guidelines for other foreign companies in Canada as well as for Canadian corporations with operations throughout the world. Many subsidiaries have taken the initiative to develop a more fulfilling role and thereby make themselves essential to their parents' globalization. Some would be extinct or insignificant today if a foreign firm had not decided they could be revived and fitted into their global master plan. Sometimes, foreign subsidiaries are better off when their ownership changes from one foreign firm to another in a different country. Some Canadian subsidiaries, like Pirelli's, are stepping stones to the United States, while others, like Siemens's Canadian operations, are viewed as part of a composite North American market that also encompasses the United States and Mexico. Finally, there are subsidiaries that are offsprings of companies partnered in international joint ventures. What follows are examples of each category.

How Two Smart Canadian Subsidiaries Benefit from Their Parents' Globalization

Garrett Canada of Toronto (aircraft environmental controls) and Klöckner Stadler Hurter of Montreal (engineers and contractors) demonstrate how Canadian subsidiaries can themselves become international players simply by riding on their parents' coat-tails. Garrett Canada is owned by Allied-Signal of New Jersey (1989 sales: $11.9 billion U.S.), a 47-country aerospace, automotive, and engineered-materials colossus. It is the world's foremost manufacturer of aircraft environmental controls, with an enormous 75 percent market share.

Thanks to the globalization of the aircraft industry, Garrett Canada has begun to sell to outside customers while continuing to supply its immediate parent, the Los Angeles-based Garrett Corporation. "Within ten years, Garrett Canada's overseas business should amount to 30 percent of revenue," predicts Vice-President Robert Polk.

Formerly a senior executive at Garrett's U.S. corporation, Polk was dispatched to Canada in 1990 with the assignment to convert the Canadian operation from merely an in-house source into an industry-wide supplier. "Although it will not be free of Los Angeles, Garrett Canada will be increasingly independent of, as well as mutually supportive to, Garrett U.S.," Polk adds.

Garrett Canada dates back to 1954 when Garrett U.S. bought an Ontario firm called Aero Sales Engineering, a sales and service organization that also made and overhauled aircraft products. Some years earlier, the U.S. company had rejected starting a subsidiary from scratch. After its purchase and renaming as Garrett Canada, the new member of the family did as asked by its parent, which handled international sales from Los Angeles. This policy made sense because the bulk of the world's aircraft construction was centred in the United States.

Today, however, this concept is outmoded now that European and Pacific Rim countries are building their own planes, and Eastern Europe is on the verge of doing so. Rather than cede U.S. business to offshore manufacturers in a quid pro quo for access to their customers, invest in overseas joint ventures, or acquire foreign companies, Garrett U.S. decided it could best increase its overseas business by having its Canadian subsidiary sell internationally as well.

Garrett Canada has found that it sometimes has an advantage over its parent for the very reason that it is a foreign subsidiary. Whereas companies manufacturing aircraft parts in other countries tend to regard Garrett U.S. as competition because its products cover a broad range, including power units and engines, they do not feel threatened by Garrett Canada since it only makes environmental controls.

"When the Los Angeles corporation had 90 percent of the Free World market, it was prudent for Canada to climb on the bandwagon, rather than lay out money to compete directly," Polk explains. "But in today's more competitive market, Garrett Canada needs to be able to sell on its own. Decisions as to whether Canada should be the sole source can be made rapidly via a telephone conversation with Los Angeles. Competitors are willing to deal directly with Garrett Canada because it already is recognized as world class in its field."

Of course, another incentive for the enlargement of Garrett Canada's role is the availability of federal government industrial research development funds, but Polk emphasizes that the company will also invest heavily itself in R&D. In turn, Canada will benefit if Garrett Canada's separate international sales effort necessitates expansion of its facilities, as the company expects will happen.

In becoming a foreign-owned subsidiary in 1979, Stadler Hurter gladly exchanged Canadian independent ownership for the financial backing and access to the world markets of Klöckner, a big German corporation. Today, the former management at Stadler Hurter has absolutely no regrets. Revenues at the renamed Klöckner Stadler Hurter have leaped to $60 million, and in 1986 and 1989 it won federal government export awards. Moreover, these gains have not been at the expense of much of its autonomy. Except for the president and controller, who are appointed by the parent company, Klöckner Stadler Hurter, which has about 250 employees, is staffed by Canadians. Yet, at the same time, it is plugged into the contacts of Klöckner's worldwide offices, including many in developing countries, prime customers of engineering and contracting services.

Stadler Hurter was well established when it decided to become foreign-owned, having been founded in 1923. Nevertheless, it concluded that to be competitive it had to become part of an international organization. "For the firm to achieve its objective of being an offshore contractor as well as a consulting engineer, it required a strong balance sheet, and service companies tend not to have these," says Alan Curleigh, vice-president, international contracts and project finance at KSH. "It regarded Klöckner as the financial godfather it needed." For its part, Klöckner, a multifaceted steel producer and industrial plant contractor, wanted an engineering company to augment its operations. "Both sides were convinced the synergy would be fantastic and it has been," Curleigh adds.

At the time of the sale, the federal Foreign Investment Review Agency still existed, and opponents of foreign takeovers of Canadian industry protested. However, Stadler Hurter convinced the agency that the Canadian companies that were expressing interest in acquiring it really only wanted to buy it in order to eliminate a competitor.

Because Klöckner is global, it now has the capability of delegating work anywhere within its family. Thus, it is up to KSH to persuade Klöckner that it is most suited for a project. Often, its winning arguments are based on sentiment, rather than cold economics: British Commonwealth links, a similar government system, or a foreign government minister who graduated from a Canadian university.

Survival through Becoming a Foreign Subsidiary

The Winnipeg bus manufacturer New Flyer Industries has climbed back from the edge of death in 1986 to robust good health today thanks to a European company that saw it not as a disaster but rather as a springboard to North American expansion. Moreover, the European company Den Ousten Bus Works of Holland was correct in its evaluation. Today, New Flyer is profitable and is Canada's third largest bus manufacturer, as well as North America's fifth. In addition, it is once again privately run; at the time of its sale, New Flyer was 74 percent owned by Manitoba's New Democratic government.

Its resurrection demonstrates the lengths to which companies sometimes have to go in their globalization quest, as well as the amount of time and effort that must be devoted to remaking a subsidiary thousands of miles away. Only a foreign company finding it difficult to enter the North American market would have been attracted by New Flyer, then known as Flyer Industries. By 1986, the company, established in 1930, had a dismal record. Not only had it lost a staggering $75 million since 1968, but its buses were also notorious for poor quality. Its only appealing aspects were its price tag—a cheap $2 million—and its proximity to the U.S. market, a nearness which met Den Ousten's globalization needs.

Founded in 1927 and still family owned and managed, Den Ousten dominates Holland's bus market both within and between cities. However, with the 1992 advent of a single European market rapidly approaching, it was concerned that it would be faced with much more European competition. Therefore, it sought to lessen its dependence on that part of the world through diversification in North America. It ruled out starting from scratch because other European bus companies had found this tactic too costly and because North American bus sales were suffering from over-capacity. Therefore, Den Ousten decided it would be better to acquire an existing facility.

Flyer's recovery was by no means instantaneous; instead, it was the result of more than a year's overhaul. The easiest step was to add "New" to its name to emphasize that it was a born-again enterprise. To Den Ousten, much of New Flyer's misery stemmed from cumbersome bureaucracy. The ratio of management to factory workers was much higher than conventional levels, with the 250 blue-collar workers just barely outnumbering the 200 in management. Initiative and enterprise were stifled by the six levels of authority between the plant floor and executive office.

Den Ousten stringently pruned submanagers and managerial assistants, replacing them with just seven department heads and one chief executive. One-fourth of the factory workforce—68 employees—was sent in groups of three for five-month immersion courses at Den Ousten's Holland facilities. On their return, they enthusiastically inducted their co-workers in the Den Ousten approach.

To overcome New Flyer's reputation for inferior workmanship, Den Ousten replaced its design with its own. Principally, it substituted its noncorroding fibreglass panels that can be sculpted to various shapes for Flyer's conventional aluminum sides. Fibreglass panels are cheaper to install because they do not require riveting, as does aluminum. Furthermore, Den Ousten expanded Flyer's product line to include articulated buses. These buses, 15 feet longer than standard size ones, can accommodate more people, yet easily turn corners because of their accordion-like joint. Another design transferred by Den Ousten is the low-floor bus, of which the entrances and exits are level with sidewalks in contrast to the usual raised floors and entry and exit steps. New Flyer's low-floor buses are used to transport baggage-laden plane travellers at New York's Kennedy Airport, and the company anticipates sales to other American, as well as Canadian, airports. North American transit systems also are expected to buy them due to an increasing number of municipalities legislating easier-to-use buses for the elderly and the handicapped.

Furthermore, New Flyer is reintroducing the electric trolley as an alternative to gas-consuming diesel buses in these days of rising oil prices. Although many cities have removed the overhead wires needed for electric buses, quite a few still retain them, including Vancouver and Toronto in Canada, San Francisco and Boston in the United States, and such countries as Thailand, Brazil, and Chile.

From the beginning of its ownership, Den Ousten has gone out of its way to keep New Flyer Canadian in its management and workforce, except for a Dutch factory manager parachuted in during the first few years of reorganization. Although it could readily have dominated New Flyer's board since it is the sole owner, it wanted to underscore its commitment to Canada through the appointment of Canadians. Therefore, it persuaded Harold Thompson, a prominent Manitoban, to become New Flyer's chairman. He is also chairman of the Manitoba Public Insurance Corporation, which operates Autopac, the province's compulsory auto insurance program. "I hesitated because of my horror over Flyer's reputation, but then agreed because I was impressed by Jan Den Ousten, who heads the Dutch company," Thompson says. Subsequently, he suggested other well-connected residents of Winnipeg for the board.

As Den Ousten expected, the bulk of New Flyer's sales are to the much larger U.S. market. However, this penetration did not just simply happen; Den Ousten made it happen, primarily through the establishment of a 50-person satellite plant in Union City, California, near San Francisco, and in Oakland—two cities identified as prime potential customers. The shells of U.S.-destined buses were made in Winnipeg, and the seats and engines installed in California. "This enabled New Flyer to provide an onsite testimonial of its competitive price and quality, thereby enhancing its chances when U.S. communities issued tenders for new buses," Thompson points out.

In 1990, New Flyer closed the California plant and shifted U.S. production to Grand Forks, North Dakota for logistical reasons. "This location is easier to monitor because it can be reached by a two-and-a-half hour drive from Winnipeg, whereas the Union City facility was several hours away by plane," explains Executive Vice-President Guy Johnson. "Also, the central location enables easier coverage of the entire United States." For example, New Flyer recently signed a contract to ship buses to Atlanta, on the east coast.

The only blot on New Flyer's recovery is one that many companies would envy: output rebounded so swiftly that the greatly reduced administrative side could not keep pace. Consequently, Johnson, formerly an executive at an Alberta recreational vehicle manufacturer, was hired in 1989 to shore up the purchasing systems, materials control, finance, and accounting. With that achieved and orders lined up a year in advance, New Flyer is a born-again company, as well as a notable example of the benefits possible from foreign takeovers.

How Globalization Can Both Help and Hinder
Foreign Subsidiaries

Becoming foreign owned is often a matter of trade-offs: security as part of a company with vast financial resources and an internationally well-regarded product in exchange for a very restricted role. Amada Canada of Mississauga, Ontario is a case in point. It is owned by Amada Company of Japan, a $3.5 billion manufacturer of sheet metal machinery used in the construction of computer chassis, electronic components, and switchgear equipment.

In the overall scheme of Amada, its Canadian operations are microscopic, accounting for just 1.5 percent of worldwide sales. Therefore, Amada Canada's role is commensurately minuscule. It is allowed to retain its profits in order to be self-sustaining, but receives no infusion of funds from its parent. It neither manufactures nor initiates designs; its role is strictly to sell. "Considering the small Canadian market, we could not be competitive in manufacturing against imports from the United States, Germany, and other Japanese companies," explains Carl Ruhe, Amada Canada's general manager. Furthermore, Amada Canada cannot sell in nearby northern American states because Amada's U.S. subsidiary opposed what it regarded as potential cannibalizing of its turf. It took this stand even though Amada Canada originated as a spinoff from it.

However, while the U.S. operation successfully flexed its muscles against its Canadian offspring, it is still just another subsidiary of the Japanese parent. Therefore, its role is not much more magnified than Amada Canada, even though it has three hundred employees compared to just 45 in Canada. In 1987, in a centralization move, Amada Japan removed Amada Canada from the jurisdiction of the U.S. subsidiary to have it report directly to Japan. In addition, Amada allocates little manufacturing to the United States since U.S. sales are a small portion—about 12 percent—of Amada's worldwide business. Instead, most manufacturing is done in Japan and by a French machinery firm called Promecam, purchased in the 1970s to give the Japanese firm a European foothold. Promecam's Quebec-based Canadian subsidiary was merged with Amada Canada, with the result that Amada's Quebec sales increased due to Promecam Canada's strong presence there.

Another example of how a foreign takeover can strengthen a Canadian company while at the same time restricting its role is provided by AEG Canada of Ajax, Ontario, about 30 miles east of Toronto. Its story as a foreign-owned company began in 1970 when what was then Bayly Engineering, a small firm established in 1947, was purchased by German electrical giant AEG-Telefunken. It was a friendly takeover because Bayly believed it lacked the financial weight to expand or weather recessions. For its part, AEG, which already had North American sales offices, wanted a manufacturing outlet, too.

Bayly was one of five potential candidates that AEG considered. Although demand was stagnant for the telephone jacks and remote-control radio equipment which Bayly made at that time, AEG chose it since its engineering skills were complementary to its own. In 1986, AEG, in turn, was purchased by Germany's Daimler-Benz Group, well known for the Mercedes-Benz automobile, as well as for aerospace and computer science products.

As a wholly owned subsidiary, AEG Canada's direction is determined more in Germany than Ontario. AEG rechannelled the manufacturing side, called AEG Bayly, into automated postal-sorting equipment, in which AEG has a 65 percent worldwide market share. However, initially it was merely an assembly operation. Only when Canada Post, a major customer, insisted that suppliers increase their Canadian sourcing content did AEG convert AEG Bayly into an original manufacturer. AEG was accustomed to this conversion, having just done the same with its Australian subsidiary in response to the demands of that country's postal authority.

But while AEG's ownership catapulted the Canadian company into a high-growth business from its previous stagnant one of jacks and telephone equipment, the relationship by no means carries over into AEG's many other activities. Instead, AEG often bypasses AEG Canada in favour of selling through other subsidiaries in Canada or through independent distributors. For example, although 100-percent-owned Modicon Canada (industrial automation) and Modcomp Canada (computer systems) are located in Mississauga, Ontario, within easy driving distance of AEG Canada, they handle their sales independently. Both are Canadian subsidiaries of U.S. firms acquired at the same time as their parents. AEG's power tools and household appliances are sold by distributors.

Until 1989, AEG Canada did handle Canadian sales of AEG's urban transit equipment. That stopped when AEG purchased Westinghouse's transportation system unit; these sales are now handled by a subsidiary of AEG Westinghouse. AEG Canada now hopes to broaden its role through partnerships with Canadian engineers capable of adapting AEG equipment to Canadian requirements.

How a Change in Foreign Owners Can Help

Business globalization sometimes seems to resemble a giant chess game with ownership of subsidiaries in a state of flux as their parents undergo mergers or acquisitions. A case in point is provided by Murata Erie North America, located in Trenton, Ontario and the largest employer there next to the Canadian Air Force Base. Originally, it was a subsidiary of an American company, Erie Technological Products. The U.S. parent was bought and sold several times and was often in financial trouble before Murata Manufacturing of Japan purchased it in 1980. The Canadian subsidiary changed ownership along with its former parent. Murata is one of the world's top manufacturers of electronic ceramic capacitors used in a wide assortment of products ranging from military equipment to automobiles and television sets.

The Japanese restored their new North American subsidiaries to health not by putting them on a short leash, but by allocating separate production functions to each and allowing considerable independence. The Trenton plant was made the sole producer for Murata of electromagnetic interference filters, which sift out static, since it already held the lead in these in Canada. Murata delegates world production assignments to its other 11 foreign subsidiaries, too. Each is responsible for its own research and development and worldwide marketing of its specialty.

Furthermore, on acquiring the Canadian company, Murata Japan spent millions of dollars upgrading the then 20-year-old factory: it installed air conditioning, new ceilings, brighter lighting, and more comfortable work benches. It also made several million dollars available for a "clean room," a particle-free environment essential for the manufacture of the delicate and intricate electronic components that the Trenton plant produces.

As a subsidiary, the Canadian company naturally still has to operate within Murata's worldwide strategy. But in day to day matters, it has autonomy. "North America has a different way of doing business than Japan, and Murata realizes this," says Paul Leger, export manager at the Canadian subsidiary. "If we are successful, it's a plus for our side; if not, we're asked for explanations." Obviously, nothing is extraordinary about this attitude—the same accounting is also part of everyday life within Canadian-owned companies.

Canadian Subsidiaries That Predate American Ones

For many overseas companies, the United States is their first and often only choice for a North American subsidiary because of its large population. But some companies prefer to start in Canada for the very reason that its market is 10 percent of that of the United States. They would rather do well in a smaller marketplace than do battle with giant U.S. corporations. Only after they have a strong footing in Canada do they consider a U.S. presence. Such is the process exemplified by Pirelli, an Italian tire and cable company that makes $7 billion (U.S.) in revenue and has operations in five continents.

Pirelli's cable group, which makes power and telecommunication cable as well as building wiring, has plants in 12 countries. Its Canadian branch, begun in 1953, was the first foreign cable operation opened by the company in a quarter century. Pirelli Cables waited until 1978 to establish U.S. operations, having used the interim period since 1953 to go into Mexico, Peru, and Australia. The company started off in power cable production in Canada and the United States. Then in 1972, it opened a communications cable facility in the Vancouver suburb of Surrey. Today, it specializes in optical fibre, which conveys far more messages at greater clarity and speed but much lower cost than conventional copper cable.

For 13 years the Surrey plant was Pirelli's sole North American communications cable factory. But by 1985, its substantial exports to the United States prompted the opening of an outlet there in Lexington, South Carolina. Surrey's head engineer was placed in charge of its development. Since the United States is a much bigger market, the American factory has moved ahead of Surrey's in volume. Because it produces power cable and building wire as well as optical fibre, Pirelli chose it as the site for a new research and development centre, instead of Surrey. However, Surrey continues to have its own engineering design staff. "Whenever Lexington gets new equipment, we remind it of its origins," Shawn Davison, the marketing manager at the Surrey facility, says with a smile.

Pirelli has sound reasons for two North American optical fibre facilities. One plant can take over if the other is shut down by a strike or natural disaster, and their deliberate location at opposite ends of the continent prevents costly shipping duplication. Surrey supplies the western United States, but the Lexington facility does not ship to eastern Canada. Head office does not want it to cut into Surrey's sales in the much smaller Canadian market, and it wants its Canadian customers to regard it as a good local citizen. Pirelli ranks second in Canada in optical fibre sales after Northern Telecom and third in the United States, a much bigger and more open market. In Canada, Pirelli virtually is locked out of optical fibre sales in Ontario and Quebec because Bell Canada, the telephone service supplier in those provinces, principally buys its cable from Northern Telecom, its equipment subsidiary.

While the Surrey and Lexington plants live in harmonious North American co-existence, internationally it is a much different story. Surrey is just one of Pirelli's worldwide family of optical fibre producers. All these brothers and sisters are made to compete fiercely against one another for transactions. When Pirelli's Cable Export co-ordinating office at Milan headquarters receives an order, it requests quotations from all the cable facilities. It also takes into consideration geographic proximity to customers to determine from which point transportation costs would be cheaper. Price, however, is the most important factor in Cable Export's decisions.

Even though Canadian wages exceed those in less expensive Pirelli locations such as Mexico, that does not place Surrey at a disadvantage since labour accounts for only 10 percent of the production cost of optical fibre, according to Davison.

Canadian Subsidiaries as Part of the North American Strategy of Overseas Companies

The Canadian subsidiaries of overseas corporations are emerging from the background into the foreground as their parents turn their attention to North America for much of their future growth. Many regard Canada as a gateway to the entire North American market, both in the wake of the Canada–U.S. free trade agreement and in anticipation of a U.S.–Mexico–Canada common market similar to the post-1992 unified Western European marketplace.

Siemens, the German electrical engineering and electronics giant with 1988–89 sales of $39 billion, typifies this reverse pattern. It is the world's fifth largest electrical and electronic firm, after IBM and General Electric of the United States and Hitachi and Matsushita of Japan. But it has reached that position primarily by concentration on its home country and the rest of continental Europe. Nearly half of its revenue is derived from what was West Germany and almost another 30 percent from elsewhere in Europe. The United States accounts for 11 percent ($4.3 billion) and Canada for 1.3 percent ($500 million).

Siemens pins much of its hope for doubling its sales by the end of this decade on North America. "Siemens wants to sustain its share in the European sector of the economic Triad of Europe, Japan, and North America, as well as catch up with its competitors in North America," says Gerd Hufnagel, manager, public relations, of Siemens Electric Ltd., the company's Canadian arm. "North America is the biggest market for our type of products. The U.S. market alone is ten times bigger than Germany's. By contrast, Japan's is four times greater. Thus, the U.S. market dictates the pace of development, and we must be close to U.S. customers to know what they want. Further, to remain price competitive, Siemens needs the sort of volume shipments the U.S. can provide."

While Canada figures prominently in Siemens's North American strategy due to the free trade agreement, similarities that Siemens perceives between Canadian and European work habits and business styles also play a role. "Canadians tend to be more loyal to their employers and more patient regarding compensation and career advancement," observes Hufnagel, who worked for Siemens in Germany and the United States before being posted to Canada. "Conversely, Americans are more accustomed to the hire and fire method and to quitting halfway through a project. Moreover, although productivity and the quality of workmanship are lower in Canada than in Germany, they can surpass U.S. performance. For example, we relocated production from a New Orleans plant to Canada because of that facility's bad quality and productivity." An additional Canadian attraction is the use of the metric system, also employed by Siemens's design headquarters in Germany. The United States is one of the few places that has not switched from the imperial to the metric system.

Siemens is interested in Canada for its own sake as well as for its proximity to the U.S. market. It has a longtime presence dating back to the turn of this century when it opened its first Canadian office. Its Canadian plants manufacture switchgear, electronic and transportation components, as well as hearing aids and lighting products for commercial, automotive, industrial, and scientific use. The Canadian subsidiary has spearheaded Siemens's North American light rail transit (LRT) business. Its current president, William Waite, born in Ontario and a Siemens employee since 1963, won Siemens's first major Canadian LRT orders, in Edmonton and Calgary, shortly after his 1975 transfer back to Canada from the company's head office in Munich. He became president of the Canadian operations six years later. Siemens Canada also has mandates from head office to make motor controls and power distribution systems for pulp and paper, oil and gas, mining, material handling, and utility businesses in Canada and around the world.

Siemens intends to grow in North America, as it has recently been doing in Europe, primarily through mergers, acquisitions, and strategic partnerships with competitors. President and CEO Karlheinz Kaske has vowed that Siemens "will look at every ship that floats by." The first major North American "ship" acquired by Siemens since Kaske's pledge was California telephone equipment manufacturer Rolm Corporation, purchased in 1989 from IBM. In 1990, it kicked off its Canadian takeover drive with the purchase of Magna International's electric motor division, reflecting head office's selection of automotive electronics as a new growth area complementary to Siemens's traditional activities.

Siemens has ample funds for its acquisitions drive, partly because it has not wandered into unrelated, less profitable diversification as have many of its rivals, and partly because it pays a lower dividend rate than many. Siemens specializes in capital goods—

equipment and machinery subsequently used in the production of consumer goods. Philips, Europe's largest electronics group, is struggling to recover from its first-time-ever dismissal of a chairman (in July 1990), layoffs of more than fifty-five thousand people, a substantial profit decline, and a massive paring of its product mix. It was making a huge array, including lamps, stereo equipment, compact discs, clocks, vacuum cleaners, printed circuit boards, and military machinery.

Not only is Siemens more focused, but it is also in a higher growth sector. Over the next few years, the worldwide market for capital electrical and electronic goods is predicted to grow by 7 percent annually, compared to 4 percent for consumer ones. Furthermore, consumer electrical and electronic goods are a bigger financial drain on a firm because much more money must be expended on marketing to build buyer awareness. Moreover, if just one line fails, it can have a devastating impact on the entire company. Philips is a case in point. Its unhappy chain of events began with a drop in its sales of semiconductor circuitry and computers.

Siemens has plenty of money for expansion since it pays much lower dividends than most North American corporations feel obliged to dispense. This practice is common in Germany (and many other countries, notably Japan) where corporations prefer to plough back profits into further development. Indeed, despite its tight-fistedness, Siemens's dividend rate is above the average for German publicly held companies. In that its stock so far is only traded on the Frankfurt and London stock exchanges, Siemens has seen no need to revise its strategy. Moreover, its shareholders seem content to wait for long-term results, rather than the instant gains popular in North America.

Having pledged itself to increased internationalization, Siemens can be expected to step up its acquisitions in Canada as well as the United States, especially since its Canadian sales already are growing at a faster clip than overall results. For those concerned about becoming a takeover target, Siemens stresses its reputation for retaining employees, generous stock options, medical and pension benefits, and the type of career advancement opportunities possible in a large, worldwide company. Its foreign divisions are encouraged to send staff to training programs, including a German language immersion course, at Siemens's Munich headquarters. Reflecting its globalization, the company favours a multinational executive mix. For example, five of its U.S. operations are run by

Americans, four by Germans, and one each by Canadian, Austrian, and Dutch nationals.

Canadian Subsidiaries That Are Part of International Business Alliances

The increasing number of international alliances between foreign companies also can inject foreign investment into Canada as a side effect, as illustrated by Halla Climate Control Canada of Belleville, Ontario. Opened in 1989, it is the first foreign subsidiary of a joint venture formed in 1985 by the Ford Motor Company of the United States and the Mando Machinery Corporation of South Korea for the production of automotive climate controls. Mando is a leading South Korean automotive-parts manufacturer.

Their partnership began with a modest $4 million in capitalization; that amount has since grown to $40 million. Worldwide sales had reached $150 million (U.S.) when the Canadian branch was opened. The main plant is in South Korea and locally managed, with the exception of five Ford engineers who assist in technical and quality control matters. Joint ventures between foreign companies, and often between competitors, are becoming prevalent in the car industry both to reduce individual financial loads through cost sharing and to leapfrog protectionist barriers.

Despite its brief existence, Halla Korea has become the main supplier of automobile air conditioners to Hyundai, Korea's leading carmaker. It also has a contract with Kia, another Korean auto firm in which Ford has a 15 percent interest. The Hyundai connection, however, brought Halla to Canada. Asian car parts suppliers frequently accompany their customers across the Pacific in order to protect their business from overseas competitors. Just ten months after Hyundai opened its Canadian plant in December 1988, Halla's Canadian transplant was also in operation. Although Hyundai is located in Quebec, Halla deliberately settled in Belleville because it is equidistant between Hyundai's plant in Bromont and car makers in Detroit to which Halla hopes to also sell ultimately.

Halla's establishment of the Canadian subsidiary was an act of faith, considering that the worldwide glut of automobile production is particularly pronounced in North America. Moreover, Halla does not expect to reach its maximum production capacity until 1994, the same year that Hyundai expects to be in full swing. Nonetheless, Ford and Mando went ahead with construction of the Canadian facility in order to be near Hyundai. Ford and Mando did, however, minimize their risk by starting with a small plant.

Should business boom, it can be easily expanded onto now vacant land also owned by Halla. The factory currently is only an assembly operation. According to managing director Young Cho, at least three hundred thousand units in annual volume would be required for conversion to full-scale manufacturing; currently, the factory has the capacity for only one hundred thousand units.

As Halla Canada is still in its early stages, it is being shepherded by Mando and Ford expatriates. Cho was marketing manager at Mando and one of the first Mando executives transferred to the fledgling Halla in Korea. Four other Halla-Korea representatives from the engineering and financial sides were also sent to Canada. Ford contributed only one person—a marketing analysis supervisor who oversees financial and business planning. Although no date has been set, both the Korean and Ford personnel plan to depart eventually, and Halla will be run by Canadians.

Japanese–Canadian Business Relations

Japan is by far the biggest offshore buyer of Canadian goods. In terms of dollar value, Canadian exports to Japan slightly exceeded the combined total to the largest customers after the United States and Japan: the United Kingdom, Germany, and South Korea. Two-way trade between Canada and Japan is nearing $20 billion, compared to $12 billion in 1985, and Japanese investment in Canada leaped from $2.3 billion in 1985 to more than $4.7 billion in 1990.

However, in the context of total foreign Japanese investment, Canada ranks low. Only about 3 percent of Japan's direct overseas investment is here, compared to around 45 percent in the United States. Therefore, it was front page news when the Japanese Ministry of International Trade and Industry released a report in 1990 favouring Japanese investment in Canada. The report was based on the findings of a business delegation that visited Canada a year earlier. The highly complimentary remarks were in stark contrast to lukewarm evaluations given by previous fact-finding groups in 1976 and 1986. In an effort to capitalize on the good impression, the federal government is providing funds for scientific and technical co-operation, as well as for Japanese language training programs for business people, and the government's first permanent Asian-Pacific exhibition centre for new Canadian exporters.

The emphasis on science and technology reflects Canada's desire to be much more than a supplier of natural resources to Japan. Canada's three major exports there are coal, wood pulp, and softwood lumber. By contrast, its three biggest imports from Japan are automobiles, telecommunications equipment, and electronic computers. Manufactured end-products represent less than 7 percent of Japan's purchases from Canada. Nevertheless, there is a ray of hope that this imbalance will diminish, based on the increase from 37 percent a decade ago to about 46 percent now in the proportion of processed, "value-added" goods shipped to Japan. For example, while Canada formerly exported only logs to Japan, now it sends window frames, prefabricated housing panels, and furniture kits.

How much of this increase in value-added exports can be attributed to Canadian initiative and how much to profound changes in Japan's economic patterns is debatable. But certainly it could not have occurred without these alterations in Japan. This process is summarized by Hiroyoshi (Mike) Tsuchiya, executive vice-president of Mitsubishi Canada, one of the ten largest exporters of Canadian goods to Japan. He says: "A century ago, Japan built houses with its own lumber. When it ran short of indigenous resources, it began to import lumber from the northwest United States and western Canada, although it still used Japanese labour. However, during the last decade, the number of skilled labourers in Japan decreased because today's more affluent generation prefers to become lawyers. Also, while the emphasis of Japanese industry throughout most of the 1980s still was on 'heavy, thick, long and big' manufacturing such as steel and ship production, today it is on 'light, thin, short, and small' high-tech items. Thus, whereas Japan's need used to be for raw materials that it then processed, today it has to import them in the form of semi- or completely finished goods."

In its diversification from investment in Canada's forestry and mining industries into a broad range of value-added activities, including chopstick manufacturing, meat processing, canola oil production, and pulp mills, Mitsubishi Canada exemplifies this evolution. It is also a co-partner with its parent, Mitsubishi's U.S. subsidiary, and Stelco in a newly opened $200 million mill that produces rust-resistant steel sheet for cars made by American automakers as well as by Asian transplants.

Mitsubishi's first major investment in Canada was in 1966 in Crestbrook Timber (now Crestbrook Forest Industries) located in the East Kootenay forest region of British Columbia. At that time, Crestbrook was a small logging, sawmill, veneer, and plywood company with big ambitions. It wanted to become a fully integrated forest products company that produces pulp, also, but it lacked the millions of dollars that a pulp mill costs. Since its need for money coincided with Japan's desire for natural resources, Crestbrook elected to trade its independence for the cash that would make its dreams come true. Thus, it sold half its shares to Mitsubishi and Honshu Paper Company, a leading Japanese manufacturer of corrugated paperboard liners, in return for their paying the mill's $43 million construction cost.

When the mill was completed in 1968, it was the largest joint venture to that date between Canadian and Japanese firms. Today, Mitsubishi and Honshu each own 32 percent of Crestbrook, which continues to sell to them at a slight discount. In 1989, in a reassessment of Crestbrook's 1984–86 income tax returns, Revenue Canada disallowed a portion of the discount, thereby increasing Crestbrook's income for tax purposes. The government also assessed nonresident withholding tax on the amount of the increase on the grounds that a portion of the sales discount constituted a benefit to shareholders who were also sales agents. Although Crestbrook has appealed the reassessment, it expects similar ones for each year since 1986 until the issue is resolved.

In any event, Crestbrook is not the exclusive supplier to Mitsubishi and Honshu. "Our output isn't big enough," explains James Black, manager, traffic and pulp sales co-ordination. Also, the mill only produces pulp for kraft paper, a tough dark brown paper primarily used for wrapping and making bags, whereas Mitsubishi and Honshu make all types of paper. Therefore, they have to find the pulp for these elsewhere.

As regular customers, Mitsubishi and Honshu have provided stability to Crestbrook, even in its darkest days in 1985 when it suffered an $8 million loss. They continued to support Crestbrook because its woes were not solely internally caused; lower prices were also to blame. The backing of the two Japanese investors enabled Crestbrook to spend a record amount on capital improvements that year, despite its red ink. These expenditures increased production, improved quality, and reduced costs, with the result that Crestbrook returned to profitability in 1986. With sales of $262 million in 1989, it now ranks about sixth in size among British Columbia's forest producers and around twentieth in Canada. Crestbrook and Mitsubishi are planning a joint venture $1.3 billion bleached kraft pulp mill and fine paper complex in north-eastern Alberta that will be the world's largest. It's output will be 1,500 metric tonnes per day.

Mitsubishi's other major investment in a Canadian natural

resources company is its 12 percent interest in Westar Mining of Vancouver. Mitsubishi buys a portion of Westar's coal and sells it internationally, principally to Japan, but also to 19 other countries.

While maintaining its interest in Canadian natural resources, Mitsubishi Canada is becoming a manufacturer as well. In 1990, it opened the world's largest chopstick plant in northern British Columbia at Fort Nelson. Although aspen, a wood suitable for chopsticks, grows in the Fort Nelson area, that was just one reason why Mitsubishi located the factory there. The other reasons tally with Japan's outward search for processed goods. "Labour costs are steep in Japan, and there is a shortage of skilled workers," says Takao Tashiro, project planning and co-ordination department manager at Mitsubishi Canada. Neither problem existed in Fort Nelson, where there was little industry and high unemployment. For it, the chopstick plant is a godsend; furthermore, as it goes into two shifts a day, it will provide even more job opportunities.

Another example of Mitsubishi's value-added sourcing is its interest in an Alberta plant that crushes rapeseed into canola oil. In the past, Japan tended merely to import the rapeseed and crush it itself. In addition, for a decade Mitsubishi has had a 20-percent interest in Lakeside Farm Industries, a large Alberta cattle grazing and meat processing operation. That investment typifies the long-term strategy for which the Japanese are famous: not until April 1, 1991 did Japan abolish its quotas on beef imports. Moreover, compared to Australia, which supplies 52 percent of Japan's beef imports, and the United States, which sends 42 percent, Canadian beef is virtually unknown to the Japanese. Furthermore, Japanese consumers prefer beef with a high fat content, whereas Canadian beef is known for its leanness. However, Canadian efforts to persuade the Japanese that low-fat beef is also tasty are beginning to pay off with much greater sales. If this trend continues, Mitsubishi's patience will be rewarded.

An estimated twenty-five to thirty thousand Canadians work for the three hundred Japanese firms in Canada. While most are increasingly appointing Canadians to senior positions, their head offices continue to send over some of their own executives to act as a link.

For example, at Mitsubishi Canada, the chairman is Canadian. Of the 15 departments at head office, eight are managed by Canadians and seven by Japanese. Tsuchiya, the executive vice-president on loan from the Tokyo head office, sums up the reason why some areas remain Japanese-run at Canadian affiliates. "Perhaps the Japanese proportion at Mitsubishi is too high, but Canadians need more exposure to the Japanese style of management," he says. "Mitsubishi Canada culturally and managerially is Japanese-oriented, with the decision process conducted on the Japanese consensus basis rather than the Canadian method of dictation by the boss."

A major reason why Canada is attractive to Japanese investors is that Japanese-bashing is much more muted than in the United States. Still, there is some, which can irritate Canadians working at Japanese firms in Canada as much as it does the Japanese.

"I dislike it when people refer to Honda of Canada as a foreign car manufacturer. The Big Three—General Motors, Ford, and Chrysler—are foreign-owned, too; yet they are not thought of that way," says Arnold Norris, a Canadian who is Honda of Canada Manufacturing's vice-president of general affairs. "When I said that to a newsmagazine reporter, he changed the phrase to 'offshore manufacturers.' So I set him straight about that, too, by telling him I don't have to cross an ocean to come to work."

He is firmly backed by Honda of Canada Manufacturing's president, Hiroshi Hayano, previously executive vice-president of Honda's U.S. plant. "Honda of Canada is not a puppet or branch organization, but an autonomous one that operates independently and self-reliantly, which is the way it should be," he comments.

On the other hand, here is the reaction of a Canadian who has been with a Canadian–Japanese joint venture throughout its more than 20 years' existence and is now a vice-president. Emphasizing that his is "a story of observation, not bitterness" and that he chose to remain with the company, he says: "The Japanese are kind, clean, nice people with a good sense of humour and a liking for golf, but they are a closed society. At our company, the Japanese representatives do not make a move without checking with Tokyo because they dread making decisions that could jeopardize their upward career path.

"Moreover, this practice of avoiding tough decisions is perpetuated by their sending over people for a short time, as a stopping point on their hoped-for ascent of the corporate ladder. If you are a customer of a Japanese firm, it's wonderful, and if you are a supplier, it's not bad, but if you are a minority partner in a joint venture—as is the case with our firm—it can be awful. I have files full of projects and ideas that went nowhere because the imported Japanese management feared making decisions. In my opinion, we lost opportunity upon opportunity as a result."

Counterbalancing his remarks are those of Carl Ruhe, general manager of Amada Canada. "Canadian companies acquired by Japanese firms must adjust themselves to differences in management style," he notes. "The biggest difference is that Canadians are accustomed to decision making by one individual, whereas the Japanese prefer group consensus. Thus, they take longer to reach decisions.

"The Japanese are investing money, creating jobs, and treating their employees better than fairly. For Canadians to resent that is unfair. My question to such critics is 'Why do you wait for others to invest? Why don't you invest money yourself?' "

As for the Japanese, they perceive a distinct difference between what Canadians and Americans value most dearly. Observes Mitsubishi's Hiroyoshi Tsuchiya: "Canadians believe in fairness, Americans in liberty. In its pursuit of liberty, the United States tends to interfere as a 'policeman,' a concept with which other countries are not always comfortable. As for Canadians, because they treasure fairness, they tend to spend an exhaustive time making certain that everyone is treated fairly. That's a beautiful concept, but internationally it is not always acceptable because others get impatient with the delays that result."

Tsuchiya then goes on to emphasize what the real considerations should be in Canadian–Japanese business relations: "When I consider the merits of partnerships with Canadian firms, my foremost yardstick is whether such partnerships will best meet the needs of the market and contribute to the flow of commodities and products. I don't think of each side as Japanese and Canadian. Rather, my concern is whether they will be good natural partners, and hence increase Mitsubishi's competitiveness."

Whether investment in Canada best meets their needs in this era of business globalization is being considered carefully by all foreign investors, and what they decide will have an enormous bearing on the country's future. How some Canadian subsidiaries are forcing their owners to decide in Canada's favour is discussed in the following chapter.

C H A P T E R

7

World Product Mandates

"World product mandates aren't given; they have to be won."

Brian McGourty,
Chairman, President, and CEO,
Honeywell Ltd.

I t was the sort of slightly bizarre order that a company the size of Camco, with more than $500 million in sales, could have been tempted to dismiss arrogantly. Camco, the appliance division of General Electric Canada, is Canada's largest manufacturer of refrigerators, ranges, microwave ovens, dishwashers, and laundry washers and dryers under the brand names GE, Hotpoint, Moffat, and McClary. The unusual order came from a Taiwanese customer. Not only did he request that Camco supply him with washers covered in a bamboo wood grain finish, but he also stipulated that Camco inscribe the Chinese symbol for washer plus his name and a drawing of his face on each machine.

As a multimillion dollar company, Camco could have told him either to accept Camco's standard models or take his business elsewhere. But despite its size, Camco knew it could not afford such high-handedness in this era of globalization when a competitor anywhere in the world might be only too happy to oblige the customer. Thus, without hesitation, it did exactly as asked in order to have a world product mandate for his business.

Camco's ready compliance illustrates the survival tactics that foreign-owned subsidiaries in Canada must employ in these extremely competitive days of globalized business. The toppling of tariff walls throughout the world is rendering obsolete the traditional methods of international business expansion: branch plants that churned out a broad range of products originated and developed at their parent's head office hundreds or thousands of miles away.

In today's liberalized trade environment, international corporations no longer have to maintain a worldwide network of branches in order to circumvent protectionist duties. Therefore, if they believe it makes economic sense to do so, they can close foreign operations just like a number of U.S. companies have done in Canada in the aftermath of the Canada–U.S. free trade agreement. Moreover, it stands to reason that as corporations go global, they will do their utmost to avoid wasting money through duplication of product lines in many countries. Thus, to continue to exist, foreign subsidiaries in Canada will have to transform themselves from small-scale versions of their parents into world-class companies that deserve world product mandates.

Sometimes referred to as "missions," "focused manufacturing," or "centres of excellence," world product mandates are a form of niche strategy. They range from sole production of a limited number of items for worldwide sale by a corporation to total responsibility, starting with research and development and proceeding to manufacturing and marketing. The economies of scale they create enable the corporation to reduce prices, thereby enhancing its competitiveness. For foreign subsidiaries, they epitomize the expression "less is more": although a smaller assortment of products is made, output is greater.

"In today's world, subsidiaries will not get anything by waiting for it to drop out of the blue into their laps; yet, I am concerned that many branches in Canada are not being sufficiently aggressive," warns Grant Murray, vice-president, corporate relations at IBM Canada. "Canadian managers must make their case more strongly than before to win against their American counterparts who are accustomed to pursuing opportunities very vigorously. Canadians can compete in any industry, provided they set about to do so."

Winning world product mandates is a formidable challenge for foreign subsidiaries in Canada. Despite numbering among the country's largest corporations, they constitute but a fraction of the size of their parent's total empire. Nevertheless, astute foreign-owned subsidiaries in Canada are turning Canada's prime disadvantage—its small market—into "special leverage" for obtaining world mandates.

The smallness has forced Canadian companies to become skilled in small-to-medium-volume production runs and to develop the flexibility for extensive variety. Camco demonstrated these capabilities in filling the order for its Taiwanese customer. Furthermore, the Canadian subsidiaries do have certain strengths that offset the attractiveness to their parents of shifting Canadian manufacturing to countries where the cost of labour is low. "Engineering processes are of high quality in Canada, and the workforce is better educated and more stable than in Mexico, which has lower wage rates but much higher employee turnover," points out Stephen Snyder, Camco's president and CEO. "Besides, materials tend to account for a greater proportion of costs than labour."

For Canada, the winning of world product mandates by foreign-owned subsidiaries is both good and bad. On the plus side, mandates can spark a surge in exports, increase local research and development as well as manufacturing and employment and also prompt the upgrading of designated facilities. For instance, world product mandates have more than doubled the export volume of Honeywell's Canadian operations since 1986. In addition, IBM Canada's decision to open a plant in Bromont, Quebec, which at first specialized in typewriters and now makes computer circuits, triggered the development of a Quebec high-tech centre in this community 50 miles south of Montreal. Today, Bromont's industrial strip also contains a General Electric aircraft engine components plant and Hyundai's car plant.

However, the limited scope of the world product mandates forces foreign-owned subsidiaries to import more, including some items they used to manufacture but lost to sister companies elsewhere. For example, Honeywell's Canadian subsidiary formerly made 75 percent of the products it sold in Canada; now that proportion is just 25 percent. "We're manufacturing more, exporting more, and importing more," says Peter Rankine, vice-president and general manager of Honeywell's Canadian residential and building controls group, the principal exporting division of the subsidiary.

Furthermore, in survival of the fittest behaviour, companies discard secondary items so as to concentrate on world product mandates. That can cause much hardship because the plants that made these items are closed, their workers lose their jobs, and their suppliers are deprived of contracts. Camco, for instance, has reduced its number of suppliers from twelve hundred in 1983 to six hundred and fifty today, and by the time its restructuring is completed later this decade, the number will likely be halved again. In another example of the shrinkage caused by the mandate process, General Electric Canada shut a Montreal lighting factory that the company describes as "old with a creaky elevator and no longer efficient." But the closure was counterbalanced by the installation of $40 million in new equipment at the company's Bromont aircraft parts plant.

World product mandates also are forcing executives at some Canadian subsidiaries to relinquish much of the considerable autonomy they enjoyed in the days of the traditional branch plant. In a global business, there can only be one decision centre and that is at head office. While executives whose authority has declined try to persuade themselves it is a natural consequence of being part of a successful global team, in their hearts they miss the power.

These sentiments are well summed up by Robert Gillespie, executive vice-president of GE Canada: "We are proud that GE Canada builds all the mid-sized dryers for GE. We agree it is an excellent idea that GE Canada should sell its specialty silicone products all over the world and that the blades and vanes for certain GE plane engines be made in Bromont, Quebec. But the quid pro quo is that we are having to share more of the Canadian management with our global counterparts in GE." Consequently, GE plant managers in Canada no longer report to the Canadian office; instead, their supervisors are the 14 strategic business unit managers located at GE's U.S. headquarters, who oversee GE's major businesses worldwide. They are all American because even though GE is stepping up its global activity, it still is predominantly a U.S. enterprise.

Not having control over manufacturing deprives GE's Canadian executives of much of the usual role of management. They are left with responsibility for employee career development and benefits, government and public relations, and bank borrowing. Pierre Bisaillon, manager of the Bromont aircraft engine parts plant, praises the new system for plugging the Canadian operations directly into "the manufacturing orientation of the Americans while still making available the Canadian head office's strong business sense and long-term outlook." However, executives at other Canadian subsidiaries, such as Du Pont, Honeywell, IBM, Edwards (owned by General Signal), and Allen-Bradley (owned by Rockwell International) still have considerable latitude.

What follows are the reasons for—and strategies behind—the world product mandates of a cross-section of foreign-owned Canadian subsidiaries. Edwards demonstrates the importance of such charters to a subsidiary's survival. Upjohn Canada exemplifies how world product mandates can keep a subsidiary running in Canada at a time when other foreign-owned companies in its industry are departing. Honeywell Limited demonstrates how Canadian subsidiaries can transform themselves from miniature versions of their parents into self-sufficient research and development, manufacturing, and marketing mandate centres.

IBM Canada shows the importance of aggressiveness by a long-time subsidiary to prevent being overlooked. Du Pont Canada highlights the often unique status of Canadian subsidiaries in a foreign owner's empire, as well as the restructuring necessary to become even stronger. GE Canada's Camco division and Bromont aircraft parts plant, along with Allen-Bradley Canada, spotlight how Canadian subsidiaries can emerge the winners in the intense around-the-world competition within a global corporation for mandates. Lastly, Pratt & Whitney Canada highlights how world product mandates are affected by a parent company's overall strategy.

Edwards: How World Product Mandates Can Save Canadian Subsidiaries

That world mandates can spell the difference between life and death for foreign-owned companies is not melodrama but the stark truth. But to achieve such charters, subsidiaries sometimes have to go so far as to reorganize their product lines completely, revise all job descriptions, retrain their entire workforce, including those in manufacturing, testing, sales, and service, as well as re-educate customers. Moreover, during this transition, they must obtain the co-operation of employees, naturally concerned about the impact on them of this extraordinary break with tradition, as well as keep the business running smoothly.

Such was the complex manoeuvre successfully accomplished between 1983 and 1986 by Edwards, a wholly owned unit of General Signal of Connecticut, a major manufacturer of electrical transportation controls and signals.* Edwards now has the mandate to make and sell worldwide the corporation's computer-based fire alarm detection equipment. Its revenue has risen by 10 to 15 percent annually since the transition, and its metamorphosis proves that a Canadian subsidiary can reverse the traditional dependence on a U.S. parent. Its achievement is even more remarkable because it could not narrow its product base, unlike other mandate-winning subsidiaries. Instead, the nature of its business demands that it continue to produce several thousand items to meet both safety and decorative needs. For example, many devices are available in more than one colour.

Therefore, how Edwards accomplished its transformation with a minimum of disruption is a useful case history for other subsidiaries already immersed or on the brink of similar circumstances. Edwards's saga begins with its establishment in 1923 in Canada as a sales office, the conventional initial thrust of U.S. corporations into Canada. As was usual with such branches, Edwards took several decades to evolve into manufacturing. It began to assemble a limited number of items in the 1930s and to manufacture on a small scale in the late 1940s. In 1952, it moved into the nucleus of its present site in Owen Sound, Ontario, northwest of Toronto in the Georgian Bay recreational area. At that time, it had one hundred employees. Over the succeeding years, several plant expansions were added, and employment now totals eleven hundred. By the end of the 1970s, the firm was proclaiming itself to be Canada's major producer of fire alarm systems.

Nevertheless, Edwards was like an apple with a rosy skin but a worm-eaten core when its present general manager, Brian Veale, assumed his position in 1980. Although Edwards seemed healthy, its position was precarious because it had not kept pace with technology. It was still producing electromechanically operated alarms while rivals were switching to computer-based systems. "Edwards was faltering and its survival depended on getting the right resources into place," Veale says. With his background in computer circuitry, Veale himself "was unafraid of technological change."

His formidable challenge was to instil the same fearlessness throughout the company and to disperse innate hostility at

---

General Signal's 1989 sales were $1.9 billion U.S.

Edwards's U.S. parent. Eventually, it forged ahead to become the U.S. parent's supplier of computer-based alarm devices. For American companies, accustomed to the opposite procedure, a success of this kind can be ego deflating. Edwards did encounter what Veale describes as "controlled rivalry," but it persevered, aware that the U.S. operation still had lots of other products to make.

The theme of Veale's argument to General Signal was that Edwards must modernize or die. "We are in a field with many competitors; therefore, if we do not have state-of-the-art manufacturing, the market will be eaten by other firms," he stressed. He further pointed out that the modernization would strengthen Edwards not only domestically, but also globally, which would be important in the future. "Most businesses are going global; if we don't, we will be in deep trouble," he warned.

Impressed by his bluntness, General Signal readily agreed "that we needed to invest substantially to gain ground," Veale continues. That left him with the task of persuading the unionized plant that while Edwards would go out of business without the new technology, its installation "would not eliminate positions, but on the contrary would spur growth." Like other executives before and since, Veale found that "purchasing new equipment is the simplest part of such a transition; the hard part is to obtain workers' cooperation."

Since Edwards is one of the few big employers in Owen Sound, where the population is around twenty thousand, its employees had a profound incentive to go along with the changes. Few alternative employers existed. Nevertheless, Veale wanted the workers to feel that they, as well as management, were important participants in the change. Thus, he formed joint consulting committees which met regularly throughout the process, thereby maintaining harmony. The workers had to acquire many high-tech skills ranging from computer-aided design to the operation of computerized systems for price quotations, component sequencers, test equipment, and punch presses and brakes. Employees unwilling to learn the new skills were assured they could retain their traditional jobs because Edwards still would be making enough other products—primarily signals, varying from hazardous-location warning devices to electric buzzers and industrial sirens and clocks—that would not be subject to the technological changes.

Considering the massive preparation required for Edwards to qualify for a product mandate, Veale wisely decided not to try to handle it all himself, but instead to make use of readily available outside expertise. With the assistance of the Ontario government's Ministry of Colleges and Universities, he devised a four-year apprenticeship program. He asked acquaintances at Litton Systems Canada (aviation equipment) to instruct on soldering techniques. So that female employees could balance career and home life, Edwards participated in an Ontario government program, run by the Ministry of Skills Development, that enables workers to learn an electronic trade enough through a combination of on-the-job training and home study. It also booked daycare facilities for employees' children and arranged a supplementary emergency babysitting service. These efforts resulted in Edwards winning an Ontario government employment equity award.

Upjohn Canada: How Product Mandates Keep a Subsidiary in Canada

Unlike some prominent U.S. pharmaceutical drug companies that have closed their Canadian operations in the wake of the U.S.–Canada free trade agreement and consolidated operations at home, Upjohn has elected to stay in Canada. Upjohn Canada ranks eleventh in an industry that is 85 percent foreign-owned and is one of only two major patent prescription producers to make generic as well as brand name drugs. (The other firm is Syntex.) Generic drug companies make cheaper versions of prescription drugs when patents expire.

The Upjohn Company, headquartered in Kalamazoo, Michigan, is perhaps best known for Kaopectate, an antidiarrhea medicine; Rogaine, an antibaldness treatment; and Motrin, a pain reliever. It has elected to keep open its Canadian subsidiary, established in 1935, despite industry-wide pharmaceutical sales in Canada accounting for only 1 percent of the world's total and the Toronto plant currently operating at less than full capacity.

Its reason for continuing to maintain its Canadian subsidiary is that Upjohn Canada is its largest foreign subsidiary except for one it has in Japan. Moreover, Upjohn Canada's sales and earnings per employee rank among the highest of any Upjohn subsidiary, according to Peter Croden, president and general manager of Upjohn Canada. This accomplishment stands out in Upjohn's worldwide operations because, unlike the United States, Canada has socialized medicine and stringent health care price controls.

But while Upjohn Canada is carrying on, it is doing so on new terms. Prior to the free trade agreement, the Toronto plant made products primarily for the Canadian market, standard procedure for Canadian branches of U.S. companies. Since then, as part of an overall reorganization of activities by Upjohn to reduce production costs throughout North America, sterile products once made in Canada are being shifted to Upjohn's Kalamazoo headquarters. In turn, a number of capsules and tablets are being transferred from Kalamazoo to Toronto. Out of a total Upjohn Canada workforce of 420 people, two dozen worked in the sterile manufacturing department and have been retrained for capsule and tablet production.

Upjohn Canada has earned high marks within the company for its initiative in generics and research as well as for its cost control leadership. Croden also says Upjohn Canada was about 18 months ahead of its parent in implementing quality improvement programs and "just-in-time" manufacturing scheduling to minimize inventory costs.

Although a strong opponent of generic drugs, like most of Canada's pharmaceutical industry, Upjohn Canada wanted to be part of what is the fastest-growing segment of the North American pharmaceutical market. Thus, in the mid-1980s, Robert Durham, Upjohn Canada's general manager at that time, formed a generic division called Kenral. Today, Kenral is one of Canada's largest generic drug companies, marketing Upjohn products no longer under patent, as well as products licensed from other companies.

Upjohn Canada's clinical drug research is conducted in a unique manner both within the Upjohn family and within Canada. Established in 1983, the clinic is affiliated with the University of Western Ontario and located in Victoria Hospital, a 950-bed teaching hospital in London, Ontario. The clinic also works in association with four other nearby hospitals, several research institutes, and a regional cancer centre. The company intends to double its research spending in Canada by 1993.

In cost controls, Upjohn Canada has a distinct advantage over its U.S. parent. As only one of hundreds of employers in Toronto, Upjohn does not bear the burden of the city's economic well-being. Therefore, it has always kept its employment numbers lean. By contrast, the parent company, as the economic backbone of Kalamazoo, a much smaller community, tended to overemploy. "Even when times were tough, it felt obliged not to lay off employees," Croden says. "Thus, Upjohn's overall sales per employee are lower than at most other pharmaceutical companies around the world."

The job security was a blessing to employees, but dividend-hungry shareholders complained that this paternalism dragged down earnings. Because Upjohn wants to remain independently owned, it must prevent its shareholders being wooed away by a lucrative takeover offer. Consequently, it is downsizing—or as its executives euphemistically say, "rightsizing"—the company's workforce to improve profit margins. Upjohn Canada avoided this problem by externalizing as many administrative functions as it could, including printing, travel arrangements, and advertising. The money saved is redirected into research and development.

Honeywell: From Branch Plant to World Product Mandates

Like many American firms, Honeywell initiated its globalization in Canada; its Canadian division, established in 1930, was its first foreign subsidiary. Today, just over 60 years later, the Canadian operation, like most U.S. subsidiaries in Canada, is a comparatively small part of the total operations of its parent company. Honeywell is now active in 90 countries and derives the bulk of its international sales from Europe, followed by Asia. In this it typifies the global pattern of U.S. corporations in recent years. Thus, while Canadian nationalists are concerned about the extent of American control of our economy, Canadian subsidiaries of U.S. companies worry as to how to remain vital to their globe-trotting parents.

For many, like Honeywell Canada, the solution is world leadership in a few products rather than continuing as a full-product duplicate branch plant for which the need is vanishing in this globalized era. Honeywell Canada originated strictly as a distributor and then progressed into a branch plant to eliminate payment of cross-the-border duties and, more significantly, to deal directly with the Canadian market. Like its many American counterparts, Honeywell had discovered that the United States and Canada are not identical and, therefore, American products do not necessarily succeed north of the border.

Until 1970, Honeywell Canada sold only within Canada. Then it realized that in order to obtain the economies of scale requisite for cost competitiveness, it had to export because the Canadian market was too small for mass production on a scale similar to that in the United States. Casting about for what to sell, Honeywell settled on hot water heating zone valves and Great Britain as the place to sell them. The United Kingdom needed such valves, since it was in the process of installing hot water heating. Moreover, Commonwealth preferential duties made purchases from Canada appealing. From Honeywell's viewpoint, the valve was a low cost export initiative, being easy to make and light in weight to ship. Today, Honeywell Canada also sells the valves to the United States, continental Europe, and Asia. Buoyed by its success with the valves, the subsidiary went on to export fan limits, devices that shut off hot-air furnace fans when a cut-off temperature is reached, as well as electric heat controls.

Due to the valves, fan limits, and electric heat controls, Honeywell Canada had begun to transform itself from a mirror image of its parent to an indigenous Canadian manufacturer with its own export customers. By the early 1980s, 75 percent of what it made was of Canadian origin rather than clones of U.S. products. Nevertheless, the subsidiary had not obtained any world product mandates. Therefore, as it had all along, it continued to take the initiative to achieve its objective.

In 1985, Honeywell Canada hired a management consultant to examine its operations and report on how they could become even more competitive. He suggested the rationalization of product lines to best-sellers in order to create the economies of scale that would justify a substantial outlay on worldclass computer-integrated equipment. Such equipment, he noted, would place the Canadians on a par with competitors' technology. At that time, Honeywell Canada was manufacturing 11 product lines. With these supportive outside expert recommendations, the Canadian executives went to the U.S. parent's head office in Minneapolis to present their case for mandates.

Why, they asked, should a company in a market one-tenth the size of that of the United States make the same things as its American parent? Would it not be preferable, they argued, to dole out the products to the place most equipped to make them? Certainly, they added, Honeywell Canada had proved its skill in zone valves, fan limits, and electric heat controls.

Their logic prevailed. The United States took away most of the overlapping products. Canada was left with world mandates for the zone valves, fan limits, and electric heat controls. The U.S. fan limit assembly line was dismantled and shipped to Canada. "We lost many products but gained in volume," remarks Peter Rankine, vice-president and general manager, residential and building controls group. For example, whereas Honeywell sells fifty thousand zone valves in Canada, its worldwide volume exceeds one million.

As companies go global, co-ordination is essential. At Honeywell, each country's subsidiary retains responsibility for sales within its borders. However, representatives from subsidiaries elsewhere with world mandates can take care of customers' technical problems in those products.

The local heads of each division meet two to three times annually to discuss major global issues. The meetings rotate around Honeywell's 90-country network and are chaired by the host country's executives. These conferences are supplemented by get-togethers between engineers and production managers from around the world to exchange technical information and standardize processes to the extent that local voltage and regulatory differences permit. The mixture of centralization and decentralization reflects Honeywell's belief in "glocalization"—think global but act local. "Head office determines what businesses the company should be in and what markets to serve, but how to do it is left to each country," Rankine says.

Like any winner of mandates, Honeywell Canada wants more. These will have to be developed within Canada because no other subsidiary will want to relinquish its assignments. Therefore, to increase its business, the Canadian subsidiary is spending much more on research and development, focusing on items with global potential. "No business in Canada today is exempt from the context of globalization," states Chairman, President, and CEO Brian McGourty.

The transformation from a miniature carbon copy of its parent into a world mandate company has paid off handsomely for Honeywell. Three hundred jobs were created and export revenues soared by 50 percent. Although rationalization also caused a jump in imports, their increase is substantially lower than that in exports.

IBM Canada: Carving Out a Major Role through Mandates

IBM Canada practises what it preaches: it believes Canadian subsidiaries should hustle for prominence instead of lazily waiting for crumbs tossed out by their parents. IBM Canada ranks sixth in size among its parent's 128 foreign subsidiaries and is one of only eight with manufacturing and research and development facilities.

Moreover, much to its pride and delight, the Canadian branch is the only IBM foreign subsidiary that reports directly to head office.

The aggressiveness of the Canadian outfit dates back to its earliest days. It is IBM's oldest foreign subsidiary, having been established in 1911, the same year its parent was incorporated under the name Computing-Tabulating-Recording Company. The Canadian subsidiary is responsible for the IBM name, having dubbed itself International Business Machines in 1917. It was not until 1924 that the U.S. headquarters took over the name as its worldwide one. Although the Canadian outfit traditionally has been managed and staffed by Canadians, it did not obtained its unique direct line to head office in Armonk, New York until 1990. Before that, IBM Canada was just one of several subsidiaries reporting to the "American Group," a division also encompassing Latin and South America. IBM also has a Europe-Africa-Middle East region, headquartered in Paris and an Asia–Pacific Group run from Tokyo.

According to Grant Murray, vice-president, corporate relations at IBM Canada, the subsidiary's status was upgraded because it was judged "mature enough to run its own affairs" without a middleman between it and head office. In addition, the Canadians and Americans speak the same language and have similar economic systems, making it easier from them to understand one another. By the same token, the Paris office is mostly staffed by Europeans and the Tokyo one by Japanese, Australian, and Hong Kong nationals. For IBM Canada, the direct link reinforces the considerable degree of autonomy that it has long had and enhances its opportunity of obtaining a sympathetic hearing of its needs, wants, and problems by the top echelon at IBM.

However, the switch probably would not have occurred without the recent delayering of management at IBM which occurred in an effort to rid the company of stifling bureaucracy. Murray describes this old system as "management by contention," whereby the number of approval levels encouraged risk avoidance and hence sharp disagreements because enthusiasts blocked by junior naysayers believed they had no choice but to take even the most straightforward issues all the way up the hierarchy.

The Canadians have proved their leading edge talent in management methods, retraining procedures, technology, and manufacturing. Visitors to IBM Canada's Markham, Ontario headquarters quickly perceive one striking management innovation when they walk onto the executive floor—very few secretaries. Their almost total absence, except in offices of the most senior executives, stems from a company decision in 1986–87 to allocate more of the work-force to customer relations so as to ensure continued client loyalty and satisfaction.

The secretaries were transformed into "information and market-ing specialists" and the people for whom they had worked were instructed to use electronic phone mail and internal computer memos rather than resort to reams of paperwork as in the past. Now, if they need to send letters to the outside world, they give them to central word processor pools. For a company in the fore-front of high technology it was about time that it made greater use of its own tools. Furthermore, through redeploying its secretaries, the Canadian subsidiary was able to adhere to its practice, unbro-ken since its establishment, of not laying off its employees. Conse-quently, in the late 1980s when the parent company was reducing worldwide employment by some fifty thousand positions and many companies in Canada were also downsizing their work-forces, IBM Canada employees were secure in their jobs.

In another imaginative solution to the issue of retraining, IBM Canada recently shifted three hundred people from its Toronto plant, which had a manpower surplus, to its short-of-labour labora-tory, which is also in Toronto. Although the plant workers were unskilled in the lab's programming techniques, as a paternalistic employer, the company preferred to invest in their education in such skills rather than replace them. However, because of the number of workers involved, it lacked the in-house resources. The novel solution was to devise a curriculum in conjunction with Ryerson Polytechnical Institute of Toronto, which Ryerson's fac-ulty taught in its classrooms. "This approach halved the normal retraining time and attracted so much interest throughout IBM worldwide that many other facilities incorporated the techniques in their own retraining programs," Murray says.

IBM Canada's lab is the second largest software R&D facility within the IBM family although the revenue of the entire Canadian operation is only a tiny portion of the whole. This distinction bolsters the Canadian operation's future, because the development of software applications could, in theory, be done almost anywhere since it depends on human, not natural resources. But it also puts the Canadians on the defensive, as they must constantly come up with bright new ideas to enhance their reputation for innovation. One such idea, developed in consultation with the Metropolitan Toronto Police, is computer imaging that depicts what a child missing for several years would look like today, as well as the probable appearance of a masked robber minus his disguise.

From its outset, IBM Canada was determined to manufacture rather than be a sales outpost, but until the 1950s it was an assembly operation "putting tops on bottoms," in Murray's phrase. Today, as part of IBM's globalization, the Canadian operation's plants in Toronto and Bromont, Quebec each have product mandates. The Toronto facility specializes in memory cards and power systems. It developed a process enabling more functions to be packaged on the cards; for example, one model can hold up to 250,000 pages of typed information. Bromont is the sole North American manufacturer of advanced computer circuit components. Its surface-mounted plastic modules contain very high density memory chips and are designed for installation on electronic cards used in many IBM products. Ninety percent of its output is exported to IBM plants in the United States and the rest to European and Japanese facilities.

The Bromont plant's evolution demonstrates how agile a foreign subsidiary must be in adjusting to changed circumstances. It began in 1971 in typewriters, a product far removed from computer circuitry, but then a company staple. In what is common practice in transnational companies, IBM Canada traded its production of magnetic typing cards to its U.S. parent in order to get more typewriter manufacturing volume. As a result, Canadian typewriter production tripled and the longer production runs substantially reduced costs. But as the years passed and word processors started to overtake conventional typewriters, IBM saw no point in continuing to split its typewriter production between the United States and Canada and consolidated it in the United States.

For IBM-Bromont, what seemed to be a crippling loss turned out to be a gain. Since it no longer had to manufacture a product with poor prospects, it could fight for one that was on the leading edge of technology—the advanced computer circuits. In its favour was its proximity to an American IBM plant just 85 miles south in Vermont that is a principal IBM customer for such components. In line with IBM Canada's policy of retraining instead of replacing, Bromont put its employees through a nine-month in-house course to transform them from typewriter to computer experts. To convert and expand the facilities, IBM Canada has invested about $349 million in Bromont since 1981.

A world product mandate is not a lifetime sinecure; instead, it must constantly be re-earned, as IBM's Bromont plant shows. It has retained its charter through increasing workplace efficiency. It improved its productivity by 50 percent largely through more comfortable working conditions, including better lighting, the playing of background music, and a variety of workbench heights and widths to accommodate different body shapes. Additionally, it diagnosed each production stage to determine how to reorganize the total process by levels of complexity and thereby reduce defects.

The Bromont plant's survival, through its swift gear shift, not only helps IBM Canada but also benefits Canada, according to Michael Wong, the plant manager. "In 1971, our plant had three hundred employees; today there are sixteen hundred and we plan further expansion," he says. "Also, we are augmenting Canada's technical prowess by producing high value-added technology within Canada and we are providing considerable business to Canadian suppliers."

But he cautions that success such as this should not deteriorate into dangerous complacency. "Nobody gave us our mandate; we've had to fight for everything we've got and without continuous improvement, we could, theoretically, lose our business," he notes. "Moreover, we not only have to compete against other IBM sites making similar components, but also against vendors eager to sell to IBM. A mandate is not a God-given right to exist; competitive services and products are vital, too, to survival."

Du Pont Canada: Restructuring to Be Stronger

Despite its relatively small size, Du Pont Canada always has enjoyed special status in its parent's gargantuan worldwide empire. While parent E.I. du Pont de Nemours ranks ninth in size among U.S. corporations and twenty-sixth worldwide, with 1989 sales of more than $35 billion (U.S.), its Canadian subsidiary places only eighty-third in Canada, with 1989 sales of $1.4 billion (Canadian). Worldwide, Du Pont employs close to 146,000 people; Canadian employment is just over 4,100. Nevertheless, owing to historical reasons and its recent self-initiated overhaul, which catapulted it well ahead of the rest of the company in return on equity and productivity, Du Pont Canada has every reason to be confident that it will retain its unique position.

Historically, it is significant as one of Canada's oldest foreign subsidiaries and as Du Pont's first step outside the United States.

It originated in 1862 as a Canadian-owned enterprise called the Hamilton Powder Company, since Hamilton, Ontario was its founder's home city. Fifteen years later, Du Pont acquired a 70 percent interest, thereby marking its initiation as an international business enterprise. It now derives 45 percent of its revenue from outside the United States.

Today, Du Pont Canada is the only foreign Du Pont subsidiary that is not wholly owned. Instead, 25 percent is held by Canadian investors. By contrast, the Canadian subsidiaries of such other big U.S. corporations as General Motors, IBM, Safeway, Dow Chemical, Woolworth, K-Mart, and General Electric are wholly controlled by their American parent. In further acts of independence, Du Pont Canada has had its own research and development centre since 1956, derives one-third of its sales from products that it developed, and retains about 85 percent of earnings for reinvestment in Canada. All its senior officers are Canadian and of its 12-member board, only two are not Canadian: the vice-chairman and the chief financial officer of the parent company.

On the other hand, in 1989 Du Pont Canada's chairman and CEO was made international group vice-president of Du Pont worldwide, the first time a non-American has held the position. "We believe Du Pont Canada proves that the modern multinational corporation should delegate as much independence as it can to regional operations," says James Stewart, a senior vice-president of the Canadian subsidiary.

But in this era of globalization, Du Pont Canada cannot rely on sentimentality for preservation of its special status. Rather, it must continue to earn it. Therefore, in the early 1980s, 15 senior Du Pont Canada executives began to prepare their company for the future. For their consultations to be constructive, they determined they would not be self-laudatory because such behaviour perpetuates stale methods. Instead, they vowed to expose what was wrong with the way they managed. They knew improvement was imperative as the firm's profits had not been in the top 25 percent of Canadian companies throughout the 1960s. Moreover, although free trade with the United States was not yet on the horizon, the company was certain that competition would become increasingly international due to declining tariffs and increasing globalization of trade. "We knew that the days of the branch plant had passed, and that if we were going to survive and thrive we would have to become world competitive," Stewart says.

The think tank concluded that world competitiveness could

only be achieved through streamlining Du Pont's portfolio and capitalizing on its strengths in specialty businesses with higher profit margins. "We decided not to waste our time trying to improve weak businesses, a trap into which many companies fall," Stewart continues. "Instead, we decided to concentrate on strengthening businesses, which were already potentially strong, on a world basis, had attractive growth likelihood, and would reward our technological capabilities."

To obtain a sharper focus and subsequently keep itself on track, the company framed a two-sentence directional statement intended to be simple to understand and mobilizing in its thrust. The first sentence describes core values: "safety, concern and care for people, protection of the environment, and personal and corporate integrity." The second reflects the profound redirection deemed necessary. It says: "We are committed to becoming a more market-driven, customer-oriented, self-managed organization, dedicated to quality and innovation and committed to achieving continuous improvement, as measured by our relative competitive position."

Copies of this statement are located throughout Du Pont's plants and its head office in Mississauga, Ontario. Then, in 1987, as Du Pont neared the completion of its restructuring, it commissioned a sculpture for its lobby that dramatizes its mission. Called *Daedalus and Icarus*, the sculpture depicts the famous Greek myth with the father and son in modern clothing. It reminds employees and visitors of the power of imagination and innovation (Daedalus) as well as the sin of pride in not using technology carefully (Icarus). According to the legend, when Icarus disregarded his father's warning not to fly too close to the sun with his wax wings, the sun melted them and he plunged to his death.

To become more market driven and customer-oriented, Du Pont vigorously compared itself with world competitors, not just Canadian ones. This assessment helped it to separate businesses that it felt had a strong future from the rest of the lineup. Subsequently, it closed or sold 10 of its 31 product lines, even though they comprised more than 25 percent of sales. It also ruled out any further building of facilities scaled to the Canadian market alone, a sharp break with its traditional branch plant mentality. Vowing never again to invest in anything that was not competitive globally, the company went so far as to shut a big, new, multimillion-dollar polyester filament plant in Quebec, which it judged as below the world standard and therefore noncompetitive.

Like other foreign-owned subsidiaries in Canada, Du Pont

decided to take advantage of the flexibility and specialization that the country's small market encourages. Moreover, as Stewart notes, these characteristics "reinforce the need to become internationally competitive." Du Pont Canada, for example, defeated a European subsidiary's bid for the world mandate to produce Lycra XA, a fibre for disposable diapers, by its agility in bringing it from the development to the test stage within just a few weeks. In that disposable diapers are under attack by environmentalists, they are not a "huge business opportunity," Stewart concedes, but Du Pont Canada's speed in developing "Lycra XA" proved to Du Pont worldwide "how fast we are on our feet."

Du Pont Canada also invented tamperproof, recyclable individual portion pouches for liquids such as milk and juice and is Du Pont's worldwide producer of them. The pouches have come to be widely used in schools' milk and juice programs for students. Furthermore, Du Pont Canada has a world product mandate for 2-litre packages of salad dressing, mustard, and condiments designed for restaurants. They snip open the bags and squeeze the contents into their own dispensers.

Moreover, as part of its changeover, Du Pont is spending money to make money, doubling its R&D budget and tripling that for market research since 1984, as well as spending more than $600 million on plant modernization and automation, beginning in 1987. True to its pledge that it would only invest in world competitive operations, it recently completed a world-scale hydrogen peroxide plant in Alberta that doubles its Canadian capacity, brings its production costs in line with those worldwide, and exceeds the output of its U.S. parent.

The company's redesign has gone far beyond paring its product lineup to pruning the number of management layers from 11 to 6 so as to eliminate time-consuming bureaucratic snags that can prevent the winning of world product mandates such as "Lycra XA." For example, the chain of command used to wend its way from site managers to division managers and upward to the vice-president of manufacturing, a senior vice-president, the vice-chairman, and finally the chairman/CEO.

Two positions, those of vice-president, manufacturing and division manager were eliminated. The site managers now report to the senior vice-president in charge of manufacturing who, in turn, goes straight to the chairman/CEO or, if he is unavailable, to the president/chief operating officer. In addition, site managers' authorization over capital expenditures was raised to $200,000 from

$30,000. Streamlining the reporting system has made the site managers, the front line in any corporation, "more business oriented," according to Stewart. "By broadening the spans of control, we have forced people into distinctive and additive jobs," he explains.

This system of leaner management combined with greater responsibility extends to the plant floor. For example, facilities that formerly had one supervisor for every 20 people, now have as few as two for 50. Employees can now arrange customer calls, production schedules, and training on their own, rather than get bogged down in a time-wasting review process.

While this self-management encourages creativity, initiative, and flexibility, it also means that most employees are now performing several functions. For example, the executive assistant to the chairman, the president, and the company policy committee is, in addition, a member of the five-person corporate planning department. In turn, that department has one secretary instead of one for each member. As a reward for working more efficiently, company employees share in profits related to gains in return on equity. Half the employees own Du Pont Canada shares, too.

Du Pont's willingness to shed years of tradition so as to be world competitive has paid off handsomely. Its return on equity now meets or exceeds that of most major Canadian corporations. Furthermore, it is well on its way to becoming even more of a global company. Its exports in 1990 were more than two-thirds greater than in 1989, despite the high Canadian dollar, and were a marked improvement in comparison to 1989's 21 percent increase over 1988. Export gains now far outpace overall corporate growth, and the company expects this trend to continue.

Allen-Bradley Canada, General Electric Canada: How Canadian Subsidiaries Win Company-Wide Battles for Mandates

Because world product mandates are earned, not given, intense internal corporate rivalry for them often occurs. Subsidiaries that emerge victorious from these family feuds have proved they have the fortitude to do well against worldwide contenders. "Canadian subsidiaries have to press their point of view and retain a high profile so as not to get lost in the shuffle as their parents go more global," warns William Hetherington, president and CEO of Allen-Bradley Canada. "In the rationalization of manufacturing that globalization entails, there is the potential to be a winner or a loser, and nobody wants to be a loser."

Here is how Allen-Bradley, Camco (General Electric's appliance subsidiary), and GE Canada Aircraft Engines became winners.

Allen-Bradley Canada

A leading supplier of industrial automation systems and controls, Allen-Bradley Canada was established in 1954 as the Canadian branch of Allen-Bradley U.S., which was founded in the late 1800s. In 1985, the five trustees who then controlled Allen-Bradley were sued for not sufficiently diversifying the company and they decided to sell the business. It was bought by Rockwell International, well known for its work on the American space exploration program.

At the time that Rockwell acquired Allen-Bradley Canada, Canada was Rockwell's largest customer outside the United States. Rockwell's other Canadian interests include automotive parts and telecommunications equipment.

Just prior to the Rockwell takeover, Allen-Bradley Canada, independently of its parent, developed medium voltage controls for industrial electric motors, thereby diversifying the company into a product that records a strong $300 million annually in worldwide sales. At first, the Canadians passed on their technology to Allen-Bradley U.S. But just as it had outdistanced its parent in creativity in this area, Allen-Bradley Canada quickly surpassed it in revenues for the controls, out-selling the U.S. operation by a ratio of 4:1.

Having demonstrated its ingenuity and marketing superiority, Allen-Bradley Canada pressed for a world product mandate in these controls. "Because we had done well and our American counterparts hadn't, we were able to convince the U.S. head office that we could make a total success in North America and the rest of the world," Hetherington says with pride. Hence, production of these voltages was centralized at Allen-Bradley's Cambridge, Ontario headquarters. Subsequently, it parlayed this triumph into leverage to obtain further mandates.

When Rockwell International purchased Allen-Bradley, it did not withdraw any mandates from the Canadian subsidiary. In fact, Rockwell granted it special status because it is Rockwell's largest Canadian subsidiary. Allen-Bradley Canada is the only Rockwell Canadian subsidiary with its own board of directors, and Hetherington is the sole representative from these satellites on Rockwell Canada's board.

In theory, a foreign subsidiary in one part of the world with a mandate should be able to count on its sister companies around the world to sell its products with enthusiasm. But as Allen-Bradley Canada glumly discovered, being part of a global corporation can be a marketing drawback rather than an asset. "For instance, the salespeople in Australia were only familiar with lower voltages used in computers and were frightened of our product," says William Torrance, vice-president, sales and marketing. "Also, they lacked customer contacts for our higher voltages. Therefore, we had to educate them as to how to sell these items."

Camco

In 1980, when Camco began to export, General Electric, its U.S. parent, regarded it somewhat as a competitor. "It wanted to keep all the export appliance business to itself," recalls Claude Ménard, Camco's export program manager. "It was concerned that Camco would endanger its export sales; instead, we increased total volume by focusing on special product sales, thereby freeing the U.S. facilities to concentrate on mass production."

Undaunted by its parent's hostility, Camco went ahead, and its export volume has soared from a scanty $100,000 in 1980 to more than $30 million today. Most of the exports are shipped from Camco's Montreal plant where the company's washer, dryer, and dishwasher business has been centralized since 1983. The factory exports 15 percent of its output, primarily to the United States, the United Kingdom, Australia, and Taiwan.

Since its parent left Camco to sink or swim on its own, Camco had to rely on its own resources to develop export business. Like many companies in Canada, it turned to both the provincial and federal government trade departments for advice as well as for financial assistance to attend international trade shows. It also employed the tried-and-true argument of many Canadian companies that as smaller enterprises they can offer more flexibility than mass producers. "We stressed our willingness to make as few as one thousand units, whereas our parent is uninterested in orders of under five thousand," Ménard says.

That willingness prompted the unusual Taiwanese order, with the client's face depicted on each machine, as well as one from a United Kingdom firm for washing machines with lid locks to comply with British government accident-prevention regulations. "It was an order for only about three thousand machines and no U.S. company was interested because they believed the low quantity did not warrant the expense required for the special design. But we at Camco were accustomed to modest production runs due to our experience in Canada's specialized, small marketplace," Ménard says. Camco devoted six months to design such machines and subsequently obtained the leading market share in top load machines in the United Kingdom. Now that British consumers are showing a preference for front load washers, Ménard expects Camco's U.K. sales to shrink, but its track record there is helping Camco sell these machines elsewhere in the world where they are becoming popular.

In 1984, a sale to a GE distributor in Australia of a premium model washer with a complete range of features brought matters to a head between Camco and its U.S. parent. Because GE declined this specialized order, the distributor turned to Camco, thinking he was keeping the business within the family. However, those familiar with company politics will not be surprised that GE was upset that Camco obtained the order. It believed its subsidiary had insubordinately engaged in one-upmanship, whereas Camco maintained it had helped GE by retaining the business.

When both sides calmed down, they realized a crossroads had been reached. Camco could establish its own worldwide sales force, or it could appoint GE as its sole distributor in return for certain manufacturing concessions by GE. They agreed on the latter option, and Camco received world mandates in non-North American power voltages and specialized production runs. Camco now provides special voltages to 30 countries and makes such specialty items as gas dryers and small electrical ones.

For the Montreal factory to be flexible and multifunctional and thereby earn its mandates as well as a respected position in the GE empire required an entire overhaul of Camco's methods. Other foreign-owned subsidiaries should pay heed because their survival may well depend on similar measures. In 1980, when Camco first considered going global, it assembled no fewer than two hundred units at a time. Today, it specializes in swift response, custom-made orders, sometimes for just one machine. "The plant has the flexibility to produce a made-to-order machine the day after the request is received and to ship it the following day," Ménard says.

This flexibility stems from Camco's multifunctional product lineup. The 60 models are grouped into six families for which two-thirds of the parts are identical. Moreover, so that completion is not slowed by supplier delays, Camco reduced the variety of components that it needs and thereby the number of suppliers.

For instance, it now gets only five types of timers, yet retains its reputation for flexibility because they can be used on ten different models. "Thus, our production has ceased to be tied to the longest lead time of a supplier," Ménard says.

Furthermore, Camco's inventory control is flexible. Unique, low-priced "cosmetic" items such as knobs are stocked in large quantities, whereas bigger, more expensive ones like motors, of which Camco uses four types, are scheduled for just-in-time delivery. To retain its grip on its mandates has also involved substantial investment in upgrading facilities. Between 1986 and 1990, the Montreal plant, purchased back in 1948 by GE, spent $30 million on new equipment.

Camco's world mandate success is also due to a productivity improvement program launched in 1981 as its export program got fully underway. To improve productivity, Camco increased workers' opportunities for direct participation in the plant's well-being. Its system is based on the much admired and imitated Japanese technique of workplace democracy. Several management layers, including superintendents, were removed while workers were trained in multiple skills and grouped in teams. Quality circles also were established, but participation is voluntary, and so far only one-third of the workers take part. As an example of their value, Ménard cites the packaging quality circle which formed a joint committee with a supplier to improve its products. "Management ordinarily might just have changed suppliers," he comments.

Now that Camco has forced its parent to recognize its worth, they work together smoothly. Montreal managers and their counterparts at GE's Kentucky appliance plant speak daily, and Camco is linked by computer to GE's sales offices around the world. "GE may not have been a believer in Camco a decade ago, but it certainly is now," Ménard says proudly.

GE Aircraft Engines

In 1981, as Camco was in the early stages of its fight against GE's American appliance division for world product mandates, a similar in-house power struggle broke out over the establishment of GE Aircraft Engines Canada in Bromont, Quebec, GE's first non-American aircraft component facility. To prove its worth, the Canadians realized they could not merely equal the Americans; they had to outclass them.

The Canadians, however, could rightly claim that they did not solicit the mandate but inherited it as part of GE's international ambitions. GE's global strategy calls for beefing up aircraft engine and electric power-turbine businesses, in which the high entry costs serve as a fortress against foreign competitors. By contrast, consumer appliances are more vulnerable to low-cost imports. As part of its strategy, which has widened its worldwide aircraft engine market share from 20 to 45 percent, GE wanted to sell engines for CF-18 fighter planes to the Canadian government. The government, however, decrees that as an offset to defence purchases from foreigners, they must do some production in Canada.

GE acquiesced and built a $110 million plant at Bromont that makes compressor airfoils for a GE engine used to power Boeing 737s, the Airbus A-320 and A-340, and some McDonnell Douglas planes. Airfoils help maximize engine thrust. The Bromont plant has only a partial mandate; the design and testing are done in the United States by GE.

At the time that the Canadian plant was planned, these particular airfoils were being made at GE's Rutland, Vermont facility, only 70 miles south of the Quebec–U.S. border. GE's corporate planners decided that Rutland should relinquish this work because it had sufficient demand for other products to make up for the loss. They attempted to soothe Rutland by saying it would no longer be squeezed for space. Rutland was not pacified. Although the ill-will is brushed off today as "friendly competition," it actually was more like a civil war. "Some people there wanted us to fail and felt we were taking jobs and money away from their place," says Bromont plant manager Pierre Bisaillon.

GE Canada realized that for Bromont to outclass GE's American engine plants it would have to depart from GE's conservative, hierarchical management style. In a bold experimental approach for GE, Bromont organized its workers into multiskilled teams and gave them extensive powers, including the establishment of schedules as well as quality and productivity goals. They also were given a say in hiring, training, and salary reviews. The results are impressive: extensive gains in productivity, low absenteeism, and a far better quality record than the average for the industry. So successful was Bromont that GE incorporated many of its features into "Work-Out!", a company-wide program introduced some years later and aimed at increasing productivity through eliminating unnecessary work.

Thus, like Camco, GE-Bromont could be said to have proved its worth in spite of, not because of its U.S. parent. Moreover, Bisaillon points out that Bromont's success is good for the self-confidence of French Canadians in that "it proves they can do well and therefore creates pride."

Pratt & Whitney Canada: Trade-Offs for World Product Mandates

Pratt & Whitney Canada typifies the extent to which foreign-owned subsidiaries in Canada have matured, especially during the last 40 years, as well as to how much their fate continues to be intertwined with the rest of their family. Although the Canadian subsidiary was established in 1928, it was confined for nearly a quarter of a century to the sales and service of products made by its American parent, United Aircraft Corporation (now United Technologies). Finally, in 1951, the subsidiary persuaded its parent to allow it to manufacture on the grounds that it would enhance its competitiveness in Canada.

But the co-operation was grudging considering that in its early years as a manufacturer, Pratt & Whitney Canada's Montreal factory was a shoestring operation, notwithstanding the substantial financial resources of its parent. The factory was so strapped for money that it moved parts from one shop to another on a child's sleigh and heated airplane cylinder heads and luncheon pork and beans in the same oven. Nevertheless, it was determined to flourish, and by 1953, its first full year of production, it had sales of $8.4 million.

Today, its sales top $1.5 billion and it is the world's leading producer of small gas-turbine aircraft engines for which it has a world product mandate from United Technologies. The mandate is all-encompassing, including research, design, manufacturing, and marketing. Small gas-turbine engines are used in regional commuter aircraft business jets and helicopters. Until Pratt & Whitney Canada introduced gas-turbine engines in 1963, piston engines were standard on aircraft. Since the 1960s, gas-turbine ones have captured the majority of the aviation market, and Pratt & Whitney Canada now exports more than 85 percent of its production to 20 countries.

It owes its pre-eminence in this segment of the aircraft parts industry to several factors: access to the technological expertise of parent Pratt & Whitney in the United States, Canadian government financial assistance, and its own enterprise. It spends 19 percent of its revenue annually on R&D, far more than the national average of just over 1 percent of gross domestic product. Its lab employs two thousand, making it the largest R&D facility of foreign-owned subsidiaries in Canada and the country's biggest nongovernment lab after Bell-Northern Research.

Although Pratt & Whitney Canada took nearly four decades to exceed $1 billion in sales, its objective is to reach $2.5 billion by the end of the 1990s. According to its strategy, that increase will come from new products, new foreign customers, additional service centres throughout the world, and a transatlantic alliance formed in 1990 by parent Pratt & Whitney. It handed over 20 percent of its equity to Motoren-und Turbinen-Union (MTU), the aero-engine subsidiary of Daimler-Benz in exchange for a similar interest in MTU.

Their partnership is intended to challenge co-operative arrangements between General Electric and Snecma, the French state-owned aero-engine manufacturer, and between Rolls Royce of the United Kingdom and BMW, the German luxury car group which originated as an aircraft engine firm. Pratt & Whitney and MTU preferred partial ownership of each other to a full merger in order to reap the advantages of sharing technologies and strategies without having to relinquish their separate identities.

This deal will have a mixed impact on the Canadian subsidiary. On the plus side, the first new engine that the partners plan to build is one for regional jet aircraft, the type in which Pratt & Whitney Canada specializes. In that the development costs are estimated at a steep $1.4 billion, the partnership makes sound economic sense, since the financial risk will be split rather than borne singly. In addition, the arrangement eases concerns about selling to a possible post-1992 Fortress Europe hostile to outsiders who merely export and do not invest. "Unless a North American company is solidly entrenched there with people and facilities, it will be increasingly difficult to sell anything," reasons Gilles Ouimet, executive vice-president of Pratt & Whitney Canada. The company expects the connection with MTU will result in increased sales in Europe. Only 27 percent of its production is now exported to Europe; the bulk goes to the United States. MTU and Pratt & Whitney also plan to work together to sell engines to the Soviet Union.

However, the sharing entailed in this arrangement has its downside. To succeed, this partnership must integrate relevant production and strategic planning. This consolidation likely will lead to a decline in the workforce at Pratt & Whitney Canada over and above layoffs in 1991 amounting to 12 percent of the workforce, in response to the recession, as well as a further 13 percent reduction by 1995, due to greater use of teamwork and automation.

Clearly, world product mandates have a paradoxical impact on foreign subsidiaries, making them more self-reliant, yet perpetuating their dependence on their owners. Nevertheless, because of their cost-saving value, they are becoming part and parcel of the increasing globalization of business. Consequently, our country's economic future depends to a large degree on foreign subsidiaries here becoming world product mandate champions.

C H A P T E R

8

The Soviet Union: Opportunities and Problems

"Bureaucracy is the chief minefield in doing business in the Soviet Union: 99.5 percent of the bureaucrats only have the power to say 'no' and just half of one percent can say 'yes.'"

Peter Kazarian,
Executive Vice-President,
Seabeco Group

Nineteen ninety-one started off with a big question mark regarding Canadian—and all foreign—investment in the Soviet Union because of dismay over its political and economic turbulence. The question mark was in sharp contrast to the surge in foreign investment there in 1990. Some disenchanted Canadian companies have withdrawn after only a brief tryout, but others are not only staying, but expanding. What is likely over the coming years is that foreign business people will be dealing more with the individual republics than with the central government, as the republics' drive for independence intensifies.

The chief economic lures of the Soviet Union are that it is one of the world's largest untapped markets and it also contains the biggest oil reserves outside the Middle East. Westerners are eager to develop USSR oil as an alternative to Middle East supplies, especially in light of 1991's Persian Gulf War. In addition, they are tantalized by the prospect of selling to the 280 million people in the USSR—80 percent of Eastern Europe's population. Soviet citizens have hoarded an estimated $500 million worth of rubles because of a scarcity of goods to buy. That is half a trillion dollars worth of unsatisfied consumer demand—a seller's paradise—especially as all the Soviet republics are hungry for a vast range of products.

While Canadian businesses are latecomers to much of the global economic arena, many are on the ground floor in the Soviet Union. They can be found in almost every economic sector: construction, oil drilling, pulp and paper machinery, fast food, office equipment, and real estate. Indeed, Canadians are so interested in the prospects in the USSR and the rest of Eastern Europe that the federal government has had to redeploy 20 of its foreign service officers from Western to Eastern Europe to handle the volume of inquiries, its first ever major aggregate shift of staff.

According to federal government statistics, while just over six hundred Canadian companies now export to Eastern Europe, two thousand more are interested. The USSR is the leading attraction, with four hundred Canadian firms now exporting there and close to another eighteen hundred interested.

Although foreign companies can now set up wholly-owned subsidiaries and hold a majority interest in joint ventures, like business people elsewhere in the world, most Canadians prefer to export to the USSR rather than establish onsite operations. There are very good reasons for the hesitation. Foremost, while "perestroika" (economic restructuring) has created enormous potential for foreign businesses, its implementation has been slow and confused. Moreover, it is not a place for the faint-hearted owing to a labyrinthine bureaucracy, underdeveloped infrastructure (up to three days to place an overseas call, for example), low productivity, and scanty commercial protection legislation. Furthermore, the ruble is not convertible into "hard currency" dollars and probably will not be for most of this decade. Consequently, repatriation of profits is a major headache. How Canadian companies cope with these problems is described later in this chapter.

To do business in the Soviet Union requires large doses of the three P's: patience, perseverance, and persistence. "Business people cannot expect a windfall in the Soviet Union in return for spending only $2,000 on the groundwork," advises Edward Belobaba, international trade partner at the Toronto office of the law firm of Gowling, Strathy and Henderson. It has drawn up contracts for a number of Canadian manufacturers and developers now doing business there and recently opened a Moscow office. "Instead, business people must set aside at least $50,000 to $75,000 for four to five trips," Belobaba continues. "Nor should they rely on a Russian-speaking Soviet emigré. Instead, they should hire legal counsel because, although the USSR lacks toilet paper and toothpaste, it does not lack rules. Indeed, there are many by-laws covering zoning, historical monument protection, and so on, for which legal advice is essential." Legal expertise also is vital, since many Soviet negotiators, new to the world of free enterprise, must be educated about such concepts as profit and loss, licensing, the responsibilities of boards of directors, political risk insurance, sophisticated financing, brandname protection, and distribution methods.

"For their part, Western business people have some major misconceptions about the Soviet market," cautions John Nodwell, who has been doing business there for 20 years. His firm, Calgary-based Canadian Foremost, has sold high-mobility all-terrain vehicles for oil and mineral exploration to the USSR since 1968, three years after Nodwell, then in his mid-twenties, established the firm. He continues: "Westerners believe that because the USSR is changing to a free market system, it will be easier to do business there than it was before perestroika replaced central planning. But in actuality, it will be harder during the transition," he says. "Although Westerners see a demand for their particular product or service, there literally is a need for every product and service. Therefore, the Soviets must assign priority as to what they can pay for first."

Further advice is offered by Stephen Plummer, industrial division and aviation services director at IMP Group of Halifax, which has hotel and aircraft hangar joint ventures with Aeroflot, the Soviet national airline. "Usually, little is achieved during the first five trips," he says. "The easiest thing for the Soviets to say is *nyet*. Thus, just when you think a deal is finalized, the Soviets tend to have an eleventh-hour change of heart."

His sentiments are echoed by the experience of Calgary-based Canadian Fracmaster, which makes oilfield servicing equipment. It took the firm five years—from 1983 until 1988—to make its first Soviet sale. What clinched the deal was Fracmaster's agreement to be paid in oil, which it sells in Western Europe, instead of hard-currency dollars, since the Soviets prefer not to deplete their limited hard-currency reserves. Fracmaster's president, Ron Bullen, persevered because he believed sales in the USSR and elsewhere in

Eastern Europe would compensate for declining business at home due to the slump in Canada's oil development industry. Subsequently, Fracmaster has sold to other Eastern European countries, primarily Yugoslavia.

Canadians possess numerous advantages in doing business in the Soviet Union and Eastern Europe in general, according to Belobaba. "First, there are close heritage ties between East Europeans and Canadians because many Canadians can trace their ancestral roots to Eastern Europe," he says. "Second, there is geographical affinity; both Canada and the USSR are cold-weather countries and have Arctic boundaries. Third, Eastern Europeans have high regard for Canadian hockey. Fourth, Canadians do not have to shed many years of ideological Cold War baggage, as do the Americans. Fifth, there is a determination not to miss the boat on this market, as Canadians have elsewhere. Typically, Canadians are first to be second, but not in this case."

His statement is supported by the quick networking that occurred among Canada's corporate titans after the USSR started to relax its foreign investment rules in December 1988. Within months, 31 foremost Canadian companies established the Canada–USSR Business Council in conjunction with the USSR Chamber of Commerce and Industry. Olympia & York Developments' chairman, Albert Reichmann, is the Canadian co-chairman of the Council. O&Y is erecting a $250 million, 60-floor office tower in Moscow that will be the tallest building in the USSR.

Other Canadian founding members include Abitibi-Price, Gowling Strathy and Henderson, Lavalin International, McDonald's Restaurants of Canada, Magna International, Noranda Forest, and Northern Telecom. In November 1989, the Council helped organize a 250-member trade mission to Moscow, the largest Canadian business delegation ever to travel abroad. It scored a further coup when Prime Minister Brian Mulroney agreed to head the mission.

It was McDonald's Canada, not its U.S. parent, that introduced the hamburger chain into the Soviet Union. The opening of its first restaurant in downtown Moscow in early 1990, the culmination of 14 years of negotiations and preparations, received worldwide media attention. The nine hundred-seat outlet attracts mile-long queues.

What follows are the Soviet strategies of a cross-section of other Canadian firms: an exporter turned joint-venture participant, a real estate developer, an entrepreneur, a company that both trades and invests, and a construction machinery supplier turned project manager. Two high-technology arrangements are described, too. In addition, this chapter describes a Canadian firm that was established expressly to import a wide range of Soviet merchandise from clothing to pianos and scientific instruments.

The Exporter Turned Joint-Venture Participant

In 1966, one year after he founded Canadian Foremost, John Nodwell began to explore the possibility of selling his firm's all-terrain vehicles to the Soviet Union. He reasoned that its topography requires such equipment for oil and mineral exploration. It took until 1968 for him to make his first sale. But placed against the time frame leading up to Foremost Progress, a joint venture formed 20 years later, that first transaction seems like an overnight deal. It took eight years for the joint venture to inch from the discussion stage to a partial and ultimately full joint venture. In the final six months, however, the negotiations sped along due to the advent of perestroika. While many of today's Soviet-bound businesses have a Russian linguist on staff, Nodwell has succeeded in the USSR without learning the language, a difficult challenge because its Cyrillic characters bear no resemblance to the English alphabet.

Foremost Progress was formed for the express purpose of manufacturing the Yamal, a machine designed by Canadian Foremost for hauling equipment over swampy and rugged ground. With a carrying capacity of 70 tonnes, it is one of the world's largest all-terrain vehicles. Although the Soviets build some all-purpose land transport machinery, they have nothing comparable to the Yamal. Its production is split between Canadian Foremost's Calgary facility and the USSR. The Canadian plant makes the cab, cargo deck, and drive train, and the Soviets, the suspension and tracks. The vehicles are assembled in their country of destination. So far, two prototypes are in use in northern Siberia. Nodwell says the Yamal is also suitable for oilfield and mineral exploration work in Canada, Alaska, and the Antarctic.

Because the Soviet manufacturing is carried out in existing factories, Foremost Progress sidestepped the usual poor infrastructure nightmares encountered by joint ventures starting from scratch. Nor did Canadian Foremost have the normal headache of Westerners in sorting out reputable from dubious Soviet entrepreneurs; in this confused era of decentralization, everybody claims to have a relative with good connections. As it is an enterprise of the Soviet Ministry of Oil and Gas Construction Industries, Canadian Foremost's partner is definitely well connected.

But Foremost Progress has not been able to avoid a problem enmeshing most joint ventures: how to plan ahead during perestroika's massive transformation of the economy. "Our partner and the joint venture's Soviet suppliers and customers are part of this vast transition during which it is more difficult to pin down business and to identify who has hard-currency foreign exchange," Nodwell says. "The system of central planning and state organizations was not easy, but it was an established single market. Under perestroika, Foremost Progress has to deal with three sets of customers: the State, a whole new range of independent enterprises, and foreign oil and gas companies setting up operations there." It is from these firms that Foremost Progress expects to earn most of its hard-currency foreign exchange. Although Canadian Foremost handles worldwide marketing of the Yamal, the joint venture does have an eight-person administrative staff in Moscow, all of whom are Soviets.

Canadian Foremost deliberately minimized its risk by confining Foremost Progress to one type of vehicle and splitting production between existing Canadian and Soviet facilities. Moreover, the incoming oil companies will shortly provide it with business. Therefore, Nodwell can afford to be patient. But he warns other Westerners to be aware that the "USSR is a complex market in which it takes much time to develop business."

Real Estate

IMP Group was chosen by Aeroflot to be its partner in hotel and aircraft hangar joint ventures because two of IMP's diverse activities—hotel management and aircraft ground handling—met Aeroflot's needs. IMP owns a Holiday Inn in Halifax and provides ground services for Aeroflot at Newfoundland's Gander Airport. It also runs North America's largest fisheries supply business.

The Aeroflot-IMP joint venture, a 50:50 partnership, called Aeroimp, began with Aeroflot's request that IMP complete a 450-room Moscow hotel started by Aeroflot 11 years earlier. Aeroflot halted construction after finishing just the outer shell and the windows because of a shortage of materials and skilled tradesmen. Yet it insisted that IMP take just two years to do the interior, including the installation of mechanical and electrical devices, and all furnishings. To overcome the material and labour problems,

IMP imported workers from neighbouring countries and materials from across Europe. It also dispatched 15 Canadians as supervisors. Its methods worked: the first phase of the hotel opened in January 1991, only a few months behind schedule. The second phase is targeted for completion by the end of 1991.

Stephen Plummer of IMP says IMP proceeded with the project notwithstanding the hotel's snail's-pace history, because "it is a good commercial opportunity and we have a good partner." The hotel, called the Moscow Aerostar, is assured of business since the demand for first-class accommodation in the USSR far exceeds supply. Therefore, Aeroimp can count on high occupancy rates and can charge up to U.S. $300 a day for a room. Such stratospheric rates are common at Moscow's very few luxury hotels. Moreover, although more quality hotels are under construction, demand is sufficiently high to absorb all the new space. IMP's reason for building the hotel in two phases was to ensure sufficient cash flow from the outset. Plummer predicts the pent-up demand for quality accommodation will make the hotel profitable within just three years, way ahead of the normal timetable in North America.

In these early, confused days of perestroika when outside invest-ors have difficulty determining who is responsible for making decisions, sorting out problems, and taking action, IMP is fortunate in its partner. Aeroflot is one of the most powerful Soviet organiza-tions; moreover, as it flies worldwide, it is familiar with the capitalist credo of profit and loss. Thus, IMP did not get bogged down in checking out its partner, as do many Westerners. In addition, IMP estimates that food, linen, and other supplies will have to be flown in for ten years until Soviet products prove reliable; consequently, being partnered with an airline that can bring in the provisions fast and in refrigerated compartments, if necessary, is certainly an asset. Furthermore, Aeroimp was able to tie its hotel reservation bookings into Aeroflot's computerized ticket system.

Plummer estimates that it will take up to five years for the Aerostar employees to be sufficiently trained to qualify as senior managers. Meanwhile, 20 veterans from outside the country hold the positions. The rest of the four hundred employees are Soviets. On hiring them, IMP made what may seem a peculiar stipulation to those unaccustomed to the USSR: it insisted that none have prior experience at other Moscow hotels. "We wanted to avoid bad habits," Plummer comments. Horror stories are common about poor service at government-run Soviet hotels.

IMP does not have an exclusive arrangement with Aeroflot, but its willingness to take on the white elephant Moscow hotel earned it an ongoing relationship. The Aeroimp joint venture plans further hotels throughout the USSR and is helping the Soviet Ministry of Civil Aviation modernize its hangars. According to Plummer, they are now "of World War II vintage and, therefore, in great need of up-to-date fire fighting, mechanical, and electrical equipment." As Aeroimp imports most of the equipment from Western Europe, the Canadians are in the unusual position of negotiating on behalf of their Soviet partner against Western companies. IMP is teaching the Soviets about packaged deals, consortia, and other complex Western business methods.

The Entrepreneur

Torontonian Geoffrey Carr-Harris, a linguistics graduate turned businessman, formed his firm, Phargo Management and Consulting, expressly to do business in the Soviet Union. Since 1989, he has opened one venture after another: the country's first nongovernmental printing shops, computer stores, merchant banking, and medical instruments. His initial print shop, opened in 1989, was the first Western franchise operation in the USSR. In North America, Phargo is the exclusive distributor of *The Soviet Trade Directory*, 737 pages of information on 25,000 Soviet enterprises, and *Information Moscow*, a detailed, unofficial phone book. The city has no official telephone directory.

Carr-Harris personifies Canadians whose heritage gives them a link to the Soviet Union. In this case, because his grandfather was born there, he decided to study linguistics in the Soviet Union in the mid-1970s when he was in his early twenties. He married a Soviet citizen and returned to Canada. Subsequently, he developed many contacts during vacations with her family and through trade shows and delegations to the USSR that he helped organize.

Consequently, he was positioned to move when Soviet Leader Mikhail Gorbachev began to relax rules regarding Western investment. Carr-Harris's choice of printing shops as his initial venture was a bold decision, since at the time censorship of all printed matter had been the law for 66 years and possession of a photocopier required a special government licence. Nevertheless, he was convinced that there would be substantial volume from embassies and the growing influx of Western businesses which were having their stationery, sales brochures, business cards, and invitations printed in Western Europe or the U.S. and airfreighted to Moscow. In addition, he wanted to be well established in advance of the removal of the restrictions so that his firm would be familiar to Soviet agencies and individuals.

With this in mind, Carr-Harris applied to a global printshop franchisor, Arizona-based AlphaGraphics Printshops of the Future. AlphaGraphics has stores in the United States, Canada, Britain, and Hong Kong and is 25 percent owned by R.R. Donnelly & Sons, a large U.S. printing company. Carr-Harris requested that the franchise encompass all of Eastern Europe, not just the Soviet Union, because his goal is to cover the entire region. Tracking down a Soviet partner proved much more difficult. From 30 possibilities, he settled on Kniga Publishing House, owned by the Soviet State Committee for Publishing, Printing and the Book Trade. As their joint venture was formed before foreigners could control more than 49 percent, Kniga owns 51 percent and Phargo, 49 percent.

Phargo invested $300,000 in equipment and another $100,000 in working capital. Kniga paid the local startup costs and provided a 20-year lease for the first shop located in Moscow's downtown core. AlphaGraphics received a general licence fee from the joint venture and gets a percentage of gross revenue. In turn, the venture charges licence fees and royalties to its local franchisees. Within five years, the venture expects to have 25 stores across the USSR.

The shops are equipped with computers programmed in English and Russian for graphic design and desktop publishing, as well as with high-speed printers, printing presses, typesetters, and binding equipment. By persuading his partner that the desktop machines, which cost $10,000 to $100,000, perform on a par with multimillion dollar presses, Carr-Harris kept his investment to a level that he could afford and also reduced the amount of store space required. To offset import costs for high quality inks and paper, which are in short supply in the Soviet Union, the prices that the stores charge are double those at AlphaGraphics' U.S. outlets. Because there is little competition and the stores provide rapid service, their fees are not criticized. The stores are open seven days a week; they give two-day service but, if crucial, do the work instantly. That is a marked improvement over the four weeks that government-owned printers quote for "rush" jobs.

Besides stationery, the venture prints paper tray liners for McDonald's, children's games, postcards, and an eight-page summary of the Los Angeles Times that the newspaper transmits via AlphaGraphics' facsimile network to which the Soviet stores are linked. Due to the time difference between Moscow and Los

Angeles, the 250 diplomats and officials in Moscow who subscribe to the summary receive their copies hours before the paper's home-town buyers. The venture has generated further business through reprints of books on Russian folklore and traditions to which Soviet citizens previously had limited access. According to Carr-Harris, the first edition of one hundred thousand copies sold out over-night, even though it was priced at five times what a state-owned company would have charged. However, the 20-ruble price was far less than the up to 300 rubles charged shortly afterwards on the black market. More recently, Kniga began publishing its own weekly report on business developments in the Soviet Union.

Before forming Phargo, Carr-Harris was a partner in a Toronto computer store chain, during which time he exported some com-puters to the Soviet Union. That gave him the idea for his second Soviet-based franchise—a chain of computer shops. In this instance, he was not a pioneer. He deliberately avoided early entry because before perestroika all exports and imports were channelled through monopolistic central government and foreign trade orga-nizations. Carr-Harris believed he could negotiate better terms in the decentralized perestroika era in which all state organizations can deal directly with the West.

Although not first, Carr-Harris spotted a chance for niche leader-ship in high-end, full-support computer systems for sale to minis-tries, institutes, and banks that can afford expensive equipment. Moreover, since he did not have to install equipment and since he supplies computers mostly to order instead of maintaining inven-tory backlogs, he is able to gain back his investment more quickly than with the printing shops. Through ploughing back the money, he expects to develop this chain more speedily.

As with the print shops, he struck a deal with a major U.S. franchisor and asked for the franchise for all of Eastern Europe. The franchisor is MicroAge Computer Stores, a fast-growing chain with seven hundred stores worldwide. Carr-Harris scored a further coup when IBM appointed his franchise as its first authorized Soviet dealer.

About six months after the first computer stores were launched, Carr-Harris branched into merchant banking. Just as he had begun preparations for the printshops in advance of Soviet laws being changed to allow private printing operations, Carr-Harris laid the groundwork for his merchant bank prior to Soviet legislation per-mitting individuals to own shares in Soviet companies. As with the printing regulations, Carr-Harris helped the Soviets to rewrite their investment laws. He expects private share ownership to boom because Soviet enterprises are cash starved while Soviet citizens are cash rich, owing to a lack of goods and investment opportunities on which to spend their savings. According to Carr-Harris, at least five thousand Soviet enterprises are in immediate need of outside equity.

As Carr-Harris illustrates, there are multiple opportunities in the Soviet Union and each can serve as a building block to the next. For example, through engineers and technicians whom he met while forming the computer store chain, Carr-Harris set up another joint venture that produces an ultrasonic device for glaucoma treatment. The new company is 100 percent owned by the computer stores' parent company, and Carr-Harris hired the management, rented the factory, and supplied the office equipment. "There are two main reasons for doing business in the Soviet Union—the resources in the ground and the resources in people's heads," he says.

"The Soviet Union has extremely capable engineers, scientists, computer programmers, and architects, but they tended to hold onto their ideas because they believed the State did not pay enough for inventions. They are now champing at the bit to implement their ideas. However, as in the case of the glaucoma technology, they lacked the infrastructure for production as well as the legal knowledge about licensing and joint-venture terms." Ultimately, Carr-Harris hopes to act as a matchmaker between Soviet high-tech specialists and Western firms prepared to invest venture capital in new USSR enterprises.

Although Phargo's eclectic Soviet activities may seem to be devoid of a unifying theme, they actually are very much united by Carr-Harris's formulas for success: management control and conducting business in both rubles and hard currency dollars. Both formulas somewhat flout conventional procedures. Many joint ventures are headed by Soviet entrepreneurs with good connections, and the majority are in hard currency only since rubles are not freely convertible.

Carr-Harris believes the appointment of Soviets as top managers "can be dangerous to a venture's stability because Soviet entrepreneurs, while energetic, tend to be deficient in management skills. Sometimes, Westerners have had to liquidate ventures solely to get rid of the director. By contrast, franchising depersonalizes a business because dependence is not placed on one person." As for the financial side, Carr-Harris comments: "My golden rule is to spend dollars to make dollars, rubles to make dollars, and rubles to make rubles." What he will not do is spend dollars to make rubles. He continues: "That's suicide and is the cause of failure at many joint ventures. Rubles are not real money."

His golden rule explains why prices at the printing and computer stores are quoted in hard currency, but employees and local suppliers are paid in rubles. The shops do make an exception and accept rubles from major Soviet customers such as charities, state enterprises, and ministries. On average, rubles account for 20 percent of revenue. To make rubles from rubles, Carr-Harris reinvests the money in fledgling high-tech industries such as the factory making glaucoma detection equipment.

He regards these investments as a stake in the future. "In Western jargon, I use rubles as cheap junk bonds to invest in strategic projects or to undertake leveraged buyouts of private Soviet cooperatives," he says. "My willingness now to invest rubles means that I shall have a pool of loyal talent when rubles become convertible. Moreover, when the technology reaches worldclass status, I'll be in a position to charge hard currency for it."

The Trading and Investment Company

Seabeco Group is a Toronto trading and investment company that specializes in business development in the Soviet Union. Ninety percent of its activity is there; the rest is in Europe, the Far East, South America, and Israel. It has a broad assortment of activities underway in the Soviet Union ranging from real estate development to car battery production and luxury tourist trains.

Seabeco's chairman Boris Birshtein, attributes his firm's success to years of careful cultivation of the right contacts. "In the Soviet Union, it's not so much what you know but whom you know," he points out. "It is particularly important in this decentralized era of perestroika when it takes newcomers to the USSR a long time to identify who really has the power to make deals. It is not a place for the meek. For the average small Western businessman, it is an extremely difficult place in which to get started. Deep pockets and lots of patience are essential because beginners often lose money before they make it. This happens because they must learn what not to do as well as what to do."

Birshtein built up his contacts during nearly a decade of trading activities prior to perestroika's debut. He exported textiles, shoes, electronic goods and computers, helped construct a hotel in Leningrad, built a sports clothing factory in the Ukraine, and traded in metals. Through this wide variety of activities, he met many Soviet citizens and became knowledgeable regarding their business mentality. Such familiarity is the cornerstone of his ease in "penetrating the minefields." Birshtein comments: "To be successful in dealing with different countries, business people must understand the mentality, culture, and needs and be prepared to spend a lot of money on visits to acquire that understanding."

Seabeco looks for partners who are acquainted with the Western business style, principally with its emphasis on profitability. For instance, one of its partners is the huge Trade Union of the USSR, which describes itself as representing 180 million Soviet workers. But Birshtein willingly admits that his judgement is not infallible. He withdrew from two joint ventures because they were unsuccessful.

He says the lessons that he—and others—can draw from these failures is that investors should be prepared for setbacks and know when withdrawal is better than continuing to struggle futilely. "I can't blame the closure of those ventures on our partners, since they were not bad," he says. "It was our mistake for having made too fast and emotional a decision."

Seabeco and the Trade Union are engaged in several enterprises. They converted a Moscow guest house into a deluxe hotel called Spros, that some Western travel commentators rate as one of the city's finest. They also operate tours for executive groups and plan a charter tourist and cargo airline. Also in tourism, but with another partner—the Moscow Railway—Birshtein is converting two trains once used by senior Communist Party officials into a Soviet version of the famous Orient Express. He is refurbishing the compartments opulently and installing a casino, bars, and an elegant restaurant.

With Exide Corporation of the United States, the world's leading manufacturer of car batteries, Seabeco is modernizing existing Soviet battery plants and building new ones. When the project is completed in 1995, it will consist of 13 plants capable of an annual production of twenty million batteries. Sixty percent are intended for Soviet cars and the rest for export. According to Birshtein, local purchases will be high because current Soviet production is small and of poor quality.

Seabeco's biggest Soviet project is a $500 million, nine-hectare (about 22-acre) real estate complex in downtown Moscow. It will contain a five hundred-room hotel, a separate apartment-hotel, an office tower, a shopping plaza, a furnished media centre, parking lots, two theatres, and a congress hall. Because of the project's scope, it took Birshtein several years, until late 1990, to negotiate land leases and arrange the financing.

In addition to direct investment, Seabeco acts as a consultant to other Canadian businesses interested in the USSR. For example, it served as the marriage broker for a Canadian light bulb manufacturer that wanted to build a Soviet-based plant. In Seabeco's projects, Birshtein stipulates that much of the revenue should be in hard currency. For example, 70 percent of the Moscow complex is earmarked for foreign customers; the other part is primarily for local use. With the battery plants, local sales in rubles will cover operating costs.

The Construction Machinery Firm

Aluma Systems of Toronto, the world leader in lightweight aluminum shoring products used in construction, originally planned simply to sell and rent in the USSR through a marketing joint venture. It wound up as the onsite project manager. How this came about demonstrates why doing business in the Soviet Union is not for the fainthearted.

But first, a quick sketch of Aluma. It is a division of Tridel, a large Toronto-based construction firm and real estate developer. In 1989, preparatory to its move into the Soviet Union, Aluma hired Peter Antonoff, who is fluent in Russian, as its USSR liaison officer. Antonoff typifies capable, young multilingual Canadians who are being entrusted with extensive business responsibilities largely because of their foreign language skills. He interprets at negotiations, is the onsite intermediary between Canadians and Soviets, oversees equipment shipments, and even makes hotel and restaurant reservations.

Aluma is interested in the Soviet Union largely due to its huge housing shortage and the government's pledge that every family will have an apartment by the year 2000, instead of sharing as many do now. In Leningrad alone, where Aluma started in the USSR, the annual quota is 850,000 apartment units. Over and above, there is very high demand for office space from both Soviet enterprises and Western companies, many of which now have their offices in hotel rooms owing to the acute shortage of commercial accommodation.

The Leningrad joint venture, formed in October 1989 with a division of the Leningrad State Construction Company, increased its equity by $1 million early in 1991 for a total of $3,240,000 in equipment and cash. It rents equipment in rubles and hard currency, but only sells it in hard currency. Early in 1991, it made its first big sale—$750,000 worth of machinery to a Moscow construction group for the building of an office tower. It has plans to expand further through distributorships, beginning with four cities including Moscow.

While Aluma is doing well in the USSR, it had to overcome massive bureaucracy and workers' apathy. At the outset, it realized it had become involved with the unusual when its Leningrad partner went, as required, to register the venture with the Soviet Ministry of Finance. The ministry does not have enough staff to deal with the applications for joint ventures with which it is swamped. Moreover, as Antonoff wryly comments, those staff members that it has "have no great urge to work quickly because, as with everything in the Soviet Union, there is no incentive to work harder. Civil servants are paid little and so don't bend over backwards to work quickly."

Fortunately for Aluma, its Leningrad partner is the type that likes to get things done without delay and will step on toes, if necessary. Thus, the partner's representative camped out for one and a half weeks at the Ministry, in order to get the documents stamped. Consequently, only four months elapsed between the signing of the agreement and government approval. That is speedy by Soviet standards. By contrast, business registration can often be done in less than an hour in Canada.

The next obstacle was local bureaucratic opposition to Aluma's construction methods. Aluma designs buildings around its techniques; the Leningrad building authorities wanted to reverse this procedure. "In effect, what they were trying to do was to fit a size ten foot with a size eight shoe," Antonoff says. For instance, the city demanded that Aluma install hallway crossbeams every 20 feet. Yet the crossbeams would have had no structural value, and the cost and construction time would have been increased substantially. Considerable discussion ensued until Aluma won out.

Once construction began, Aluma's problem was getting its labourers to work. A Soviet joke neatly sums up the dilemma: "We pretend to work and you pretend to pay us." As wages are low, so is productivity and the venture's labourers brought this attitude with them. "They would sneak off to smoke, flit from one task to another rather than focus on completion of each production phase, not turn up some days, and worked at a much slower pace than their Canadian counterparts," Antonoff says. The venture pays well by Soviet standards: 600 rubles* a month compared to average monthly salaries of 140 rubles for doctors. However, the buying power of the 600 rubles is limited owing to the severe shortage of consumer goods. Just one pair of shoes on the black market costs that amount.

It was primarily the labour situation that prompted Aluma to broaden its role from the rental and sale of equipment to onsite project management. It began to oversee hiring and to implement tighter supervision. As an ultimate measure, it threatened to fire workers who continued to be overly slow. Since the lineup of Soviets eager to work at high-paying joint ventures is long, the workers took the threat seriously. Aluma also dispatched Canadian staff to train the Soviets, and brought nine Soviets to Toronto to study Canadian methods firsthand and to indoctrinate their fellow workers on their return home. When they were about to leave, Aluma gave them a small amount of Canadian currency. They all bought video cassette recorders and portable stereo decks at Canadian stores.

These purchases prompted Aluma to alter its productivity-based bonus program. When bonuses were paid in rubles, they had little impact on output because the scarcity of Soviet merchandise negated their value. To instill "a sense of dreams and aspirations," Aluma revised the program so that a certain portion of their salaries was assigned a foreign currency credit applicable to catalogue purchases. While the training and incentives are beginning to take effect, Aluma estimates it will have to continue its direct involvement for several years. "After all, 70 years of communism have left their mark," Antonoff notes.

Another worry of Aluma—and of other ventures with expensive equipment—is its protection against theft. Aluma's concern stems from the attempted theft in 1990 by two teenagers of the Canadian and Soviet flags atop a 15-metre (49-foot) high pole and some tools from a rooftop shed. Fortunately for the venture, the youths were caught by a guard. Afterward, Aluma fenced in its site and hired a patrol of several guards. The project is insured against robbery, but Aluma wants to avoid jacked-up premiums that tend to follow claims.

Like other Western investors, Aluma realized that it would have

---

About $280 Canadian at the official USSR exchange rate for rubles.

to forgo some of the gains normally expected early in the course of doing business. Profits on all sales and rentals are reinvested to achieve Aluma's long-term growth and to comply with Soviet restrictions on the repatriation of profits in hard currency. Nevertheless, it believes that the risks—being the first firm of its type to penetrate the Soviet Union, holding profits there instead of taking them out—are justified by its head start on competitors in a market with a tremendous need for its products.

High Technology

While most Canadian business people are devoting their energy to the sale of merchandise and real estate development in the Soviet Union, some have been quick to grasp opportunities in technology transfers and high-tech joint ventures. Two examples are provided by Stelco of Hamilton, Ontario, one of Canada's major steel companies, and by Scintrex, a company based in Concord, near Toronto, whose main products are geophysical and geochemical exploration instruments. Steltech, Stelco's research and development arm, is supplying the Soviets with technology for use in a 15-year program to shift from steel products for buildings, heavy machinery, and military equipment to an emphasis on cars and consumer goods. In return, Stelco asked the Soviets to help it improve its production of high-temperature alloys used in furnace construction and process controls.

Scintrex has formed a marketing joint venture in geoelectrochemical exploration techniques with a Soviet scientific research institute. The technology is Soviet; the idea to sell it globally is Scintrex's. The shrewd way Scintrex president, Harold Seigel, drew up the deal is instructive for other Canadian companies interested in high-tech alliances with the Soviets. First, he convinced the federal and Ontario governments, as well as most of Canada's major mineral exploration companies, to finance a $500,000 test of the technology in Canada. It detects gold and base metals under conditions unsuited to standard Canadian techniques. The Canadian test served to introduce the Soviet technology to the West, thereby overcoming any scepticism.

Imports to Canada

Much as the Soviet Union is courting foreign investment, it does not want the traffic to be entirely one way. As part of perestroika, it also is eager to promote exports, and thereby reduce its trade imbalance with much of the world. This includes Canada which, in dollar terms, sells seven times as much to the Soviet Union as it imports.

This combination of circumstances prompted the 1987 formation of the Winchester Group of Toronto solely for the purpose of developing a North American market for Soviet goods. Its goal is to be a one-stop shopping centre for Soviet merchandise. So far, its product lineup includes private label clothing; pianos; scientific instruments; railway, mining, drilling and industrial equipment; escalators; and binoculars, theatre glasses, and astronomical telescopes. Each product line is sold through separate subsidiaries managed either by an owner-entrepreneur with specific product expertise or by a partner company which specializes in the requisite product line. Winchester provides the umbrella services that they all need, including office space, warehousing, accounting, and group marketing. In addition, Winchester maintains a representative office in Moscow.

The company is the brainchild of Bruce Emonson and Charles Loewen, who bring disparate but complementary backgrounds to their novel enterprise. Emonson is an entrepreneur whose past activities ranged from television network development to the importation of loudspeakers. He also helped negotiate the Canadian introduction of the Soviet-made Lada car in the 1970s. Loewen is chairman of Loewen, Ondaatje, McCutcheon, a Toronto-based investment dealer. He is also Winchester's chairman, and Emonson is its president.

In November 1987, well before it was trendy to do business in the USSR, Loewen, Emonson, and 12 other Winchester people flew to the USSR to determine which products they would import first. They were received enthusiastically because, unlike most Westerners, they wanted to buy from, rather than sell to, the Soviets. Thus, it was an opportunity for the Soviets to make a dent in their annual trade deficit of approximately $1 billion with Canada and $2 billion with the United States. Moreover, Winchester was willing to pay hard currency, welcome news to a country with low hard currency reserves. Consequently, Winchester's problem was winnowing out those items it believed would do best in North America from the literally thousands that it was offered. In clothing alone, it received presentations from two thousand factories; from these, it designated 40 as suppliers.

By the end of 1989, its first full year of operation, Winchester was both pleased and frustrated. The pleasure stemmed from the realization that the past reluctance of North Americans to buy

Soviet products because of political reasons had waned. Furthermore, U.S. elimination of punitive import duties against Soviet goods enhances Winchester's sales opportunities in that market. But the pleasure was offset by frustration arising from the multitude of problems in doing business in the Soviet Union. These problems ranged from bureaucratic tangles to late deliveries and poor quality.

The result was that as of April 1990, when it released its 1989 results, Winchester was approximately nine months behind where it envisaged it would be when it assessed its outlook in mid-1989. In short, Winchester realized that while the long-run potential is enormous, developing business with a giant economy in a state of flux is a tremendous challenge.

Chief among Winchester's frustrations is the confusion unleashed by perestroika. While perestroika created the climate that made possible Winchester's formation, the diffuse system it also established has many Westerners, like Winchester, missing the days of Soviet central planning when they had to deal with only one contract. Under perestroika, each Soviet republic as well as private factories can negotiate directly. That means thousands of people now have the authority to say *nyet*. Consequently, confusion and paralysis reign rampant. Winchester often found itself negotiating and dealing with new groups of individuals, many of whom had no experience whatsoever in foreign trade dealings.

Sorting out that problem only served to put Winchester on the road to further annoyances—poor quality, late deliveries, and management unfamiliar with Western business methods. When they launched Winchester, Emonson and Loewen had little inkling of the host of hardships they would encounter in upgrading Soviet production and shipping to world standards. And did they undergo difficulties! Pianos had defective mechanisms, and binoculars and telescopes were shipped in unmarked crates via Murmansk instead of Leningrad (St. Petersburg), which is nearer to Winchester's facilities. Moreover, the Soviets lacked suitable bags for shipping grinding balls, drill bits did not meet specifications, the first escalator that arrived needed substantial modification, and the sewing on the initial lot of clothing was so bad that Winchester diverted it to the Soviet market.

Correction of these and numerous other flaws required ingenuity and considerable patience. For example, Winchester had heavy-duty plastic bags designed in Canada for the grinding balls. It persuaded the Soviets to ship the pianos in corrugated packaging, which is more space efficient and less costly than the wooden crates used by the Soviets. It taught the clothing factories how to preshrink and make materials colour-fast, label, and how to package in plastic. Also, when possible, it began to send merchandise by truck to Hamburg and Helsinki and ship from there instead of from the USSR.

In management, Winchester discovered the Soviets had to be educated about the concept of marketing. As Andrij Brygidr, president of Wintron, the scientific instrument wing of Winchester, explains: "Their so-called marketing departments were accustomed merely to sending out goods in response to orders. They were totally unfamiliar with the importance of product promotion and customer satisfaction. Moreover, this ignorance was widespread. Before I began guest lecturing at the University of Kiev, students there had never heard of the term, *marketing*."

He also gave a crash course in marketing to Wintron's Soviet joint-venture partner, a 30-year-old Ukrainian factory with six thousand employees. He introduced the Ukrainians to such Western procedures as sales brochures and manuals, competitor profiles, and sales meetings with distributors at which he handed out promotional hats and sweatshirts. In addition, Brygidr, who speaks Ukrainian, helped rewrite the factory's manuals to North American specifications, including different electrical standards, and made some cosmetic redesigns to enhance the equipment's attractiveness.

In North America, each Winchester subsidiary is individually responsible for its sales, but can turn to its parent company for market research and advice. The firms handle sales directly in Canada; in the United States, they use distributors. Generally, Winchester buys on consignment and pays the Soviets only when the goods are sold. This practice minimizes its risk as well as its hard-currency expenditures.

As is apparent from the experiences of the Canadian firms described in this chapter, the Soviet business style is utterly unlike Canada's. Aggravating the differences are the tiring logistics of doing business there. Due to the avalanche of thousands of tourists and business people, airline and hotel space are scarce. Consequently, hotels are known to maintain that they do not have bookings, notwithstanding their confirmations. It can take several hours to make restaurant reservations. The telephone system is so overloaded that overseas calls have to be booked days in advance. Ports are overcrowded. Whereas in Canada, the first truck rental agency contacted usually can readily supply vehicles the day after a request, in the USSR, at least five different agencies have to be approached. And so it goes.

The quickest solution to the bottlenecks are gifts. The Soviet gift system, aimed at cajoling bureaucrats into action, is distasteful to moralistic Canadians to whom such presents border on bribes. However, most see no difference between wining and dining potential and existing customers in the West and the little gifts in the USSR that serve to obligate the recipient. For example, one Canadian company succeeded in reducing its waiting time for an overseas line from three days to one hour by giving the senior telephone operator in that city a bottle of liquid paper to cover typing errors. A package of cigarettes or a bottle of whiskey removes the red tape involved in the extension of hotel reservations. Such renewals are necessary because Soviet hotels generally do not accept bookings for longer than two weeks. On the other hand, business negotiations can stretch out much longer. "Morally, giving cigarettes or liquor to get the extension is wrong, but when the choice is that or sleeping in the street, you give little gifts," a Canadian businessman says.

Westerners also are reluctant to do business in the Soviet Union because it lacks a fully convertible currency. Therefore, Westerners cannot repatriate profits in hard currency dollars. It is expected to take at least most of this decade until rubles are convertible on world foreign exchange markets. As of now, there are three government rates: the official rate of 0.56 rubles to the U.S. dollar; the commercial rate of 1.8; and the tourist special rate of 6.2. The black market rate is 20 to 25 rubles.

Those unwilling to wait until convertibility have four options: barter deals, export enhancement, import substitution, or countertrade. Barter deals entail reimbursement by other Western firms in dollars for supplies. In export enhancement, the Soviets pay a percentage on the amount by which the foreign investor is deemed to have enhanced export capability. Import substitution is a percentage paid in return for parts manufactured in the USSR in lieu of their importation from foreign investors' plants. In countertrade, foreign investors buy cod, vodka, caviar, and other Soviet delicacies and sell them outside the country for hard currency. However, supply and demand of such products is far too limited to make this a widely-practised alternative.

Overriding these concerns are uncertainties about the political and economic outlook. The paradox of perestroika is that for it to succeed, economic conditions may have to get much worse before they get better. The inflation rate is going up, not down. Lineups are longer. Shortages of food and other basic consumer products are deteriorating. As Edward Belobaba of Gowling, Strathy and Henderson, says: "Soviet citizens expected too much too quickly. The country didn't know in how deep a hole it was until it tried to climb out. It could take years, or perhaps decades, for any real improvements to materialize. The success of perestroika depends in large measure on whether the Soviet people are willing to lower their expectations in the short term, and wait out the painful period of transition."

Nevertheless, the cardinal point to remember is that the Soviet leadership is committed to fundamental reform. Where they disagree is over its speed. The Soviet atmosphere, therefore, is substantially different than in China where lack of official support for political and economical reform caused the undermining of Western investment. Also, even if more Soviet republics declare independence, they still will urgently need Western investment and goods.

At this early stage of the Soviet Union's transition from communism to free enterprise, Canadians must bear in mind that doing business there is a matter of definite short-term pain and probable long-term gain.

CHAPTER

9

Increasing Canada's International Competitiveness

"Globalization is impossible without strong productivity; productivity cannot be separated from overall strategic planning."

James Stewart,
Senior Vice-President,
Du Pont Canada

So far the tally of firms staying in Canada and making every effort to be competitive globally from their Canadian base substantially exceeds the number which have departed. Most of the more than one hundred firms that have left in the past few years moved to the United States and Mexico, where labour rates, taxes, social welfare benefits, materials, and living expenses are lower, thereby enhancing their cost competitiveness. Wages in Mexico are one-tenth of those in Canada.

"Canadians have higher expectations than they can afford. These expectations are the fundamental reason for the country's high taxes and debt load because taxation and debt financing are the only ways the government can meet the public's demands," says Paul Davidson, president of Tridon Limited. Tridon, which was one of Canada's major auto parts manufacturers and exporters, recently transferred its Canadian operations to the United States for cost reasons. "Therefore, the only way to lessen these burdens is for Canadians to be willing to reduce their expectations," Davidson continues. "Each time taxes, the cost of living, wages and production costs increase in Canada, the country becomes more noncompetitive, and if a company can't be competitive domestically, it follows that it doesn't have the foundation to be competitive offshore."

The companies determined to be competitive from their Canadian base are investing substantially in upgrading the productivity (output per hour) and quality of workmanship of their employees to offset the lower cost advantages of other nations. Fortunately for our country's future, these programs are beginning to pay off, but we still have a long way to go. Examples of these programs are provided later in this chapter, but a review of the economic strengths and weaknesses of Canada is important because these characteristics will influence whether Canadian businesses stay or leave.

Canada is one of the few industrialized nations with a trade surplus. Moreover, although at 4 percent, its share of worldwide trade seems small, its rank rose from tenth in 1979 to seventh in 1989. On a proportionate basis to the United States, the world's number one trader, Canada's performance is quite good, considering that the United States, with a greater output because it has a population ten times larger, has a 13.6 percent share.

In 1990, Canada recorded a merchandise trade surplus of $10.8 billion compared to $6.9 billion in 1989, its worst performance in a decade. However, the 1990 figure owed much of its good appearance to a one-time event—the Persian Gulf crisis, which boosted the prices of Canadian petroleum and coal products. The surplus was substantially smaller than during the peak years in the 1980s: $17.6 billion in 1982, $17.5 billion in 1983, $19.8 billion in 1984, and $16.4 billion in 1985. Of concern, too, more than half our export volume is still from natural resources notwithstanding gains in manufacturing sales.

That Canada has a surplus is due to its largest customer, the United States; in 1990, Canada had a deficit with all its major trading partners except the United States. In that 74 percent of Canadian exports are sold to the United States, Canada straggles behind all other industrialized nations in diversification of markets. By contrast, the U.S. ships only about 20 percent of its exports to Canada.

Their reliance on the United States places Canadian exporters in three quandaries. First, they are harmed when the Canadian dollar rises substantially in value in terms of U.S. currency. Economists say that Canadian exports are competitive when the Canadian dollar is around 80 cents U.S. In 1990, the dollar averaged U.S. 86 cents compared to 84 cents in 1989 and the much lower 73 cents in 1985, 72 cents in 1986 and 75 cents in 1987, the big trade surplus years Canada enjoyed last decade.

Second, Canadian exports inevitably suffer a decline whenever the United States suffers an economic recession. For example, in February 1991, Canadian car exports to the United States were at their lowest level since September 1983 due to the American economic slowdown. Third, it blinds most Canadian exporters to significant world demographic changes that indicate they should be stepping up their efforts elsewhere.

Today's global marketplace consists of 5.2 billion people. By the end of this decade, analysts estimate that it will be 6.2 billion, with two-thirds living in the Asia–Pacific region encompassing Australia, Bangladesh, Brunei, Burma, China, Hong Kong, India, Indonesia, Japan, Korea, Malaysia, New Zealand, Pakistan, the Philippines, Singapore, Sri Lanka, Taiwan, and Thailand. Yet, even though 43 percent of Canada's offshore exports go to this part of the world, Canada's share of the total Asia–Pacific import market is only 2 percent.

Those who like to plan ahead should bear in mind another equally dramatic projection. Today, the annual per capita income around the world ranges from a high of $20,000 (U.S.) in Japan to less than $200 (U.S.) in some Third World countries. (Canada's average is close to $18,000 in U.S. dollars.) But by the year 2050, when the world's population is expected to reach 10 billion, double today's total, the average worldwide income is expected to be $30,000 (U.S.) with much of the gain anticipated to occur in Third World countries. Therefore, preoccupied as they are in the aftermath of the free trade agreement with the United States, Canadian corporations that want to be prosperous in the coming century must also give thought to how to increase their Third World presence. As of now, Canadian exports to each of these countries are mostly under 1 percent of total foreign sales.

Another issue with which Canadian business must grapple is how to continue to penetrate foreign markets in view of the worldwide increase in "managed trade"—nontariff barriers such as import quotas, local content regulations, and regional trading blocs. Twenty-one of the world's 22 richest industrialized nations now belong to such blocs; the loner is Japan. Canada is one of the 21

LEADING EXPORTS

(In Terms of Dollar Value)
Most recent figures

COMMODITY	% OF TOTAL
Wood and Paper	16.2
Automobiles	12.3
Motor vehicle engines and parts	7.6
Food	6.9
Trucks	5.5
Chemicals	5.4
Metal ores	3.5
Crude petroleum	3.3
Industrial machinery	2.9
Telecommunications equipment	2.2
Natural gas	2.2
Iron and Steel	2.0
Office machines	1.8
Aircraft parts and engines	1.5
Coal	1.5
Textiles	0.4

LEADING IMPORTS

COMMODITY	% OF TOTAL
Motor vehicle engines and parts	12.7
Automobiles	8.8
Chemicals	6.1
Industrial machinery	5.8
Food	5.5
Crude Petroleum	2.7
Telecommunications equipment	2.5
Trucks	1.9
Iron and Steel	1.9
Wood and Paper	1.8
Textiles	1.7
Farm machinery	1.4
Petroleum and coal-related	1.3

Source: Statistics Canada

through its free trade agreement with the United States. A fully North American pact covering Mexico as well as Canada and the United States is also a strong possibility.

Many other factors also are responsible for the drop in Canada's competitiveness, ranging from poor productivity to high wage rates and feebleness in new business creation, innovation, and product quality. In the annual rankings of the international competitiveness of 23 industrial countries by the World Economic Forum, Canada reached an all-time high of fourth place in 1989 and placed fifth in 1990 and 1991. Canada's showing in both years was largely based on its praised standard of living. But, in economic terms, save for our banking system, natural resources, and transportation and communication facilities, Canada was judged as being unprepared for the fiercely competitive world of this decade and beyond.

The 1991 report ranked Canada only sixteenth in the crucial category of international orientation based on its dependence on one market—the United States—for export sales and on the Forum's opinion that Canadian companies are slow to adjust products to gain foreign sales. Moreover, that was a notch lower than in 1990. Except for a slight upward move in position from seventeenth in 1990 to fifteenth in 1991 in research and development spending, Canada scored either the same or worse in other critical categories. In product quality, it slipped from the eleventh spot in 1990 to thirteenth in 1991, in worker motivation, from thirteenth to sixteenth, and in productivity, remained unchanged at twelfth. Furthermore, our political stability, lauded in the Forum's 1990 report, no longer exists due to the constitutional crisis, although we are far from the chaos in more troubled parts of the world.

A further indicator of Canada's weakness in innovation is that it has only 0.3 percent of the world's total patent inventions according to the Conference Board of Canada, a nonprofit economic research institute supported by government, labour, and industry. By comparison, Japan holds 9.9 percent and the United States 8 percent. Therefore, Canada plays only a minor role in the introduction of new technologies. Moreover, according to the federal department of Industry, Science and Technology Canada, 97 percent of all technology used in Canada is imported, in large measure by subsidiaries of foreign corporations which prefer to consolidate their research and development at home. This high degree of dependence is not necessarily bad in the view of Brian McGourty, chairman, president, and CEO of Honeywell's Canadian operations. "Subsidiaries must be willing to accept technology transfers," he says. "They help develop Canadians' technical competence. It is impossible to be all things to all people owing to the huge amount of capital that would be required. Therefore, it is better for Canadian companies to focus and pick niches to which they can bring enthusiasm and excitement."

Unfortunately, studies by the Economic Council of Canada make clear that Canadian companies are not showing sufficient enthusiasm and excitement. The Council's analyses reveal that the rate of adoption of new technology is slower in Canada than in other industrialized countries. To lag behind both in creativity and in the acceptance of new technologies does not bode well for our country's competitiveness in innovation.

The blame for Canada's poor performance in productivity, product quality, and creativity cannot be placed solely on business and labour. While it is imperative that they work together to make Canadian business more competitive, Canada also suffers from a lack of government direction. Whereas other countries, such as the United States, Japan, and the European Community, are undertaking aggressive measures to augment the competitiveness of their economies, Canada has no national industrial strategy. For example, there is no Canadian counterpart to the shared effort of "Esprit" (European Strategic Program on Information Technologies), a ten-year multimillion dollar project begun in 1984 by the European Community and funded by companies and academic institutions, as well as by member governments. Esprit's purpose is to improve the competitiveness of European community countries in office systems, microelectronics, and computer design and programming.

Besides the high dollar and sluggishness in productivity and technological development, Canada's competitiveness is being damaged by the vast national debt. It saps the government's financial flexibility to make policy to help the country prosper. Although the Mulroney government's February 1991 budget promised to reduce the rate of growth in the debt through tightened controls on federal spending, the debt will pass $400 billion in the current 1991–92 fiscal year and reach $476 billion by 1995–96. That amount will be a more than five-fold increase over the total of $85 billion amassed between Confederation and 1980. Moreover, even if the debt's rate of increase does indeed slacken, it will continue to exceed half the value of the gross domestic product, twice the proportion in 1980. (The gross domestic product is the value of all goods and services produced in a country.)

In the area of international trade, the Program for Export Market Development (PEMD) did escape the cutbacks in government spending. However, its annual budget remains at $35 million, a level at which it has been since 1984–85 when it was chopped from $55 million as part of a then government restraint program. The freeze continues even though the literature of the department of External Affairs and International Trade about PEMD describes it as "the cornerstone of the federal government's export trade development support." Indeed, the program (outlined on page 7) has proved valuable in the 20 years since its 1971 creation. Sales stemming from PEMD-supported activities by the more than twenty-one thousand firms assisted exceed $16.5 billion. To spread the curtailed PEMD funds over as many companies as possible, External Affairs and International Trade has limited the number of times each firm can receive assistance. On average, about three thousand companies per year obtain PEMD money.

Not only is the Mulroney government tightfisted in the promotion of Canadian business abroad, it also has allocated extremely little money specifically for the attraction of foreign investment to Canada. External Affairs and International Trade receives $4.6 million and Investment Canada, the agency created by the Mulroney government both to review and promote foreign investment, gets only a meagre $800,000 to $850,000 for promotional purposes. In an effort to overcome this limitation, the agency pursues joint programs with the provinces. For example, it recently worked together with the governments of British Columbia, Nova Scotia, and Newfoundland to seek foreign participation in the development of ocean-related industries in Canada.

As a finale to the depressing aspects of Canada's future, an examination of what led to the departure of two well-known companies—Tridon and Varity—is worthwhile, as their diverse reasons could be used as yardsticks by other disenchanted corporations.

Tridon left because of the high cost of doing business in Canada, a familiar complaint. In addition, the bulk of its competition is in the United States, a circumstance shared by many Canadian companies. It already had a U.S. plant in Tennessee, one of the lower-cost states. Varity decided to relocate its head office from Toronto to Buffalo because it no longer was a Canadian company that sold internationally, but rather an international company that derived 96 percent of its revenue from outside Canada. Furthermore, it believed that by situating in the country where 80 percent of its shareholders reside, it would obtain a higher valuation for its stock.

As of now, Varity appears to be a unique case, since other Canadian firms which derive more of their revenue from outside than within Canada, such as Alcan and Northern Telecom, continue to keep their headquarters in Canada. But there is no guarantee that Varity will remain an exception, considering that the very nature of global corporations means that their loyalties, priorities, and headquarters cannot be tied to one country, not even to their countries of origin.

What makes the defections of Tridon and Varity more notable is that they occurred following valiant efforts to restore them to profitability. That they had to leave despite their recoveries underscores the difficulties of doing business in Canada.

Founded in 1924, Tridon is one of the world's leading suppliers of automobile hose clamps, signal flashers, and windshield wipers. By the 1980s, even though it had around $140 million in annual sales, it was losing ground to its mostly U.S.-based competitors and was profitable only due to favourable exchange rates. But when the Canadian dollar began to strengthen in the latter part of the decade, Tridon was in grave difficulty and redesigned itself to stay alive.

First, the family-owned firm sold 51 percent of its shares, in two stages, to Devtek, an Ontario-based aerospace and electronics manufacturer. Devtek's CEO was interested in Tridon because previously he had been president of Magna International, which supplanted Tridon as Canada's most international auto parts firm. In addition, costs were slashed by the removal of five management layers. Subsequently, production times were shortened, inventory levels pared, and an employee training program introduced.

All these measures returned Tridon to profitability—but only briefly; it slipped back into losses because its American competitors were undertaking the same strategies to cut costs. Combined with their lower expenses for wages, taxes, and social programs, their productivity improvement projects widened their cost competitiveness over Tridon. "By contrast, our Canadian plants were only 25 miles west of Toronto, one of the most expensive cities in North America," Davidson says. Thus, Tridon concluded that it would have no future unless it closed its Canadian operations.

Varity willingly paid a $50 million penalty to flee Canada. The money was a settlement for violating a 1986 pledge to remain in Canada, made in return for a combined $200 million bailout from the federal and Ontario governments. At the time, Varity was $2 billion in debt and on the brink of death. Although the federal and Ontario governments obtained shares in Varity in exchange for their assistance, the value of those shares is considerably less. Furthermore, the $50 million being paid by Varity is intended to cover employee severance payments and restored health and life insurance payments, as well as reimbursements to the two governments. Thus, the government treasuries will recover only a small portion of the taxpayer money received by Varity.

The pullout of Varity's head office from Canada has historical as well as economic significance. The company originated in 1847 as the Massey Manufacturing Company and Canadian historians refer to founder Hart Massey as "the first great Canadian manufacturer." Through consolidations with other firms, it later became known as Massey-Harris and then Massey-Ferguson. In its heyday, it was one of the world's largest farm machinery manufacturers and symbolized Canada's penetration of international markets. But by the 1980s, when it had changed its name to Varity, it was in danger of dying, partly due to plunging worldwide demand for agricultural equipment but more to mismanagement.

In the years following its rescue by taxpayers' money through the government aid, Varity returned to profitability by converting itself into a diversified company with most of its operations outside Canada. The farm machinery business was transferred from Canada to France and England, where the company had bought a large internationally active diesel engine manufacturer, the Perkins Group, in 1989. Varity also acquired two American automotive parts manufacturers: Dayton Walther (wheel and brake components for trucks) in 1986 and Kelsey-Hayes (wheels and brakes for cars) in 1989. Like Perkins, Kelsey-Hayes brought substantial international business to Varity. Kelsey-Hayes has plants in Europe as well as in the United States and was the first North American supplier of aluminum wheels to Japanese-based car plants.

Due to its diversification, Varity had become a profoundly different company. At the beginning of the 1980s, farm equipment accounted for 80 percent of its business (including the sale of related engines), 7 percent of its revenue was made in Canada, and 70 percent of its shareholders were Canadian. By the end of the decade, only 34 percent of its revenue was derived from agricultural machinery, Canadian revenue had shrunk to just 4 percent of the total, 80 percent of the shareholders were American, and U.S.-based Kelsey-Hayes was the company's biggest single division.

It was the shift in the shareholding base, however, that was the principal reason for Varity's move to the United States. Varity's executives were perturbed by what they considered the undervaluation of the company's stock on the New York Stock Exchange. It ranged between $2.00 and $3.75 (U.S.) in 1988 and 1989. The significance of that price range is that many large U.S. institutional investors are prohibited by their incorporating articles from buying shares valued at under $5.00 and/or from purchasing shares in foreign corporations. Those that do permit foreign share investments generally place quotas on the amount.

Varity's management also attributed the stock's low price to most U.S. stock market analysts ignoring the company since it was headquartered outside the United States. "Although Varity's revenue equalled that of the company ranked 120 in the Fortune 500 ratings of top American corporations, only one New York analyst regularly followed the stock and that was due partly to his being born in Canada," says Peter Barton, chief of strategic planning and development. Furthermore, having compared the price/earnings multiples (the ratio of earnings per share to the stock price) of Varity and other Canadian manufacturers to those of American ones also listed on the New York Stock Exchange, Varity's managers concluded that the Canadian companies tended to receive lower valuations.

Therefore, with no economic reason for it to remain based in Canada, Varity went off to Buffalo. Faced with its determination, the federal and Ontario governments decided that accepting its $50 million farewell settlement was more practical than spending years and thousands of dollars in a court fight to make it adhere to its pledge to remain headquartered in Canada.

Many companies, on the other hand, believe they can improve their competitiveness from their Canadian base, primarily through the intertwined programs of productivity improvement and increased training of employees. What follows is a discussion of each, with examples.

Productivity Improvement

Although "productivity improvement" has become a catch phrase among Canadian corporate executives, the performance of Canadian business makes clear the huge gap between words and action.

Between 1973 and 1988, Canada had the lowest productivity growth among all the major Organisation for Economic Co-operation and Development (OECD) countries. While its performance did improve slightly in 1987 and 1988, it was still lower than in most OECD nations*.

According to the most recent statistics of Industry, Science and Technology Canada, productivity in Canada grew a mere 2.2 percent between 1973 and 1988 compared to 5.7 in Japan, 4.7 in Italy, 3.7 in France, 3.3 in Germany and the United Kingdom, and 2.5 percent in the United States. Canada's percentage did rise at a greater rate in 1987 (2.4 percent) and 1988 (3.2) compared to the overall 15 years, but these increases were substantially behind those in Japan (7.8 and 7.5 percent, respectively), which remained the leader. Moreover, Canada slipped backwards both in 1989, with only a 1.7 percent increase, and in 1990, with a mere 0.7 percent gain.

Canadian business leaders regard productivity improvement as the principal antidote to the country's high labour costs which render labour-intensive companies uncompetitive internationally and consequently deter them from going global. Since labour cost competitiveness is significantly influenced by exchange rate fluctuations, Canada's wage differential has been worsened by the strengthening of the dollar in the past few years.

In 1990, when the Canadian dollar averaged 86 cents U.S., Canadian manufacturers were at a 4-percent-unit labour cost (the ratio of compensation per hour to output per hour) disadvantage versus the United States. In 1985, when the dollar averaged 73 cents U.S., one of its lowest levels in recent years, Canadian manufacturers had a nearly 16 percent advantage. Moreover, inasmuch as the cost of living, already steeper in Canada than in most countries, will rise under the goods and services tax, Canadian workers can be expected to insist on wages that keep pace. If their demands are met, the higher wages would increase production costs, further undermining Canada's competitiveness.

While the concise definition of productivity is output per hour, the Conference Board of Canada provides a broader explanation, describing productivity as the efficiency with which a company uses its labour resources and capital to produce goods and services. The board also points out that productivity encompasses quality

---

These are the most recent figures available.

LABOUR COSTS AND PRODUCTIVITY

(As of most recent available statistics)

UNIT LABOUR COSTS

(Ratio of compensation per hour to output per hour)

AVERAGE ANNUAL PERCENTAGE RATE OF CHANGE

YEAR	UNITED STATES	JAPAN	CANADA	FRANCE	GERMANY	ITALY	UNITED KINGDOM
			(on national currency basis)				
1973-88	4.5	2.1	7.0	8.5	3.6	11.4	9.9
1987	-1.2	-5.1	2.7	3.3	2.5	3.8	0.0
1988	0.3	-2.1	2.9	-1.6	-0.5	3.4	2.9
			(on U.S. dollar basis)				
1973-88	4.5	7.3	5.5	6.4	6.5	5.6	7.6
1987	-1.2	10.4	7.7	19.0	23.8	19.4	11.7
1988	0.3	10.5	10.9	-0.8	1.8	2.9	11.8

[Unit labour costs in terms of a common unit of accounting, most usually the U.S. dollar, are regarded as a better measure for international cost comparisons than costs expressed on a national currency basis.]

(cont'd)

OUTPUT PER HOUR

AVERAGE ANNUAL PERCENTAGE RATE OF CHANGE
(on national currency basis)

YEAR	UNITED STATES	JAPAN	CANADA	FRANCE	GERMANY	ITALY	UNITED KINGDOM
1973-88	2.5	5.7	2.2	3.7	3.3	4.7	3.3
1987	3.4	7.8	2.4	1.2	1.3	2.5	6.4
1988	3.2	7.6	3.2	5.3	4.6	2.9	4.9

COMPENSATION PER HOUR

AVERAGE ANNUAL PERCENTAGE RATE OF CHANGE
(on national currency basis)

YEAR	UNITED STATES	JAPAN	CANADA	FRANCE	GERMANY	ITALY	UNITED KINGDOM
1973-88	7.1	7.9	9.3	12.5	7.0	16.7	13.5
1987	2.1	2.3	5.2	4.6	3.9	6.5	6.4
1988	3.5	5.4	6.2	3.6	4.1	6.4	8.0

Source: Industry, Science and Technology Canada.

as well as quantity, and that a successful productivity program takes into account both the "hard" side of machinery and equipment and the "soft" one of the workforce.

Most corporations devoted the 1980s to hardware productivity solutions: upgrading, selling, or closing facilities. It is on the people side that they place most of their hopes for the 1990s and thereafter. A phrase coming into fashion to describe productivity goals is "becoming a Sigma Six company." It means six standard deviations from a statistical performance average, or production that is 99.99966 percent defect free, equivalent to 3.4 imperfections per million.

While definitions of productivity vary, the common denominator is that it is basic to corporate global success. Says Stephen Snyder, president and CEO of Camco: "Productivity is the key for survival in that the conventional tactics of pursuit of profits or, alternatively, of market share have built-in problems. Companies that pursue profits won't get market share, whereas those that charge very low prices will gain market share but become unprofitable. Thus, the only answer to be competitive nowadays is productivity improvement."

Despite the overall grim level of Canadian productivity, some firms are achieving annual improvement rates of as much as 6 percent through implementation of "worldclass manufacturing methods." Inspired by Japanese workplace methods, worldclass manufacturing entails shorter manufacturing lead times, an emphasis on quality, reduced inventories made possible by just-in-time deliveries by suppliers, constant training, multiskilling, and teamwork. Workers are "empowered," that is, encouraged to make suggestions as to how company operations can be improved. An optional phrase is "participatory democracy." Or, in plain English, employees are made to feel both more important and more responsible. They are also under considerable peer pressure to work at top quality and speed to support the rest of their team. Management must adjust, too, because they lose some of their supervisory authority while employees gain status.

A wall plaque in the office of Robert Polk, vice-president, Garrett Canada, neatly sums up the sentiment behind teamwork: "Not one of us is as smart as all of us." For his part, Camco's Stephen Snyder uses the phrase "a new Social Contract." As he explains: "To increase productivity and become factories of the future, corporations have to be committed to investing in the training and multi-skilling of people, as well as in equipment that will enhance employees' productivity. The traditional management-labour hierarchical processes are unsuitable for the 1990s. Instead, management must reach a new social contract with employees that provides more training, enables more flexibility, creates semiautonomous work groups, and rewards workers with gain sharing." Under gain sharing, the amount of money generated by productivity improvement is split among employees.

Money is just one of many incentives dangled before workers to encourage increased productivity and quality. Prizes are popular, too, akin to the coloured stars awarded at school to top students, as well as to the famous Pavlovian psychology theory of conditioned reflexes—automatic responses to certain stimuli. Northern Telecom, for example, recently introduced an annual corporation-wide contest for its "Recognition of Excellence" award. The award, a specially designed crystal ball, is given for "vision and intuitive knowledge" in customer service, quality, innovation, people development, staff support, and sales and marketing, as well as for the general manager of the year. In addition, the company has begun to present a "Spirit of Northern Telecom" award—a crystal shooting star—to the employee "who best embodies Northern's core values of leadership, customer orientation, teamwork, people growth, risk-taking, and innovation."

If imitation is indeed the highest form of flattery, the Japanese must feel extremely flattered that corporations throughout the world are copying their productivity and quality improvement methods. Many Canadian companies are already familiar with their procedures, but for those who are not, here is a brief summary. One of the chief points to remember is that the theory behind much of Japan's success originated with an American, W. Edwards Deming, whose ideas were regarded as heresy by his countrymen. The significance of its origin is not that it was American rather than Japanese, but that a first-rate idea was ignored by Deming's homeland. It is not surprising, then, that one of the cardinal aspects of worldclass manufacturing is to listen to employees, for they may very well have excellent suggestions.

The cornerstone of Deming's thesis, which he developed just after World War II, is "total quality control." He preached that better quality improves productivity and hence lowers prices, increases market share, and creates more jobs. Because Americans were accustomed to equating lower prices and higher market share with maximum production, they regarded Deming's philosophy as contradictory to everything they were educated to believe. Thus, for decades Deming was virtually ignored at home. Not so in Japan, which was eager to rebuild its economy after World War II and willing to accept advice from outsiders. The Union of Japanese Scientists and Engineers invited Deming to lecture to them in 1950, and the next year it established the Deming Award, the most prestigious Japanese prize for quality control. The Japanese did precisely as Deming advocated and built their economy into one of the world's strongest with the best productivity rate. "Quality is almost a religion to the Japanese," observes William Easdale, a Canadian who is senior vice-president, administration at Toyota Motor Manufacturing Canada.

The Japanese pursue a three-pronged strategy to achieve "total quality control." It consists of continuous improvement (*kaizen*), just-in-time delivery by suppliers, and teamwork. Usually, it is summarized in a catchy slogan such as Toyota's "Quality is our driving force." Continuous improvement calls for productivity to be enhanced through the detection of waste in machinery, materials, labour and/or production methods, and the development of solutions. Its linchpin is the Japanese conviction that volume gains are worthless if even a minute compromise is made in quality.

Thus, assembly-line workers are encouraged to pull a rope or press a button to stop production if they spot defects. By contrast, at North American plants halting the line can result in disciplinary action. Under the Japanese system, each worker is taught to regard everyone else on the production line not as a fellow worker but as a "customer" who should never receive a defective item.

Kaizen is much more than a way of thinking. It also consists of standardized work sheets that detail the most efficient way to perform each production step right down to the degree of arm rotation. Also, because their emphasis is on quality, not volume, the Japanese are willing to wait for months until they begin full production, so as to perfect everything, in a modern version of the tale of the tortoise and the hare. Like the fabled tortoise, the Japanese prefer to take their time and develop the skills that defeat the too casual hare.

Just-in-time delivery requires parts to be received the same day that they are used instead of stockpiling them for months. In addition to preventing overproduction and surplus inventory, the system exposes quality problems that might otherwise remain undetected and enables more cost efficient plant layout and scheduling. For instance, the Cambridge, Ontario plant of Toyota Motor

Manufacturing Canada maintains just two hours' worth of inventory and receives four deliveries daily.

The system does make manufacturers vulnerable to traffic tie-ups or accidents that delay deliveries. Also, the cost of gas for suppliers is far greater than if they were to make less frequent bulk deliveries. Another drawback for suppliers is that manufacturers tend to whittle down their sourcing to a few firms in order to ensure speedy delivery more readily. In turn, those selected face the predicament of losing much of their livelihood should the customer become dissatisfied. Some manufacturers work with suppliers to iron out problems; other have almost no tolerance for difficulties because of the harmful repercussions to themselves.

The Japanese teamwork system is nearly a classless society; outside of titles, no distinction is made between management and shop floor workers. Everyone wears the same uniform and there is no executive parking lot nor dining room. An absence of office walls in the administration area allows management by walking around. At most Japanese factories, there are only two categories of factory workers—skilled trades (such as maintenance and tool and die) and production. By comparison, some North American plants have more than one hundred job classifications.

As part of their psychology to make employees feel part of the team, the Japanese call their blue-collar workers "associates" or "team members." On average, teams consist of four to eight people, each of whom is trained to do the work of the rest of the team as well as his or her own. Each team has a "team leader" and for approximately every three teams there is a "group leader." "Associates" have the right of appeal to a peer group, should management wish to fire them. Management must appear at these reviews to justify their decision.

While the technical phrase for this system is "participatory democracy," the Japanese and other Asians with similar programs prefer to depict their organization as a big family. At Halla Climate Control Canada, a joint venture of Mando Machinery Corporation of South Korea and the Ford Motor Company, managing director Young Cho urges employees to say "my company," "my machine," "my floor," and so on to increase their commitment to Halla's success. They also have "my broom" and "my dustpan" to sweep up "my floor area" as in any family's "clean and well-organized house." Instead of leaving a mess for the cleaners, tidying up is standard practice in "teamwork" companies.

By encouraging Halla workers to plant trees and flowers in a group floral patch, paid for by the company, Cho improved the plant's landscaping while again enhancing workers' identification with, and pride in their company. In addition, cakes and gifts are given on birthdays and baseball games and barbecues are organized frequently.

The team system extends to families of "associates" by including them at social events. For example, Toyota holds occasional family parties with balloons, gifts, clowns, a magician, and a plant tour. Halla management conducts quarterly one-day brainstorming sessions with employees at a location away from the Belleville, Ontario plant. Ways to improve the company are discussed after which the workers are joined by their families for a picnic and dancing.

Even more significant to workers concerned about job security, the Japanese and South Koreans make a point of trying to avoid layoffs in slack times. They regard slowdowns as opportunities for increased training. What makes *kaizen* popular is its emphasis on people instead of machinery. As Cho points out: "A company's strength is determined by its people. People are its number one resource. North American corporations tend to have greater employee turnover than Japanese or Korean firms because many treat their workers as just another commodity. As long as people are viewed as just another factor of production, companies cannot expect greater productivity.

"By contrast, when workers are encouraged to think of a firm as 'my' company, their attitude is far different. They feel the commitment to stay and help the firm grow. It is sometimes said that Japanese hands are invisible because they move so quickly to finish a task. But Canadian workers can also be very productive, provided they are happy through having a say in what they are doing. Moreover, they are honest and capable as well as accurate in assembly work; these are important factors, too, in improving productivity."

For *kaizen* to take root at corporations depends on the desire of management to make it work, because without their commitment the concept is thwarted. "Corporation executives cannot sit back and wait for productivity to happen," stresses Grant Murray, vice-president, corporate relations at IBM Canada, one of IBM's highest output per hour divisions anywhere in the world. "Productivity improvement has to be managed from the top. Senior managers must set objectives and quantify the impact on productivity of investment decisions. For IBM, the decisive factor is whether headcount savings will result, by which I don't mean getting rid of people, but rather avoidance of having to hire more. For example, it can involve the transfer of employees to other jobs when their own disappear."

So as to "quantify" the effect of its continuous improvement programs, IBM asks workers to determine how to overcome "productivity gaps"—the difference between the amount of work assigned and the time and resources allocated to complete it. Of course, the upshot of bridging a gap is that the workers are asked to do even better in succeeding years. Underpinning this program is a redefinition of IBM's purpose, changing it from a corporation that sold products to one that is in the service business. As Murray explains: "The change in emphasis arises from everything that IBM does being related to existing or prospective customers. Thus, a sale not only involves a piece of equipment but also defect-free delivery and friendly, professional service."

An important side effect of productivity improvement is the impact on parts suppliers. To ensure better terms and faster service than one-year deals produce, manufacturers are switching to long-term contracts of five years or so, that they call "partnerships," although this is merely a descriptive phrase and not a legal actuality. But the partnerships have an onerous corollary in that manufacturers view them as an opportunity to shift the burden for the development of new products and/or fresh applications onto their suppliers. Consequently, while manufacturers are reducing their in-house engineers, suppliers are having to increase their design staff budget substantially. "Customers are becoming more demanding, and we must meet their requests to retain existing contacts and develop new business," says William Torrance, vice-president, sales and marketing at Allen-Bradley Canada, which makes industrial automation controls.

What follows are samples of highly successful productivity/quality improvement programs at the Canadian subsidiaries of Honda, Toyota, and General Electric, as well as at Northern Telecom.

For Honda Canada and Toyota Canada, superior productivity and quality are imperative for a good showing within their companies' global operations. In order to justify the hundreds of millions of dollars invested in their facilities, the Canadian branches must produce cars at costs comparable to those manufactured in Japan. In that Canadian labour rates are higher, the chief way for the transplants to bring their costs in line with those in Japan is to achieve maximum productivity.

Also, productivity and quality improvement are essential for winning approval for expansion on the ample land that Toyota Canada has available at its Cambridge, Ontario plant and Honda Canada at its Alliston, Ontario factory. As of now, full capacity at both is well below the average for the car industry. Since production began at Honda Canada in 1986 and at Toyota Canada in 1988, the Honda approach is outlined first.

Honda

It is a rare company that prominently displays a failure in its lobby. Honda of Canada Manufacturing is the exception. The only car in the waiting room at its Alliston plant is one of the parent company's first mass-produced vehicles, a 1966 model that sold a grand total of just 1,500 units.

Featuring this car seems to be a ludicrous defiance of conventional marketing wisdom. Normally, corporations attempt to sweep fiascos into obscurity with all possible haste, as the Ford Motor Company tried to do with its Edsel, the most famous ill-starred vehicle in recent automobile history. But behind Honda's flouting of the usual procedure is sound reasoning: it wants to stress that corporations can learn from failure and go on to enormous worldwide success, as it has done in the quarter century since 1966.

"I stress that I will allow failure 99 times, as long as a person learns from that failure," says Hiroshi Hayano, president of Honda of Canada Manufacturing. "One success out of a hundred tries is wonderful." As an example, he cites an incident that almost crippled the Canadian branch shortly after it opened. "Our employees, whom we call associates, are encouraged to suggest better ways of doing a procedure, and an associate in the paint department proposed what he thought would be a more efficient way of checking the dipping and coating process. It seemed like a good idea, and we implemented it.

"Unfortunately, what nobody then realized was that it required constant flows of electricity. The necessity of this regularity was discovered on a day when the plant underwent a sudden power blip, which caused a quick upsurge followed by a slump. As a result, the checking process failed, and we had to scrap the 20 cars that were undergoing the test at the time of the power fluctuation. Obviously, this loss was very costly and the person responsible for the process feared he would be fired. But I took the attitude that the experience—albeit an expensive one—was a lesson to watch parameters other than the process itself. We installed appropriate safeguards and still use the method. Moreover, we eventually promoted the associate."

The other benefit of the mishap was that it underscored for the company's Canadian workers the sincerity of the Japanese about tolerating mistakes arising from good intentions. "The big difference between the Japanese and North Americans is that the latter are profit and loss oriented, while the former are in for the long term," comments Arnold Norris, vice-president, general affairs at Honda's Alliston plant. "North Americans are reluctant to make decisions unless they are certain the result will be positive, because if they are wrong, they are often fired. By contrast, at Honda of Canada we emphasize that meetings at which negative decisions are reached can be as productive as those where approval is given."

Norris also attributes Honda's success to its classification of itself as an engineering company rather than a car and motorcycle manufacturer or a transportation company. "Consequently, senior Honda executives have always had an engineering and manufacturing background," he notes. "North American automakers did have manufacturing people as their heads in the 1950s and 1960s, but subsequently sales, marketing, and financial managers took over, and their mindset is far different from that of a manufacturing person. Just as a vice-president of manufacturing would find it hard to run a bank, it is difficult for accountants to understand the manufacturing mentality. Honda has done well because it consistently has allocated top priority to production, with marketing designated as a follow-up procedure."

Honda's emphasis on engineering is instilled throughout the company by treating administrative, as well as plant workers, as engineers. "We regard our personnel staff as human resource engineers who must fully understand the many aspects of their job, instead of just doing it by rote," Norris continues.

To stimulate employees to contribute ideas, Hayano urged employees to devise their own acronyms for participatory programs. The main program is REACH, shorthand for "recognition of efforts of associates contributing at Honda." Under this program, employees are awarded points which can be translated into dollar value for suggestions regarding safety and quality improvements. The top prize is a new Honda "Accord" car or a trip for two anywhere in the world where Honda has plants. To encourage participation, the program reserves the highest points for involvement while assigning lower marks for results.

While Honda has a high tolerance for employee errors, it has absolutely none for those by suppliers. "If just one part in a shipment is rejected by our inspectors, the supplier is regarded as having done an unacceptable job," Hayano states emphatically. "When a supplier once told me proudly that only three of the components he sent turned out to be defective, I replied that such a proportion was unacceptable for Honda's standards since we want zero defects. We expect a full commitment to 100 percent perfect components. We tell suppliers their parts must be satisfactory to workers on our assembly line and that if they are unhappy with a part, so are the quality control inspector and myself." Honda warns suppliers that should a part be defective, they must repair or replace it themselves at their own expense; otherwise, Honda will fix it at a charge of three times what it paid. "We deliberately make it tough to become and remain suppliers," Hayano says.

Toyota

The detailed planning, strict adherence to a timetable, and intensive training followed by Toyota Motor Manufacturing Canada in its three-year journey from the drawing board in 1985 to reality in 1988 are representative of the famous Japanese business style. Therefore, its evolution provides a useful blueprint for Canadian firms interested in the Japanese workplace methodology. Since the Japanese believe people are as vital to a plant's success as machinery, Toyota Canada devoted considerable care to the selection of workers for its Cambridge plant. "The Japanese approach training as an investment, whereas Canadians tend to look at it as a cost," says William Easdale, senior vice-president, administration.

Formerly vice-president of personnel and industrial relations at Boeing-de Havilland in Toronto, Easdale was the first Canadian hired for the Cambridge factory. "Therefore, when I am asked how much the training cost our plant, I answer 'Nothing'," he continues. "I point out that to us, training, like plant equipment and maintenance, is an investment, not a cost."

For assistance in selecting promising applicants, Easdale turned to the local office of Employment and Immigration Canada, a department that is frequently derided as being of little help in bringing together job-hunters and industry. "I was well aware that many people are critical of the department, but I was certain that if I were specific about Toyota's needs, the Cambridge office would be helpful—and it was," Easdale says. "Its director took on our assignment as a challenge to demonstrate its worth." The government employees saved Toyota the task of weeding out unsuitable applicants by only passing on the names of those with a high school diploma, three years' manufacturing experience, and a willingness to work in teams. Toyota was able to request a factory background because Cambridge is in Ontario's manufacturing heartland. So that applicants could decide whether teamwork was acceptable to them, the Employment and Immigration officers showed them a video prepared by Toyota on its methods.

This prescreening narrowed the number of Toyota job-seekers somewhat, but the company still wound up interviewing twelve thousand people, from which it ultimately hired one thousand. This was an arduous process because Toyota, unlike many Canadian companies, does not believe in hasty assessments. On average, it interviewed each person five times. Just by turning up, candidates demonstrated their enthusiasm and persistence. They underwent a battery of tests ranging from aptitude to spatial relationship exercises. In addition, they were organized in teams and given a problem to solve so as to determine their commitment to working together to improve operations.

When a core group of 120 had been hired, they were sent on a four-week immersion course at the Toyota plant in Japan that makes the company's Corolla, the model in which Cambridge specializes. On their return, some skilled trades (maintenance and tool and die) workers were trained for an additional eight weeks at a nearby vocational college. Then these original employees, along with dozens of Japanese trainers brought over from Toyota-Japan, educated subsequently hired workers in the Toyota way of running a factory.

Besides devoting much more time than many Canadian companies to initial training, Toyota never slackens in the education of its workers. Its college-type calendar offers a wide array of work-related courses, ranging from problem-solving to first aid, statistical methodologies, and exercises to prevent sore backs on the assembly line. Those interested in career advancement must take a minimum of 12 training sessions to become a team leader and 21 to become a group leader.

In line with the Japanese predilection for moving slowly into full operation to ensure that quality has priority over quantity, Toyota-Cambridge eased into production. The workers built cars on a trial basis for five months before the plant shifted into commercial production. Output was then curtailed to just five cars a day in one shift with half its current workforce. The wisdom of this gradualism was underscored just a few months later when the Automobile Journalists Association of Canada named the Cambridge "Corolla" the "best vehicle built in Canada" based on road tests of cars made in the plant's first 30 days of commercial production.

Today, the plant builds 260 cars each work day in two shifts, but the emphasis on quality remains with constant lectures on the subject. "We tell employees that it is okay to have a problem and that the very concept of *kaizen* is a recognition that everything can't be perfect. What is important, we stress, is to solve that problem and strive to be better," says corporate secretary Hiromichi (Mitch) Imanaka.

One of the biggest *kaizen* challenges at Toyota-Cambridge was how to expand production from fifty thousand to sixty thousand cars in 1990 with an increase of just 80 employees, bringing the total to one thousand. For this objective to be achieved, Toyota-Cambridge calculated it would have to complete a vehicle every 3.4 minutes compared to the existing four minutes, a considerable speedup in production for a car plant, even though it is a small fraction of time. Thus, the "takt time," the Japanese expression for the amount of time to complete a process that can involve several tasks, had to be decreased by 36 seconds at each stage of the production line.

The plant tackled the problem from several directions. First, teams were increased from five to six members so as to reduce the workload per person and thereby meet the 3.4 minutes deadline. In addition, the employees held brainstorming sessions for *kaizen* ideas that would save time through the elimination of bending and walking back and forth. As a result, there now are dollies conveying tools and parts that glide along grids at workstations in synchronization with each step of a production task. Other new devices that make the work easier include pneumatic platforms which lower batteries to the level of the cars for installation, thereby eliminating stretching. In reverse use, other pneumatic platforms are programmed to rise as the pile of wheel rims diminishes. "Some of the devices are rather unusual, but we figure that since employees invested time and effort on them, they will make certain their innovations work," Easdale says.

At 3.4 minutes per car, the Cambridge plant turns out fewer cars per day than Toyota's main plant in Japan which completes a car every 58 seconds. Nevertheless, on a proportional basis, the productivity of the Cambridge workers matches that of their Japanese counterparts. The rate is similar because the faster Japanese line requires far more workers, and they lack the time in which to perform as many tasks as the Canadians.

General Electric Canada

GE Canada's Bromont, Quebec aircraft engines parts plant proudly claims much of the credit for GE's worldwide "Work-Out!" program which seeks to eliminate stifling, time-wasting bureaucracy. "Today, we speak much less of organization charts and job descriptions and much more about what we call the three S's—speed, simplicity, and self-confidence," says the executive vice-president of GE Canada, Robert Gillespie.

According to Pierre Bisaillon, the Bromont plant's manager, its version of "Work-Out!" predates GE's universal program by eight years. Opened in 1981, the plant operates on what are called "socio-tech principles" whereby leading-edge robotics technology is operated by multiskilled employees grouped in largely autonomous teams. The teams set their own objectives regarding production, quality, and cost-saving.

New employees receive a one-page statement that outlines these principles under the heading, "The promise of GE Bromont." In part, it says: "By using state-of-the-art technology and advanced management methods, we promise to be a responsible leader in quality, productivity, human resources management, and profitability . . . . Each and every one of us feels responsible and is determined to stay one step ahead. Together, each day, we utilize our driving forces to achieve our goals." Much of this "utilization" is attributable to the plant's emphasis on training and communication regarding such topics as cost control, health and safety, and peer evaluation. All told, GE Bromont devotes 12 percent of each year's work time to training and communication, far more than GE Canada's current 1 percent and goal of 2 percent.

Thanks to its system, GE Bromont has a much lower absenteeism rate than the industrial average, as well as far greater annual productivity increases than the norm for Canada. It has annual gains of 6 percent compared to the 2 to 3 percent national average.

As part of its effort to increase the "speed and self-confidence" of its employees throughout Canada, GE Canada has an "Organization Effectiveness Centre" at its Mississauga, Ontario headquarters. An offshoot of the human resources department, the centre organizes a wide range of courses for which the cost is charged internally to employees' departments. The topics vary from customer service to sales and marketing, teamwork, and computer skills. The courses run from a half day in length to three days. Within these broad categories are programs on such subjects as how to run meetings (when to call them, developing agendas, setting and meeting objectives); telephone skills (courtesy, effective listening, managing irate customers); and salesmanship (planning calls, interviewing guidelines). The lessons cost GE a substantial sum of money; for example, $195 per person for the one-day meeting management skills session; $400 for the three-day salesmanship course; and $35 for the half-day telephone skills program.

Northern Telecom

Northern Telecom's program is based on "work cells," the company's expression for teamwork. Each morning the work cell's leader meets with its members to discuss objectives for that day and the preceding day's problems in order to find solutions and anticipate possible difficulties. Because work cell ideas and comments are group supported, they carry more weight and commitment than an individual's would.

In addition, the factory floor supervisor now has the authority to request managers to appear before the work cells in question-and-answer sessions, thereby making them answerable not only to their bosses but also to the teams working for them. Furthermore, the slow, sequential process from testing to production to quality control to marketing has been replaced by co-ordinating cross-functional work cells whose co-operation has resulted in substantial time savings. Consequently, Nortel can concentrate more on new ideas, increased variety, speedier production, and faster deliveries to customers—and hence, add to its competitiveness.

Training and Retraining

Besides altering workplace methods to infuse a greater sense of importance, diligence, responsibility, and discipline among employees, Canadian companies must realize how essential it is to invest in training and retraining to increase their competitiveness both at home and abroad.

Generally speaking, the larger a Canadian company, the more likely it is to have a training program, according to Statistics Canada studies. This is to be expected because bigger firms tend to have more money available to set aside for training. Indeed, according to the latest Statistics Canada survey of 746,100 firms, only 27 percent of the 82.5 percent that had fewer than ten employees said they have training programs.

Other reports bear out Statistics Canada's disheartening account. Comparisons of U.S. and Canadian spending on training and retraining have found that U.S. corporations spend four times as much, for an average of $400 per worker, than Canadian ones. Adding to the gloomy outlook are Canada's steep school drop-out rate, high degree of functional illiteracy, and shortage of skilled high-tech workers.

Only 72 percent of 17-year-old Canadians are still in school compared to 94 percent in Japan, 89 percent in Germany, and 87 percent in the United States. A 1990 survey by the Conference Board of Canada of a cross-section of 626 companies discovered that 70 percent believed they suffer due to workers' functional illiteracy. Twenty-six percent said a lack of basic skills in reading and mathematics slowed their ability to introduce new technology. Thirty-four percent reported functional illiteracy impeded training, since the launch of new programs had to be preceded by remedial reading and writing sessions so that employees could understand the courses. In addition, 32 percent observed that functional illiteracy caused losses in productivity.

As for the shortage of skilled workers, in a 1990 study of 822 high-tech companies by the Canadian Labour Market and Productivity Centre, 55 percent said they faced difficulties in recruiting and retraining scientific and technical staff and 34 percent reported the same problems with skilled trades workers. Compounding the problem is the rapid pace of technological change which outdates workers' skills every five years.

"Canada must attract, develop, and retain people with the capability to create and implement technology with excellence in order to compete against European, Asian, and American companies in the global market," urges Honeywell's Brian McGourty. "It is fundamental to the health of Canadian business that it work with the education system to motivate young people to aspire to a role in high technology."

As an example of what he advocates, McGourty cites the fast-growing newly industrialized Asian economies where busloads of young schoolchildren tour companies regularly. "Thus, at an early age, they develop a sense of aspiration and excitement about working in business," he says. Across the world in Germany, on-the-job training is combined with education at the high school level for students interested in the skilled trades. Government, industry, and labour plan the curriculum together.

But although the overall picture for Canada is poor in the area of workforce training and retraining, there are pockets of hope. A growing number of companies have "Adopt-a-School" programs whereby they provide school lectures, career counselling, and company tours to one or more schools in their district. Also, an increasing number of universities and colleges across Canada now combine academic studies with short-term workplace assignments, an idea originated in the 1950s by the Ontario-based University of Waterloo. In their early days, such courses focused on scientific and technical training; today, they also cover business and the arts.

In addition, more corporations are funding chairs in various courses and/or university-conducted research and development, lending management to help universities and colleges in their administration, and encouraging professors and students to work in business on a temporary or permanent basis. Furthermore, most of the nation's major universities now have centres for international business studies (See Appendix D, pages 256–58.)

In their concentration on upgrading workers' technical skills, Canadian corporations are, however, neglecting the equally important ability of being able to speak foreign languages. Although English is the international business language, being familiar with other languages, and not just French, is a courtesy. After all, the Japanese and South Koreans begin to study English at an early age. Moreover, as we are all aware, in much of the world English is not the native language. For example, in the unified post-1992 West European economic region, which will be the world's single richest market, 82 percent of the 320 million people do not speak English as their mother tongue.

Canadian business people are much more outward-looking than 15 years ago. Back then, it was unusual for Canadians to try to sell abroad, but today the airports across the country are crowded with Canadians going somewhere to try to sell something. Nevertheless, at their peril, thousands of Canadian business people continue to live in a cocoon, ignoring the trend of globalization in business. Besides being threatened by domestic rivals, today's company is vulnerable to attack by global predators from south of the border and from across the Atlantic and Pacific Oceans. For Canada to remain a major world trader, a national commitment must be made to improve our competitiveness in productivity, quality, and innovation. Should Quebec separate and any other provinces subsequently secede, thereby causing the end of Canada in its present form, companies preparing to operate globally and increase their competitiveness would still need to follow the same principles.

As this book has described, there are many inspiring success stories of Canadian companies that have taken the global initiative, either through exports or direct investment. Those still debating the wisdom of going global should pay heed to the wise inscription on a wall plaque in the office of Roland Pelletier, president of Quebec-based Transformateur Delta. It reads: "The future belongs to those who know an opportunity when they see it and then act upon it. Qui n'avance récule."

Appendix A

Federal Government Assistance

INTERNATIONAL TRADE CENTRES

For those new to exporting and/or those who want to find all the help they need in one place, these centres are the best places to start. Established in 1988, the ITCs are a joint program of External Affairs and International Trade Canada and Industry, Science and Technology Canada. They are staffed by federal government trade commissioners with extensive expertise in international trade. During the next few years, regional Export Development Corporation and Canadian International Development Agency offices will be relocated within or near ITC offices to enhance the "one-stop shopping" concept.

The centres help develop foreign marketing plans, identify market opportunities, recruit participants for trade fairs and missions outside Canada, arrange trade-related conferences and seminars, counsel on technology transfers and joint ventures, and provide applications for financial support through the Program for Export Market Development (see page 244). They also have a wealth of trade-related literature, including pocket-size export guides by country. These guides give a brief history of a country, national holidays when businesses are closed, hours of business, city maps, Canadian government contacts, travel tips, foreign exchange, business and social customs, and merchandising and distribution differences. In cases where specialized interpreters are required, the Canadian government embassy will assist in making arrangements.

There are 11 ITC offices across Canada:

British Columbia

900–650 West Georgia Street
P.O. Box 11610
Vancouver
V6B 5H8
Telephone: (604) 666-1444

Alberta

Room 540
Canada Place
9700 Jasper Avenue
Edmonton
T5J 4C3
Telephone: (403) 495-2944

	Suite 1100
	510–5th Street S.W.
	Calgary
	T2P 3S2
	Telephone: (403) 292-6660

Saskatchewan
6th Floor
105–21st Street East
Saskatoon
S7K 0B3
Telephone: (306) 975-5925

Manitoba
9th Floor, 330 Portage Avenue
P.O. Box 981
Winnipeg
R3C 2V2
Telephone: (204) 983-8036

Ontario
Dominion Public Building
4th Floor
1 Front Street West
Toronto
M5J 1A4
Telephone: (416) 973-5053

Quebec
Stock Exchange Tower
600 Victoria Square
Suite 3800
P.O. Box 247
Montreal
H4Z 1E8
Telephone: (514) 283-8185

New Brunswick
Assumption Place
770 Main Street
P.O. Box 1210
Moncton
E1C 8P9
Telephone: (506) 857-6452

Nova Scotia
1496 Lower Water Street
P.O. Box 940, Station "M"
Halifax
B3J 2V9
Telephone: (902) 426-7540

Prince Edward Island	Confederation Court Mall
	134 Kent Street, Suite 400
	P.O. Box 1115
	Charlottetown
	C1A 7M8
	Telephone: (902) 566-7400
Newfoundland	90 O'Leary Avenue
	P.O. Box 8950
	St. John's
	A1B 3R9
	Telephone: (709) 772-5511

PROGRAM FOR EXPORT MARKET DEVELOPMENT (PEMD)

PEMD is the federal government's primary export promotion program. It funds up to 50 percent of eligible expenses; a portion must be repaid if the activity generates export sales. All expenditures claimed under PEMD are subject to government audit and reported export sales may also be audited. About three thousand companies annually receive PEMD funds for:

- Participation in trade fairs and visits to identified markets outside Canada;
- Visits by foreign buyers and sales agents to Canada;
- Project bidding or proposal preparation at the precontractual stage;
- Establishing permanent sales offices abroad;
- Participation in trade fairs, seminars, et cetera by nonprofit industry associations on behalf of their member companies.

PEMD applicants must be registered in WIN Exports, the government's computerized international sourcing directory (see page 245).

BUSINESS OPPORTUNITIES SOURCING SYSTEM (BOSS)

Established in 1980 by the federal department of Industry, Science and Technology Canada, BOSS is a computerized data bank that lists the products, services, and operations of more than twenty-five thousand Canadian companies. The information is updated yearly. According to the government, it has more than sixty-five hundred domestic and international subscribers including purchasing departments of major Canadian and foreign companies; government economic development agencies; chambers of commerce; and Canadian embassies and consulates abroad. Both registration in BOSS and access to its data are free. BOSS companies automatically are also listed in the government's WIN Exports system used by Canadian trade development officers around the world to identify trade opportunities for Canadian firms.

For registration and subscription forms write:

Business Opportunities Sourcing System
Industry, Science and Technology Canada
235 Queen Street
Ottawa, Canada
K1A 0H5

WIN EXPORTS

The World Information Network for Exports—WIN Exports—is a computerized international sourcing system.

It currently lists over twenty-four thousand Canadian firms and includes for each: products and services available for export, foreign markets/countries in which the firm is currently active or is considering activity, and contacts within the company responsible for export activities.

All entries are accessible only to External Affairs and International Trade Canada or other trade officials active in identifying export trade opportunities.

Using WIN Exports, EAITC trade-development officers can:

- Identify Canadian suppliers able to respond to sales opportunities in the officer's territory;
- Make appropriate contacts on behalf of Canadian companies;
- Report back with advice to help them make informed decisions.

WIN Exports companies automatically receive *CanadExport*, the department's trade newsletter. If companies are registered on the Business Opportunities Sourcing System (BOSS)—a domestic sourcing system operated by Industry, Science and Technology Canada—they are automatically registered in WIN Exports.

For more information, contact the international trade centre nearest you or:

Trade Planning and WIN Exports (TPP)
External Affairs and International Trade Canada
125 Sussex Drive
Ottawa, Canada
K1A 0G2
Telephone: (613) 996-7182

EXPORT DEVELOPMENT CORPORATION

The Export Development Corporation, a federal crown corporation, provides a full range of financing, insurance, and guarantee services to Canadian exporters of any size.

EDC's export insurance programs:

- Protect Canadian exporters (and their domestic suppliers) against nonpayment by foreign buyers;
- Protect Canadian companies' foreign investments overseas;
- Protect members of a Canadian export consortium against a loss caused by the nonperformance of a partner.

With export financing, EDC enables foreign buyers to purchase Canadian products and pays the Canadian exporter directly in cash. In addition, the corporation makes it easier for exporters to get private sector financial backing by providing loan, performance, and bid bond guarantees to the financial institution providing the direct support.

For more information, contact:

Export Development Corporation
151 O'Connor Street
Ottawa, Canada
K1P 5T9
Telephone: (613) 598-2500

Or call the EDC regional office nearest you:

Vancouver   (604) 688-8658
Calgary   (403) 294-0928
Winnipeg (for   1-800-665-7871
Manitoba and
Saskatchewan

Toronto   (416) 364-0135
London   (519) 645-5828
Montreal   (514) 878-1881
Halifax   (902) 429-0426

CANADIAN INTERNATIONAL DEVELOPMENT AGENCY (CIDA)

The Canadian International Development Agency (CIDA) provides official Canadian international development assistance to some one hundred countries.

CIDA's Industrial Cooperation Program (INC) offers financial incentives to Canadian firms to develop long-term arrangements for business co-operation and to carry out project definition studies in developing countries. Support is also available for building contacts and identifying opportunities through visiting missions and seminars. To be eligible for CIDA-INC funding assistance, proposals must clearly demonstrate mutual social, economic, and industrial benefits to both the host country and Canada.

Contact:

Canadian International Development Agency
Consultant and Industrial Relations Directorate
200 Promenade due Portage
Hull, Quebec
K1A 0G4
Telephone: (819) 997-7775

EXPORT ORIENTATION PROGRAMS

External Affairs and International Trade Canada (EAITC) offers three training programs to assist small and medium-sized companies to expand into selected export markets:

1. *New Exporters to Border States* (NEBS)
NEBS is for Canadian companies which have not previously exported but which are "export-ready." Participants go to a Canadian trade office across the U.S. border for a one- or two-day "walk-through" course on the entire process of exporting. Experts give information on documentation and customs procedures, banking, insurance, agents, distributors, and other topics. Canadian trade commissioners advise on marketing strategies and help identify contacts for follow-up meetings with manufacturers' representa-

tives and potential U.S. buyers. The program pays return transportation costs.

2. *New Exporters to the U.S. South* (NEXUS)
This program is for companies that have traditionally exported to only one U.S. regional market, usually in the northern United States. Using a NEBS-style-workshop format, NEXUS provides information and contacts to help expand into other U.S. markets, particularly in the southern United States. NEXUS also usually features a visit to a local trade fair or event. The program pays return economy airfare.

For more information on NEBS and NEXUS, contact the International Trade Centre nearest you or:

United States Trade and Tourism Development Division (UTW)
External Affairs and International Trade Canada
125 Sussex Street
Ottawa, Canada
K1A 0G2
Telephone: (613) 993-5726

3. *New Exporters to Overseas* (NEXOS)
This program extends the NEBS/NEXUS concept to help exporters new to Western Europe learn the essentials of doing business there. Each NEXOS mission focuses on a specific sector in a specific country (eg., automotive mission to France, aerospace mission to Germany), and includes a visit to a major sectoral trade fair. The program pays for return economy airfare, ground transportation, and some hospitality.

Contact:

Western European Trade and Investment Development Division (RWT)
External Affairs and International Trade Canada
125 Sussex Drive
Ottawa, Canada
K1A 0G2
Telephone: (613) 996-3298

INTERNATIONAL TRADE DATA BANK

The "bank" provides up-to-date trade statistics to Canadian business, government officials, and others interested in international trade.

It stores a wide range of computerized trade information from the United Nations and can provide export and import data on 66 major trading nations, as well as for groupings such as the European Community and the Organisation for Economic Co-operation and Development. Customized analyses are prepared upon request.

Contact:

Library Services Division (BFL)
External Affairs and International
Trade Canada
125 Sussex Drive
Ottawa, Canada
K1A 0G2
Telephone: (613) 992-6941

CANADIAN COMMERCIAL CORPORATION

The Canadian Commercial Corporation (CCC), a Crown corporation, acts as the prime contractor when foreign governments and international agencies wish to purchase goods and services from Canadian sources on a government-to-government basis.

CCC identifies Canadian sources, obtains bid opportunities for suppliers, and certifies their capabilities to perform. In addition to participating in negotiations, the corporation follows through on contract management, inspection, acceptance, shipping, payment to suppliers, and collection from customs. Its participation helps to reduce the complexity of export sales for Canadian firms and often encourages foreign customers to purchase from smaller or less well-known suppliers, since buyers have the comfort of dealing on a government-to-government basis through CCC.

Contact:

Canadian Commercial Corporation
50 O'Connor Street, 11th Floor
Ottawa, Canada
K1A 0S6
Telephone: (613) 996-0034

Source: External Affairs and International Trade Canada.

Appendix B

Federal Government Awards for Exporting and Business Excellence

CANADA EXPORT AWARD

These awards, established in 1983 and administered by the federal department of External Affairs and International Trade Canada, are for excellence in increasing exports as well as for successfully introducing new export products or penetrating new markets. The judges are chosen from prominent business people. Applicants must have been exporting for three or more years and branch plants as well as Canadian-owned firms are eligible. There is no cash award; winners get to use the Canada Export Award logo during which time they cannot reapply for the award. According to the government, since 1983, 26 percent of the awards have gone to small companies (one hundred or fewer employees), 26 percent to large firms (one thousand or more employees), and the remaining 48 percent to medium-sized ones. About 12 to 15 winners are selected annually.

For applications write:

Canada Export Award Program
International Trade Centres and
   Regional Operations/TPO
External Affairs and International
   Trade Canada
125 Sussex Street
Ottawa, Canada
K1G 0G2

CANADA AWARDS FOR BUSINESS EXCELLENCE

Established in 1983 (the same year as the Canada Export Award), these awards are presented in gold, silver, and bronze for outstanding achievement in ten categories: entrepreneurship, industrial design, innovation, invention, labour/management co-operation, marketing, productivity, quality, small business, and as of 1990, environmental protection, conservation or enhancement. The winners are selected by independent private sector panels. The competition is open to all sizes and types of businesses in Canada whether Canadian or foreign-owned. There is no cash award; the winners receive plaques.

For applications write:

Canada Awards for Business Excellence
Industry, Science and Technology Canada
235 Queen Street
Ottawa, Canada
K1A 0H5

Appendix C

Provincial Trade Assistance

The provinces also offer a wide variety of programs covering participation in trade shows and missions, market development, feasibility studies, and counselling. Detailed information can be obtained from your nearest federal international trade centre and/or from the provincial trade offices listed below.

PROVINCIAL TRADE CONTACTS

British Columbia   British Columbia Trade Development
        Corporation
750 Pacific Blvd. South, Building B
Vancouver
V6B 5E7

Alberta   Department of Economic Development
        and Trade
Sterling Place
9940–106th Street
Edmonton
T5K 2P6

Saskatchewan   Department of Trade and Investment
1919 Saskatchewan Drive
Regina
S4P 3V7

Manitoba   Department of Industry, Trade and
        Tourism
4–155 Carlton Street
Winnipeg
R3C 3H8

Ontario   Industry and Trade Expansion Division
Department of Industry, Trade and
        Technology
Hearst Block
900 Bay Street
Toronto
M7A 2E1

Quebec	Ministère des Affaires Internationales 770 rue Sherbrooke Ouest 7ᵉ étage Montréal H3A 1G1 and 875 Grand-Allée Est Edifice H-4ᵉ étage Québec G1R 4Y8
New Brunswick	Department of Commerce and Technology Centennial Building P.O. Box 6000 Fredericton E3B 5H1
Nova Scotia	Trade Development Centre Department of Industry, Trade and Technology World Trade and Convention Centre 1800 Argyle Street, 6th Floor Halifax B3J 2R7
Prince Edward Island	Department of Industry Shaw Building, P.O. Box 2000 Charlottetown C1A 7N8
Newfoundland and Labrador	Trade, Investment and Promotion Branch Department of Development Confederation Building P.O. Box 8700 St. John's A1B 4J6

Appendix D

Assistance Available from Associations, Banks, and Centres for International Business Studies

CANADIAN EXPORTERS' ASSOCIATION

The Canadian Exporters' Association is a national, private, non-profit organization working towards the enhancement and promotion of Canadian exports since 1943.

The CEA consists of more than one thousand Canadian companies involved in exporting. These include firms from all sectors, such as large and small manufacturers, primary producers, consulting firms, trading houses, freight forwarders, banks, and other financial institutions and insurance companies.

CEA services include:

- A lending library containing more than five thousand texts, periodicals, papers, and market reports covering international business;
- Contacts with foreign buyers and agents, foreign embassies, and Canadian sources on export and overseas project opportunities.

Contact:

Canadian Exporters' Association
Suite 250, 99 Bank Street
Ottawa, Canada
K1P 6B9

CHARTERED BANKS

For clients, Canada's banks will:

- Appraise, advise, and submit surveys, report on market conditions, sales prospects, and import and exchange regulations in Canada and abroad;

- Prepare reports and advise on the credit status of buyers and potential buyers in foreign countries;
- Provide liaison between foreign financial assistance corporations;
- Handle and give guidance on commercial letters of credit;
- Pay or negotiate drafts drawn under letters of credit on foreign or Canadian banks;
- Collect time and sight drafts drawn by exporters on foreign importers;
- Advance money against drafts for collection or against drafts drawn under letters of credit in favour of exporters;
- Fulfill orders of exporters in their foreign exchange transactions in the principal foreign currencies for both immediate and future delivery;
- Handle foreign remittances and transfers;
- Provide liaison between federal and provincial government organizations in their various assistance programs for exporters;
- Assist Canadian companies in entering the export business.

CANADIAN MANUFACTURERS' ASSOCIATION

The CMA publishes manuals and newsletters on exporting issues and procedures. It also conducts courses on export documentation, seminars on export marketing, and organizes and escorts outgoing Canadian and incoming foreign trade missions.

Canadian Manufacturers' Assoication
Export Department
One Yonge Street, Suite 1400
Toronto, Canada
M5E 1J9

CANADIAN CHAMBER OF COMMERCE

The Canadian Chamber of Commerce and chambers of commerce and boards of trade in a number of centres carry out a broad range of activities designed to promote Canadian trade. These include: seminars and conferences providing information on specific markets; documentation services required for exporting; and programs to put Canadian companies in touch with foreign buyers.

Internation Affairs Division
Canadian Chamber of Commerce
55 Metcalfe Street, Suite 1160
Ottawa, Canada
K1P 6N4

BILATERAL TRADE ASSOCIATIONS

There are a number of bilateral trade associations which link Canadian business people with their counterparts in specific countries. A list can be obtained from External Affairs and International Trade Canada.

CENTRES FOR INTERNATIONAL BUSINESS STUDIES

Sponsored by External Affairs and International Trade Canada, the centres' main functions are:

- To train students in international trade and business knowledge and skills;
- To provide seminars, workshops, and similar functions for current managers;
- To undertake research on international trade and business questions.

British Columbia	Centre for International Business Studies Faculty of Commerce and Business Administration University of British Columbia 2053 Main Mall Vancouver V6T 1Y8
Alberta	Centre for International Business Studies Faculty of Business University of Alberta Edmonton T6G 2R6

Saskatchewan	Centre for International Business Studies College of Commerce University of Saskatchewan Saskatoon S7N 0W0
Manitoba	Centre for International Business Studies Faculty of Administrative Studies University of Manitoba Winnipeg R3T 2N2
Ontario	Centre for International Business Studies Office of Administration University of Western Ontario London N6A 3K7 and Centre for Trade Policy and Law Social Science Research Building, Room 304 Carleton University Ottawa K1S 5B6
Quebec	Centre d'études en administration internationale Ecole des Hautes Etudes Commerciales (HEC) 5255, avenue Decelles Montréal H3T 1V6
Nova Scotia	Centre for International Business Studies School of Business Administration Dalhousie University 6152 Cobourg Street Halifax B3H 1Z5

OTHER SIMILAR CENTRES

Alberta

The International Centre
The University of Calgary
2500 University Drive
Calgary
T2N 1N4

Ontario

Ontario Centre for International
   Business
Room 227A
Administrative Studies Building
York University
4700 Keele Street
North York, Ontario
M3J 1P3

New Brunswick

Centre for International
   Marketing
P.O. Box 440
Tilley Hall, Room 330
University of New Brunswick
Fredericton
E3B 5H1

and

Centre de commercialisation
   internationale
Université de Moncton
Moncton, Nouveau-Brunswick
E1A 3E9

Index

Abitibi-Price, 194
AEG Bayly, 149–50
AEG Canada, 149–50
AEG-Telefunken, 149
AEG Westinghouse, 150
Aeroflot, 196–97
Aeroimp, 196–98
Agarwal, Mahesh, 36, 66
Alberta Government Telephones, 95–96
Alcan Aluminium, 4–5, 13, 101, 113–16, 220
Allan, Alastair, xvi, 49, 54
Allen-Bradley Canada, 133, 167, 182–84, 231
Allen-Bradley U.S., 183
Allied Signal, 132, 143
Alpha Graphics Printshops, 199
Aluma Systems, 204–7
Amada Canada, 148–49
Amada Company of Japan, 148–49
American Telephone & Telegraph (AT&T), 81, 93, 98, 106
Antonoff, Peter, 204–6
Atco, 17
Atco Enterprises, 18
Atlantis Submarines International, 68–69

Barton, Peter, 222
Battiston, Donna, 62
BCE, 77, 91, 101–2, 105
Bell Canada Enterprises. See BCE
Bell-Northern Research, 105
Bell, Thomas, 127–29
Belobaba, Edward, 192–94, 212
Bergen, A.T., 50
Bergen, Terry, 50
Birshstein, Boris, 202–4
Bisaillon, Pierre, 166, 187–88, 237
Black, James, 159
BN Constructions Férroviaires et Metalliques, 107
Bombardier, 101, 107–10
Bougie, Jacques, 13

Brant, John, 18–19
British Telecommunications (British Telecom), 76
Brojde, Peter, 80
Bronfman, Edward, 101
Bronfman, Peter, 101
Brygidr, Andrij, 210
Bullen, Ron, 193
Bullock, Brian, 86–88
Business Opportunities Sourcing System (BOSS), 7, 244

CAE Industries, 133
Caisse de dépôt et placement du Québec, 133
Camco, 163, 165, 167, 184–86, 226
Canada Business Excellence Award, 22–23, 250
Canada Export Award, 22–23, 250
Canada Wire & Cable, 110
Canadian Commercial Corporation, 249
Canadian Foremost, 193, 195–96
Canadian Fracmaster, 193
Canadian Hunter, 110
Canadian International Development Agency, 247
Canadian Tire, 11, 121
Capsule Technology International (1990), 14–16
Carling O'Keefe Breweries, 119
Carr-Harris, Geoffrey, 198–202
Chemetics International, 5
Cho, Young, 156, 229–30
Chrysler Canada, 101, 141
Cognos, 71, 73–74
Controlled Environments (Conviron), 12–13, 51–52
Cook, Roy, 121–22, 124
Coradian, 94
Crestbrook Forest Industries, 158–59
Croden, Peter, 170, 172
Cunningham, Desmond, 76, 78–79
Curleigh, Alan, 3, 145

Daimler-Benz, 132, 189

Davidson, Paul, 213–14, 230
Davison, Shawn, 152
Dayton, Walther, 221
Deeks, William, 100, 111–13, 127
Deming, W. Edwards, 227–28
Den Ousten Bus Works, 145–47
Den Ousten, Jan, 147
Devtek, 220
DHJ Industries, 128–29
Diffracto, 44–46, 54
Distributors, 8, 11–13, 45, 80–81, 83, 92
Diversey, 121
Dominion Textile, 101, 126–30
Du Pont Canada, 166, 178–82, 213
du Pont, E.I. de Nemours, 132, 178–79
Durham, Robert, 171
Dyer, F. Robert, 76, 93–94
Dylex, 11, 121

Easdale, William, 228, 234, 236
Edwards, 12, 166–70
Eicon Technology, 10, 79–83
Elders IXL, 118
Eldorado Mining and Refining, 89
Electrohome, 37–39
Emco, 18–20
Emonson, Bruce, 208
Empress Software, 79, 83–84
Esprit (European Strategic Program on Information Technologies), 218
Exide Corporation, 203
Export Development Corporation, 30, 246

Falconbridge, 110
Federal Express, 97
Federal Industries, 47, 101, 121–24
Fell, Donald, 1, 13, 20–23
Fell-Fab, 1, 10, 13, 20–23
Flyer Industries. *See* New Flyer Industries
Ford Motor Company of Canada, 101, 141
Foremost Progress, 195–96
Fraser, John, 122

Gandalf Technologies, 71, 77–79

Ganong Bros., 3, 5, 8, 10, 55–59
Ganong, David, 3, 55–58
Garrett Canada, 143–44, 226
Garrett Corporation, 143–44
GE Aircraft Engines, 186–88, 237–38
General Electric, 132, 184–88
General Electric Canada, 163, 165–67, 231, 237–38
General Motors, 44, 91, 141
General Signal, 132, 167–69
Gillespie, Robert, 166, 237
Gillis, Alan, 47–48
Goertz, Gary, 123
Gowling, Strathy and Henderson, 192, 194, 212
Grace, David, 41–42

Hageniers, Omer, 45
Halla Climate Control Canada, 156–57, 229
Hamilton, Hugh, xiii, 4, 100, 103, 105–6
Handling Specialty Manufacturing, 52–53
Harper, Stuart, 5
Hatch Associates, xv
Hayano, Hiroshi, 232–34
Herring, Kenneth, 60
Hetherington, William, 133, 182–83
High technology, 70–99
Honda of Canada Manufacturing, 141–42, 161, 231–34
Honeywell, 132, 163, 165–67, 172–74, 217, 239
Honshu Paper Company, 159
Hudson, Desmond, 104–5
Hufnagel, Gerd, 153
Hurd, Dennis, 69
Hymac, 46–47
Hyundai Auto Canada, 141–42, 156, 165

IBM Canada, 71, 132, 140–41, 164–65, 166–67, 174–78, 230–31
Imanaka, Hiromichi, 236
IMP Group, 193, 196–98
Imperial Oil, 101, 133
Infotron Systems, 79
Instrumar, xvi, 48–49, 54

Intera Information Technologies, 73, 86–88
International Hard Suits, 50, 54
International Road Dynamics, 50–51, 54

Japanese investment in Canada, 157–62
Johnson, Guy, 148
Joint Ventures, 8–9, 57–58, 118–20, 156–57
Joseph, Eugene, xv, 70, 84–86

Kaizen, 228, 230, 236
Kaske, Karlheinz, 154
Kazarian, Peter, 191
Kendon, Richard, 117
Kenral, 171
Klöckner Stadler Hurter, 3, 10, 143–44
Kniga Publishing, 199
Kornatowski, John, 83–84
Krieser, Thomas, 46–47

L'Abbé, Richard, 8, 13, 35, 39–41, 45
Lafontaine, Guy, 43
Lavalin International, 194
Lavelle, Patrick, 125–26
Lee, Seung-Bok, 141–42
Leger, Paul, 151
Leningrad State Construction Company, 204
Loewen, Charles, 208
Loewen, Ondaatje, McCutcheon, 208
Lukas, Stephen, 14
Lumonics, 74–76

MacDiarmid, J. Hugh, 75–76
MacDonald, John, 104–5
MacKenzie, James, 67–68
MacKenzie, Ken, 52
MacMillan Bloedel, 110
Magna International, 53, 101, 124–26, 154, 194, 220
Management issues, 3–5, 13–14, 73–74, 82, 85–88, 91–92, 94–96, 102–5, 107–9, 111–19, 121–26, 129–30, 219–22
Mando Machinery Corporation, 156–57, 229

Marketing strategies, 1–2, 7–11, 20–22, 24–69, 73–74, 81–86, 88, 90, 97–99, 100, 103–4, 106–7, 110–13, 117–18, 120–21, 126–29
Marocco, Norbert, 61–62
Masco Corporation, 18–20
Matthews, Terry, 94
McDonald's Restaurants of Canada, 194, 199
McGourty, Brian, 163, 174, 217–18, 239
Med-Eng Systems, 8, 13, 35, 39–41, 43, 45
Medionics International, 36, 66
Ménard, Claude, 184–86
Microage Computer Stores, 200
Milltronics, 4, 12, 47–48, 122
Milo, Clive, 12
Mitel, 76, 93–94
Mitsubishi Canada, 131, 158–62
Mitsubishi Corporation (Japan), 132
Mitsui & Co. (Canada), 133
Mobile Data International, 5, 76–77, 93, 96–97
Modcomp Canada, 150
Modicon Canada, 150
Molly Maid International, 67–68
Molson Breweries, 118–20
Molson Companies, 101, 118–21
Moore, Gordon, 15
Morton, David, 13, 114
Motoren-und Turbinen-Union, 189
Motorola, 77, 97
Murata Erie North America, 150–51
Murray, Grant, 164, 175–77, 230–31

Nautical Electronic Laboratories ("Nautel") 41–43
Newbridge Networks, 93–95
New Flyer Industries, 145–48
Newtech Instruments, 90–92
Niche strategy, 35–69
Nickerson, Donald, 91–92
Nippon Telegraph & Telephone, 106
Nobbs, W. Michael, 39
Nodwell, John, 193, 195–96
Noranda Inc., 101, 110–13, 194
Noranda Sales, 100, 110–13

Norcen Energy Resources, 110
Nordon International, 88–90
Norris, Arnold, 161, 233
Northern Telecom, xiii, 4, 71, 77, 92, 98, 100–110, 152, 194, 220, 227, 231, 238
Nova Corporation, 95–96, 101, 116–18
Novacor, 116–18
Novatel Communications, 93, 95–96
Nuytten, Phil, 50

Olympia & York Developments, 194
O'Neill, W. Paul, 89–90
Ouimet, Gilles, 189

Pan, George, 117–18
Parass, Dennis, 52–53
Pascoe, F. Michael, 95
Pelletier, Roland, 43–44, 54, 241
PEMD. *See* Program for Export Market Development
Perkins Group, 221
Phargo Management and Consulting, 198–202
Philips Canada, 133
Philips, N.V., 133, 155
Pirelli, 132, 143, 151–53
Plummer, Stephen, 193, 197–98
Polk, Robert, 143–44, 226
Pollock, John, 38–39
Positron Industries, 5, 93, 97–99
Potter, Michael, 72, 74
Pratt & Whitney Canada, 132, 140, 167, 188–90
Prévost, Ed, 16, 119–20
Productivity improvement, 222–38
Program for Export Market Development (PEMD), 2, 7, 40, 219, 244
Promecam, 149
Purdie, Kingsley, 18

Rankine, Peter, 165, 174
Recherche et Développement Technologique, 43
Reichmann, Albert, 194
Rempel, Sylvia, 64, 66
Rempel, Victor, 64–65
Robinson, Kim, 121

Rockwell International, 132–33, 167, 183
Rolm Corporation, 154
Roumi, Michael, 12–13, 51
Royer, Raymond, 107–9
Rudolf Wolff, 112
Ruhe, Carl, 149, 162
Russell, William, 91

Scintrex, 207
Seabeco Group, 191, 202–4
Sears Canada, 60, 133
Seigel, Harold, 207
Shade-O-Matic, 61
Shell Canada, 133
Shermag Furniture, 59–61
Short Brothers, 109
Sico, 11, 16
Siemens, 132, 143, 153–56
Siemens Electric Ltd., 153–55
Sluggett, Glen, 4, 12
Snyder, Stephen, 165, 226
Soviet Union, doing business in, 191–212
STC, 102, 108
Stadler Hurter. *See* Klöckner Stadler Hurter
Stelco, 207
Steltech, 207
Stewart, James, 179–82, 213
Strite Industries, 37
Strite, Joseph, 37
Stronach, Frank, 126
Sumitomo Corporation, 95
Sumitomo Heavy Industries, 75, 95
Sun Ice, 62–66
Sutcliffe, David, 77, 97

Tashiro, Takao, 160
Telus Corporation, 96
Thompson, Harold, 147–48
Tilley, Alex, 63
Tilley Endurables, 62–63
Torrance, William, 184, 231
Toyota Motor Corporation, 235–36
Toyota Motor Manufacturing Canada, 141–42, 228, 231–32, 234–37
Trade Union of the USSR, 203
Training, employee programs, 238–40

Transformateur Delta, 43–44, 54, 241
Tridel, 204
Tridon, 213, 219–20
Tsuchiya, Hiroyoshi (Mike), 131, 158, 160–62

United Technologies, 188
Upjohn Company of Canada, The, 132, 167, 170–72
Upjohn Company, The, 170–72

Vahsholtz, R.J., 123
Varity, 219–22
Veale, Brian, 168–70
Virtual Prototypes, xv, 70, 79, 84–86

Waite, William, 154
Weiser, Reginald, 97–99
White, Paul, xv
Wilkinson, Christopher, 3, 5–6, 8, 58–59
WIN Exports. *See* World Information Network for Exports
Winchester Group, 208–10
Wintron, 210
Wong, Michael, 178
World Economic Forum, 71, 217
World Information Network for Exports (WIN) 84, 245
World product mandates, 163–90
Wulkan, Maks, 79–82